*Family and the law in eighteenth-century fiction* offers challenging new interpretations of the public and private faces of individualism in the eighteenth-century English novel. John P. Zomchick begins by surveying the social, historical and ideological function of law and family in eighteenth-century England's developing market economy. He goes on to examine in detail their part in the fortunes and misfortunes of the protagonists in Defoe's *Roxana*, Richardson's *Clarissa*, Smollett's *Roderick Random*, Goldsmith's *The Vicar of Wakefield* and Godwin's *Caleb Williams*. Zomchick reveals in these novels an attempt to produce a "juridical subject": a representation of the individual identified with the principles and the aims of the law (especially its respect for property) and motivated by an inherent need for affection and human community fulfilled by the family, which offers a motive for internalizing the law. The different ways in which these novels express their ambivalence towards that formulation indicate a nostalgia for less competitive social relations, and an emergent liberal critique of the law's operation in the service of society's elites.

D1785546

CAMBRIDGE STUDIES IN EIGHTEENTH-CENTURY
ENGLISH LITERATURE AND THOUGHT 15

Family and the law in eighteenth-century fiction

# Family and the law in eighteenth-century fiction

*The public conscience in the private sphere*

### JOHN P. ZOMCHICK

*Associate Professor, Department of English, University of Tennessee*

CAMBRIDGE
UNIVERSITY PRESS

CAMBRIDGE UNIVERSITY PRESS
Cambridge, New York, Melbourne, Madrid, Cape Town, Singapore, São Paulo

Cambridge University Press
The Edinburgh Building, Cambridge CB2 8RU, UK

Published in the United States of America by Cambridge University Press, New York

www.cambridge.org
Information on this title: www.cambridge.org/9780521415118

First published 1993
This digitally printed version 2007

*A catalogue record for this publication is available from the British Library*

*Library of Congress Cataloguing in Publication data*
Zomchick, John P.
Family and the law in eighteenth-century fiction: the public conscience in the private sphere /
John P. Zomchick.
p.     cm. (Cambridge studies in eighteenth-century English literature and thought)
Includes bibliographical references.
ISBN 0 521 41511 X
1. English fiction – 18th century – History and criticism.
2. Law and literature – History – 18th century.
3. Social problems in literature.
4. Individualism in literature.
5. Family in literature.     I. Series.
PR858.L38Z66 1993   823′.509–dc20     92-15796 CIP

ISBN 978-0-521-41511-8 hardback
ISBN 978-0-521-04428-8 paperback

*For my parents*
*Gloria Marie Bohner and Anthony J. Zomchick,*
*who laid down the law,*
*and for my grandmother*
*Elizabeth Bohner,*
*who took it up again*

# Contents

# Preface

In the following pages a familiar figure emerges, taking shape against the background of society's laws. I have named this figure the "juridical subject" in order to emphasize that the figure owes its coherence to a system of legal beliefs, principles, and practices, which attain frequent and clear visibility both in the society and the narratives of eighteenth-century England. Under a different emphasis the figure might be named the "liberal subject," as in a recent study by D. A. Miller, or the "subject of Providence," as in the work of Martin Battestin.[1] The proliferation of labels suggests less a historical uncertainty or critical confusion than it does a profusion of social roles and critical methods for describing them. In current critical parlance, it attests to the recognition of fragmented subjectivity as the product of modern culture. In other words, the individual – whether ideological mirage or concrete person – is rarely all of a piece. Awareness of this fragmentation, both then and now, produces the need to create a design for living. In my readings of the following eighteenth-century novels I will argue that the law provides the matrix for one such design.

Law, of course, is new neither to eighteenth-century society nor to literature. Kathy Eden has demonstrated the influence of "the methods and procedures of the law" on Aristotelian literary theory from its origins through the Renaissance.[2] Hayden White has suggested "that narrative in general, from the folktale to the novel, from the annals to the fully realized 'history,' has to do with the topics of law, legality, legitimacy, or, more generally, authority."[3] Another legal historian and scholar has written that the "traditional symbols of community in the West, the traditional images and metaphors, have been above all religious and

---

[1] D. A. Miller, *The Novel and the Police* (Berkeley: University of California Press, 1988). Martin Battestin, *The Providence of Wit: Aspects of Form in Augustan Literature and the Arts* (Oxford: The Clarendon Press, 1974).

[2] Kathy Eden, *Poetic and Legal Fiction in the Aristotelian Tradition* (Princeton: Princeton University Press, 1986), p. 6.

[3] Hayden White, "The Value of Narrativity in the Representation of Reality," *Critical Inquiry* 7.1 (1980). Rpt. in *The Content of the Form: Narrative Discourse and Historical Representation* (Baltimore and London: The Johns Hopkins University Press, 1987), p. 13.

legal."[4] I summon these authorities to indicate the obvious: law has always played an important role in society and culture. The "rules of justice," David Hume writes, are "highly conducive, or indeed absolutely requisite, both to the support of society, and the well-being of every individual."[5] Law and narrative, then, universalize experience by patterning particular events and ordering the contingencies of daily life.

Long ago Ian Watt, commenting on remarks made by Charles Lamb and William Hazlitt, noted the relation between "formal realism" and courtroom procedure. More recently, Lennard Davis and John Bender have examined the ways in which laws and theories of punishment enabled and evolved with the eighteenth-century English novel's representational practices.[6] Other critics have noted the popularity and function of criminal narratives, and even the most casual reader cannot help but be struck by the ubiquity of juridical episodes in the fiction of the period.[7] Even when the law's officers are mostly absent, as they are in *Roxana* and *Clarissa*, juridical discourse still structures personal and social relations in the narratives in a way that makes the protagonists' good fortunes depend upon each's ability first to internalize the juridical norms of public life and then to externalize them in the governance of self and – if male – family.

Although I have used an eclectic method in reading the six novels that follow, that method has been shaped by critics of bourgeois civil society. With their aid, I have sought to understand the narratives' civil and familial grammars, by which the juridical subject is doubly predicated: first, as a member of "*civil society* where he acts simply as a *private individual*, treats other men as means, degrades himself to the role of a mere means, and becomes the plaything of alien powers";[8] and second, as a member of the family, where relations are supposed to be determined by love and cooperation. This simultaneous double predication entails upon the subject the tasks of escaping domination by the public sphere's alien

---

[4] Harold J. Berman, *Law and Revolution: The Formation of the Western Legal Tradition* (Cambridge and London: Harvard University Press, 1983), p. vi.

[5] David Hume, *A Treatise of Human Nature*, ed. L. A. Selby-Bigge; 2nd edn., rev. by P. H. Nidditch (Oxford: The Clarendon Press, 1978), 3.2.2.497.

[6] Ian Watt, *The Rise of the Novel: Studies in Defoe, Richardson, and Fielding* (Berkeley and Los Angeles: University of California Press, 1957), pp. 33–34. Lennard Davis, *Factual Fictions: The Origins of the English Novel* (New York: Columbia University Press, 1983), ch. 5, esp. p. 87. John Bender, *Imagining the Penitentiary: Fiction and the Architecture of Mind in Eighteenth-Century England* (Chicago and London: University of Chicago Press, 1987).

[7] See, for example, Davis, ch. 7; and John J. Richetti, *Popular Fiction before Richardson: Narrative Patterns, 1700–1739* (Oxford: Clarendon Press, 1969), chs. 2 and 3. More recently Lincoln Faller has written about the social and ideological functions of popular rogue biographies, Newgate narratives, and trial accounts. See *Turned to Account: The Forms and Functions of Criminal Biography in Late Seventeenth- and Early Eighteenth-Century England* (Cambridge: Cambridge University Press, 1987).

[8] Karl Marx, *On the Jewish Question*, in *The Marx-Engels Reader*, 2nd edn., ed. Robert C. Tucker (New York: Norton, 1978), p. 34.

powers and of preventing their infiltration into the private sphere. What better way to escape being the plaything of alien powers than to transform an oftentimes alien juridical discourse – those laws that structure civil society's transactional market – into what M. M. Bakhtin calls "internally persuasive discourse"?[9] This merging of the private conscience and public law – the genesis of a juridical conscience – is an understandable, perhaps inevitable, response to the "merciless life" of "civil society," where (to quote Marx again) "various forms of social connectedness confront the individual as ... external necessity."[10] The law joins one to the dominant form of social reason even as it divides one from other contenders for social goods. What better way to prevent the infiltration of competition into the private sphere than to align the conscience with a protecting law?

Also underlying my examination of these narrative grammars is the assumption that eighteenth-century English society was becoming secular, resulting in the gradual supplementation of metaphysical by immanent standards of value. According to J. G. A. Pocock, for example, in the market society of early capitalism men and women "were now expected to be obsessed with what others thought of them, or might think of them" in order to maintain "credit."[11] As Sarah Scott described it in *Millenium Hall*, society had become the place where the "same vanities, the same passions, the same ambition, reign in almost every breast; a constant desire to supplant, and a continual fear of being supplanted, keep the minds of those who have any views at all in a state of unremitted tumult and envy ..."[12] That I give little attention to religious discourse does not mean that it was no longer important. As Leopold Damrosch has demonstrated, however, providential habits of thought were being secularized, often by the novelists whose realistic fictions were committed to the representation of a material world.[13] Even if belief in Providence still provides explanations and consolations, it does not provide the protagonist with as socially effective an instrumental rationality as juridical discourse can.

9 M. M. Bakhtin, "Discourse in the Novel," in *The Dialogic Imagination: Four Essays*, trans. Caryl Emerson and Michael Holquist, ed. Michael Holquist (Austin: University of Texas Press, 1981), esp. pp. 349–50.

10 The phrase *merciless life* is from Theodor W. Adorno and Max Horkheimer, *Dialectic of Enlightenment*, trans. John Cumming (London: Verso, 1979), p. 152. Marx, *The Grundrisse*, in Tucker, *Marx-Engels Reader*, p. 223.

11 J. G. A. Pocock, "Early Modern Capitalism – The Augustan Perception," in *Feudalism, Capitalism and Beyond*, eds. Eugene Kamenka and R. S. Neale (New York: St. Martin's Press, 1975), p. 79. For a strong opposing view to the secularization thesis, see J. C. D. Clark, *English Society 1688–1832: Ideology, Social Structure and Political Practice during the Ancien Regime* (Cambridge: Cambridge University Press, 1985). See also G. S. Rousseau, "Review Essay. Revisionist Polemics: J. C. D. Clark and the Collapse of Modernity in the Age of Johnson," in *The Age of Johnson*, vol. 3, ed. Paul Korshin (New York: AMS Press, 1989), pp. 421–50.

12 Sarah Scott, *A Description of Millenium Hall* (New York: Penguin Books, 1986), p. 61.

13 Leopold Damrosch, Jr., *God's Plot and Man's Stories: Studies in the Fictional Imagination from Milton to Fielding* (Chicago and London: University of Chicago Press, 1985).

Unlike religion, law holds out the promise of mastering changing social relations. I have chosen to look at the law as an ordering discourse of and in the early novels' social worlds.

It may be useful at this point to indicate my debts to and differences from three earlier studies that take up the problems of individualism and the novel. Ian Watt's classic *The Rise of the Novel* is an obvious point of departure. But whereas Watt explores the consequences of economic individualism on the plot and characters of the novels he studies, I focus on the adaptive functions performed by juridical individualism in conjunction with the family. Watt notes that "[t]he fundamental tendency of economic individualism ... prevents Crusoe from paying much heed to the ties of family ..." For *Roxana*, however, juridical discourse creates its most powerful effects through the family. And although in his chapters on Richardson, Watt devotes considerable attention to "private experience" and family life in an England increasingly devoid of "any permanent and dependable network of social ties," he overlooks the juridical habits of thought that inform the conflict between Clarissa and her family, and that link Lovelace to the Harlowes.[14] By focussing exclusively on the effective powers of juridical discourse, I hope to reveal its specific instrumental functions in the construction of the subject of individualism, which Watt defines eloquently if incompletely in this still influential and admirable work.

More recent studies of the novel have continued Watt's examination of its origins and effects. Michael McKeon, for example, has explored "how the external social order is related to the internal, moral state of its members"; that is, with problems of social status based on the contingently antithetical attributes of birth and merit.[15] In McKeon's dialectical model, the novel provides a staging ground for the conflict between aristocratic and progressive ideologies, from which emerges a conservative ideology that partly negates and partly subsumes elements of each. By drawing upon an impressive array of historical sources and modern commentary, McKeon shows that the novel belongs in that moment of capitalist ideology that legitimated unlimited accumulation.[16] But because his interests are primarily synthetic and because he is interested in establishing both the novel's origins and its progress toward cultural and aesthetic legitimacy, he often overlooks the particular narrative means by which the sometimes errant and always desiring individual is subjected to the law. I shall examine closely the enabling functions of market society's juridical discourse, as those functions are themselves explored in the narratives of the day.

[14] Watt, *Rise of the Novel*, pp. 66, 185.
[15] Michael McKeon, *The Origins of the English Novel, 1600–1740* (Baltimore and London: The Johns Hopkins University Press, 1987), p. 20.
[16] McKeon, *Origins of the English Novel*, pp. 202–3.

In his recent work on penal and narrative discourses, John Bender describes how both discourses "manipulate identity by recomposing the fictions on which it is founded."[17] Influenced by a concept of power stemming from Michel Foucault, Bender argues that "[b]oth the realist novel and the penitentiary pretend that character is autonomous, but in both cases invisible authority is organizing a mode of representation whose way of proceeding includes the premise, and fosters the illusion, that the consciousness they present is as free to shape circumstance as to be shaped by it."[18] Bender's focus on the techniques that account for power's efficacy leads him to represent the individual as an object inscribed by an increasingly anonymous and invisible social authority. By dwelling on the way in which the penitentiary and the novel attain their ends "obliquely – not by intimidation but by inspection, not by force condensed into awe but by the manipulation of consciousness through time," Bender must necessarily overlook the aspects of juridical discourse that have not been incorporated into a totalizing regime of discipline and punishment.[19] I will argue that the mature juridical subject is both an object of visible and invisible forces of power as well as a subject empowered by her or his internalization of that same law. In short, I want to contribute to a rehabilitation of the subject (without losing Bender's powerful critique of social discourses of power) as an active agent capable of carving out a space of freedom and enjoying it.

The first chapter of this work introduces a number of key historical and methodological points for the discussion that follows. Thereafter, I devote each chapter to a reading of one novel in order to follow in some detail the construction of the juridical subject. I have chosen novels whose protagonists show little or no propensity to criminal acts in order to emphasize the law's effects upon the nominally law-abiding. And when the issue of criminality arises, as it does in *Roxana, Clarissa*, and *Caleb Williams*, I show it to be peripheral to the forces that inform character.

I begin with Daniel Defoe's *Roxana* because the heroine of that work relies on express contracts and a contractual mentality in order to realize her desires and – simultaneously – to distance herself from family ties that bind her in unacceptable ways. Contract promises Roxana the freedom from necessity that all Defoe's protagonists seek. And yet, unlike his other protagonists, she finds such freedom ultimately insufficient. The next chapter on Richardson's *Clarissa* continues the examination of contractual relations. Rather than being freed to pursue her own interests by the contract, Clarissa finds herself redefined by her family's politically and economically motivated contracts. In this instance, custom and traditional expectation on the one hand and new instruments for the realization of

---

[17] Bender, *Imagining the Penitentiary*, p. 38.    [18] Ibid., p. 212.    [19] Ibid., p. 218.

desires on the other fall into conflict. The third chapter, also on *Clarissa*, examines Lovelace's intellectual and practical debt to the same law that he ridicules. A civil antinomian, Lovelace's conscience is as dependent upon juridical discourse as are those of the social climbers whom he despises.

In the next three chapters, the law serves a more positive and enabling function, even when and sometimes because it is the object of criticism. The young hero of *Roderick Random* learns to renounce the satisfactions of personal vengeance in order to enjoy the pleasures of an eroticized domestic life. Vengeance is irrational, unless it is achieved through the law. Fielding's *Amelia* takes up where *Random* leaves off. Instead of renouncing satisfactions that are associated with aggression and violence, the already married Booth must renounce – or at the very least curb his desire for – the promiscuous satisfactions of the public sphere. The law punishes Booth for being economically and emotionally incontinent. Only when he attempts to direct the law's powers against the family's larcenous maidservant does he learn to subject his impulses to a newly acquired public conscience. Goldsmith's *The Vicar of Wakefield* continues the theme of juridically inspired self-restraint further. Primrose, the *paterfamilias* at a later stage of life, struggles to maintain his authority in the face of challenges from within and outside of the family. The outcome of that struggle is rendered especially difficult because the narrative represents personal desires as always subject to dangerous exploitation in a market society.

Finally, I end the study of law and character in relation to civil society and family with a work from which family is largely missing, subsumed into a master–servant or guardian–ward relationship: William Godwin's *Caleb Williams*. The anarchist philosopher's novel describes the destructive and deconstructive powers of the public conscience. Rather than containing personal pleasures as it does in the middle three novels of the study, the juridical discourse in Godwin's novel destroys the self that it is meant to constitute. Of all the novels in this study, *Caleb Williams'* treatment of the law is most critical. But in a sense the study ends where it began, at an intimation of the inadequacy of regulating human actions solely through juridical means, whether those means be the contracts that Roxana strikes or the inquisitions that both Caleb and his adversary launch against each other.

In the following pages, I have sought to practice what John Brenkman has called a "critical hermeneutics ... [that] engages the text in a counter-movement to domination, but without thereby releasing the interpreters from the tasks of ideological critique and historicizing analysis, including the task of measuring the distance and historical difference between societies."[20] I have tried to be faithful to this task by holding up to

[20] John Brenkman, *Culture and Domination* (Ithaca and London: Cornell University Press, 1987), p. 233.

critical scrutiny the narratives' self-in-construction and the imagined
world that this self desires to inhabit. I have assumed that narrative
presents a dialectic between the languages of freedom and necessity, desire
and law. Even if the reciprocal effects of each term upon the other are
undeniable, there is no reason to suspect that authority and compulsion
always overcome the wish to be free, nor that free choice is merely an
ideological illusion.[21] In an *Enquiry Concerning Political Justice* William
Godwin writes that "[w]e inhabit a world where sensations do not come
detached, but where everything is linked and connected together."[22] In
such a world, it seems unlikely if not impossible that the subject should not
but long for a commodious life and the means to realize that longing.
Therein lies the dual movement of freedom and necessity, of desire and law
(as the guarantor of merit and enjoyment). At the same time, Godwin
continues, "no man ... can pursue his private conceptions of pleasure,
without affecting, beneficially or injuriously, the persons immediately
connected with him, and, through them, the rest of the world."[23] If we
readers of eighteenth-century novels have the same desires for a commodious life today, it may be that we have less a sense of the way in which our
pleasures – supported by a juridical discourse – impinge upon the rest of
the world. I have looked closely at these texts in order to bring to light both
the pleasures and the pains of desire and self-regulation as they are
imbedded in cultural longings for freedom and community, the irrepressi-
ble and renewable resources of social life.

[21] See Bender, *Imagining the Penitentiary*, p. 212, for the argument that "development" of character
is an effect of discursive power on the subject of narrative.
[22] William Godwin, *Enquiry Concerning Political Justice*, ed. Isaac Kramnick (Harmondsworth:
Penguin Books, 1976), p. 390.
[23] Ibid., p. 392.

# Acknowledgments

The writing of this book was made possible in part by financial support from the Leopold Schepp Foundation for Boys and Girls while I was a graduate student at Columbia University, which also generously supported the project in its initial stage; and by summer grants from The John C. Hodges Better English Fund of the Department of English, University of Tennessee; a University of Tennessee Graduate School Faculty Research Grant, and a National Endowment for the Humanities Summer Stipend.

This project began as a Ph.D. dissertation under the guidance of John H. Middendorf at Columbia University. I owe him a continuing debt for his support and encouragement over the years. While at Columbia I also benefitted from the suggestions of Michael Seidel, Ann Van Sant, Fred Keener, and Laurence Dickey. I have been fortunate to find equally interested and insightful friends and colleagues at The University of Tennessee, Knoxville. This is a better book because of conversations with Allen Dunn, Jim Gill, Bob Gorman, Bob Leggett, Lea Ann Leming, and Rob Stillman. I owe a special debt of thanks to Jack Armistead, who read parts of the manuscript, encouraged my continuing work on it, and guided me through the tenure process. I wish also to thank Paula R. Backscheider, Cathy Matson, Larry Rothfield, and James Thompson, all of whom read either parts or all of the manuscript and made valuable suggestions for revision. The readers for the Press, who remain unknown to me, helped me to shape and clarify its central argument. I owe a large debt to John Richetti, the American editor of this series, who offered invaluable encouragement along the way. I also wish to thank Howard Erskine-Hill, the British editor of the series, for his suggestions; Kevin Taylor, for his editorial assistance and support; Susan Beer, for her efficent and friendly copy editing; and Lynn Hieatt, for guiding the manuscript through production. Finally, Sarah Elizabeth Matson Zomchick changed my thinking about law and family in ways that I have yet to realize fully but that I hope will benefit her in the years ahead.

# 1

# Introduction

For *Law*, in its true Notion, is not so much the Limitation as *the direction of a free and intelligent Agent* to his proper Interest, and prescribes no further than is for the general Good of those under that Law.

John Locke, *Two Treatises of Government*, 2.57.348

## I The novel, the law, and the juridical subject

In times of change (no matter how gradual that change may seem to our postmodern sensibility), when all that is solid melts into air as easily as Moll Flanders' husbands or Captain Booth's money, intelligent agents seeking proper interests need direction. Early modern England was such a time, experiencing a number of modest and not-so-modest "revolutions" in which law played a directive part. There was a revolution in historiography that generated new interest in describing and explaining continuity and change, custom and innovation over time.[1] There were the political revolutions that generated new theories of power and authority.[2] And there were the commercial revolutions that generated new forms of social life.[3] Just as the law played a directive role in the constitution of these new forms of social life, so too it played a formal role in one of the last revolutions of the early modern period: the revolution in literature that endowed the novel with the legitimacy that would lead to its hegemony in nineteenth-century culture. In history, in politics, in economics, and above all in the sense of what it means to be human, law shaped,

[1] See J. G. A. Pocock, who writes that "the historical thought of seventeenth-century England ... acquired much of its special character and its power over the English mind from the presence and nature of that uniquely English institution, the common law." *The Ancient Constitution and the Feudal Law: A Study of English Historical Thought in the Seventeenth Century. A Reissue with a Retrospect* (Cambridge: Cambridge University Press, 1987), p. 31. See also T. F. T. Plucknett, *A Concise History of the Common Law*, 5th edn (Boston: Little, Brown, 1956), pp. 48–49.

[2] Pocock, *Ancient Constitution*, pp. 301–2. Plucknett, Concise History, p. 51. Howard Nenner, *By Colour of Law: Legal Culture and Constitutional Politics in England, 1660–1689* (Chicago and London: University of Chicago Press, 1977), *passim*.

[3] Joyce Oldham Appleby, *Economic Thought and Ideology in Seventeenth-Century England* (Princeton: Princeton University Press, 1978). Christopher Hill, "Sir Edward Coke – Myth Maker," in his *Intellectual Origins of the English Revolution* (Oxford: Clarendon Press, 1965).

1

empowered, and authorized. In quite specific ways the law helped to produce an internally coherent and self-regulating subject, ready to claim the natural rights which belong by definition to a juridical subject.

To say that the law produces a subject of rights may seem to contradict the notion that rights exist independently of any and all social formations. And yet, in order to arrive at a theory of rights, it is necessary to postulate a situation in which those rights are denied to an individual: that is, it is necessary to live in society already, for in a fabled state of nature freedom is a state of being rather than a right. Rights emerge from relations within a social collective at a time when the collective confronts problems of power, authority, and order as a collective. At the same time, rights belong to the individual, whose relation to the collective is usually described in terms of duty. In the pages ahead I shall argue that as the novelists of eighteenth-century England create the juridical subject in their fictions, they contribute to the creation of the modern, secular subject of rights whose ethical nature is both product and producer of the peculiar traditions of English law.

The novel and the law, then, will be treated as partners in forging a modern "collective consciousness." As the novelists encounter the new and recall the old, they hammer their representations upon the anvil of the law in order to create what Philip Corrigan and Derek Sayer have called the "'permissible' parameters and forms of individual identity" in the modern nation state.[4] To assert that all forms of identity in the novel carry the law's imprint is not to contest the uniqueness of experience or of individual character. Rather, it is to assert the influence of the collective on character as well as that of character – however it is imagined – upon the collective. The law's deep engagement with individual and communal life makes it one of the few common points of identification in a collective that otherwise establishes strong ideological barriers between public and private life. Clifford Geertz has called law "not a bounded set of norms, rules, principles, values, or whatever from which jural responses to events can be drawn, but part of a distinctive manner of imagining the real... [Law is] local knowledge not placeless principle ... constructive of social life not reflective, or anyway not just reflective of it ..."[5] Eighteenth-century novelists can no more imagine character without law than they can imagine a society without conflicts.

Geertz's dictum on the law reminds us of its rootedness in the material life of the collective. Although one risks effacing the particularity of

[4] Philip Corrigan and Derek Sayer, *The Great Arch: English State Formation as Cultural Revolution* (Oxford: Basil Blackwell, 1985), pp. 5–6. The authors have taken the term *collective conscience* from Durkheim.
[5] Clifford Geertz, *Local Knowledge: Further Essays in Interpretive Anthropology* (New York: Basic Books, 1983), pp. 173, 218.

material conditions by generalizing about them, it is still to possible to say that the "local" character of the law is distinguished by its dual nature as both instrument of protection and oppression. In a time when periodic criminal epidemics led the law-abiding citizen to fear for his or her safety if not the end of civility itself, how to reassure that citizen that she or he will continue to enjoy the commodious life that all seek?[6] In an address to the Grand Jury of Westminster on 24 April 1728, Sir John Gonson declared that "all Vice, Immorality, and Profaneness should be suppress'd." Gonson believed that "All Manner of Wickedness, even in those Instances, when it doth not directly injure any private Person, nor disturb the publick Peace, has an ill Influence upon Society, tends to make Men bad Subjects, and worse Neighbours, and indisposes them for the due Discharge of the Relative Duties of Life."[7] Some twenty years later Henry Fielding was expressing the same fears and giving the same charge. Fielding tells the grand jurors that "so hungry is [the people's] Appetite for Pleasure, that they may be said to have a Fury after it ... [T]he Rod of Law, Gentlemen, must restrain those within the Bounds of Decency and Sobriety, who are Deaf to the Voice of Reason, and superior to the Fear of Shame."[8]

I have quoted from Fielding's and Gonson's more or less formulaic addresses to the assembled grand jurors to demonstrate that positive law can afford protection from those who "are so apt to violate those equitable Laws [of Nature] to gratify their Passions and corrupt Inclinations; and, when left to the boundless Liberty, which they claim from Nature, ... would be ... Plundering the Acquisitions of another ..."[9] Positive law, however, also raises the question of boundaries in another sense; namely, those bounds which it must respect if it is not to become oppressive. The fear of a tyrannous and oppressive law is part of the English libertarian tradition, with its jealously guarded civil freedoms, clearly expressed by the writers of Cato's Letters: "neither has the Magistrate a Right to direct the private Behaviour of Men; nor has the Magistrate, or any body else, any Manner of Power to model People's Speculations, no more than their Dreams."[10] The magistrate must respect the private lives of British subjects. The law should protect, but it should not intrude. Even an absolutist like Thomas Hobbes believes that the "use of Lawes ... is not to bind the

---

6  For the connection between crime and economics and crime and peace, see J. M. Beattie, *Crime and the Courts in England, 1660–1800* (Oxford: Clarendon Press, 1986), pp. 213–37.

7  Sir John Gonson, *The Charge of Sir John Gonson, Knt., to the Grand Jury of the City and Liberty of Westminster*, 4th edn (London, 1740), pp. 13–14.

8  Henry Fielding, *A Charge Delivered to the Grand Jury, at the Sessions of the Peace Held for the City and Liberty of Westminster, etc. On Thursday, the 29th of June 1749* (London, 1749), pp. 52, 54.

9  Gonson, *Charge of Sir John Gonson*, pp. 99–100.

10  John Trenchard and Thomas Gordon, *Cato's Letters: Essays on Liberty, Civil and Religious, and Other Important Subjects*, 6th edn., 4 vols. (London: 1755; rpt., New York: Da Capo Press, 1971), 2:246.

People from all Voluntary actions; but to direct and keep them in such a motion, as not to hurt themselves by their own impetuous desires, rashnesse, or indiscretion, as Hedges are set, not to stop Travellers, but to keep them in the way."[11] Direction, not bondage, is the best way to secure social order.

One can, in fact, use Hobbes's metaphor above in order to plot social relations as a journey, dynamic rather than static, and thus in need of guidance. If we did not know it already, Henry Fielding reminds us in his farewell at the opening of the last book of *Tom Jones* that journeys and narratives are very much alike, involving the experience of movement (mental or physical) and change over time and through space. The eighteenth-century novel, J. Paul Hunter has argued, provides guidance to both the callow and the curious.[12] Viewed in this way, law and narrative both stand as references, guides for adjudicating between personal desires and social demands – the latter understood in the double sense of personal demand for society and social demands upon person. In this study I will argue that in the period before the development of professionalized social and human sciences (whose role in the creation of a discursive and obedient subject has received much recent critical attention), law provides narrative with local knowledge aimed at the satisfaction of an individually experienced and yet eminently social desire.[13]

It is difficult to speak of social and cultural consequences of modernization without also invoking a now-lost face-to-face social order or a soon-to-be-gained utopia of freely realized individual potential. I shall try to avoid both extremes in the discussion that follows, even if at times I find it necessary to speak of loss and gain in ways that sound nostalgic or utopian. Fundamental to this study is the premise that an expanding market economy changes the ways in which collective and individual life are experienced and imagined. On the one hand, there are positive consequences of change, such as greater freedom for the individual. Writing about the relation between Protestantism's individual conscience and capitalism, Christopher Hill notes that "in a society where custom and tradition counted for so much, this insistence that a well-considered strong

---

[11] Thomas Hobbes, *Leviathan*, ed. Richard Tuck, Cambridge Texts in the History of Political Thought (Cambridge: Cambridge University Press, 1991), 2.30.239–40.

[12] J. Paul Hunter, "'The Young, the Ignorant, and the Idle': Some Notes on Readers and the Beginnings of the English Novel," in *Anticipations of Enlightenment in England, France, and Germany*, eds. Alan Charles Kors and Paul J. Korshin (Philadelphia: University of Pennsylvania Press, 1987), pp. 268–74. See also *Before Novels* (New York: Norton, 1990), chs. 10–11; and below, ch. 5, n. 46, for a discussion of pilgrimage in the novels of Fielding and Smollett.

[13] For a summary of recent work on discursive constructions of the subject, see Anita Levy, *Other Women: The Writing of Class, Race, and Gender, 1832–1898* (Princeton: Princeton University Press, 1991), ch. 1., and p. 133, n. 6. For a study that looks at the role of the nineteenth-century novel in policing behavior, see Miller, *The Novel and the Police*, ch. 1.

conviction overrode everything else had a great liberating force."[14] On the other hand, there are negative consequences such as those described by Jean-Christophe Agnew in his reflections on an increasingly unregulated market economy in England from the sixteenth century onward: "When freed of ritual, religious, or juridical restraints, a money medium can imbue life itself with a pervasive and ongoing sense of risk," Agnew comments, "a recurrent anticipation of gain and loss that lends to all social intercourse a pointed, transactional quality."[15] The transactional quality described by Agnew appears in many places, not least notably in Thomas Hobbes's definition of the human being as essentially characterized by "a perpetuall and restlesse desire of Power after power, that ceaseth onely in Death ... because he cannot assure the power and means to live well, which he hath present, without the acquisition of more."[16] Thus, I assume a material connection between human character and the experience of a market economy, a relation that leads a number of early modern thinkers to find a reflexive competitiveness in human nature.[17] I am not assuming that human character can be understood only in relation to economic practices; rather, I assume that those practices exist because they produce and are produced by certain habits of action, including the ways that desires are gratified or denied. This assumption entails another: a tendency within English society to rationalize behavior in order to "maximize its profit," to reward it with commodious living. *Rationalization* need not be pejorative, the reduction of all social practices to rule and figure (although it often carries the utilitarian sense of calculation); it also means taking the best that tradition has to offer and making it into a system that can guide one through the challenges of the changing world. According to Daniel Boorstin, some such idea led Blackstone to write the highly influential *Commentaries on the Laws of England*.[18]

The extent to which the patterning and regulating of human desires is necessary depends to a large degree on sociopolitical attitudes. For Gonson and Fielding (quoted above) the necessity is great. In the mind of

---

[14] Christopher Hill, "Protestantism and the Rise of Capitalism," in *Essays in Economic and Social History of Tudor and Stuart England, in Honor of R. H. Tawney*; rpt. in his *Change and Continuity in Seventeenth-Century England* (Cambridge, Mass.: Harvard University Press, 1975), p. 88.

[15] Jean-Christophe Agnew, *Worlds Apart: The Market and the Theater in Anglo-American Thought, 1550–1750* (Cambridge: Cambridge University Press, 1986), p. 4.

[16] Hobbes, *Leviathan*, 1.11.70.

[17] Andrezj Rapaczynski writes that for Hobbes, Locke, and Rousseau the "first, spontaneous form of social interaction, at least insofar as it transcends the confines of the family, is not cooperation but *competition* ..." *Nature and Politics: Liberalism in the Philosophies of Hobbes, Locke, and Rousseau* (Ithaca and London: Cornell University Press, 1987), p. 9. Adam Smith, of course, finds the propensity to truck, barter, and exchange – transactional behavior – a fundamentally human trait as well.

[18] "Blackstone ... [took] for granted that since the law was worth studying, it must be capable of being rationalized and reduced to principles." Daniel Boorstin, *The Mysterious Science of the Law* (1941; rpt. Gloucester, Mass: Peter Smith, 1973), p. 20.

Bernard Mandeville, desires (the motor of competition) should be free to further the general good by promoting trade, which he calls the "Principal, but not the only Requisite to aggrandize a Nation." In continuing his thought, however, Mandeville notes that "there are other Things to be taken care of besides. The *Meum* and *Tuum* must be secur'd, Crimes punish'd, and all other Laws concerning the Administration of Justice, wisely contriv'd, and strictly executed . . . the Multitude must be aw'd, no Man's Conscience forc'd . . ."[19] Mandeville's prosperous state arises from a vigorous trade supported by law and what today would be called ideology. Rather than relying on the coercive power of the law to maintain social order and the fine distinctions of *meum* and *tuum*, Mandeville recommends other means of controlling the multitude for whom, in the words of R. S. Neale, "[p]roperty *was* the material basis of civil society and its alienating consequences constituted the network of social relations."[20]

Property presupposes settled conceptions of *meum* and *tuum*. Those settled conceptions, in turn, presuppose a psychological distance between individuals, or what John Brown calls "a kind of regulated Selfishness, which tends at once to the Increase and Preservation of Property."[21] Property begets selfishness, which begets more property, which requires yet more selfish care, and so on. Of the getting of goods there is no end, even for the devout, as Max Weber noted long ago.[22] Ways of reconciling the fury after accumulation (and whatever pleasures, spiritual or otherwise, that it brings) with the general good and with a shared sense of human identity has remained an ideological project since the eighteenth century.[23] It can be read quite clearly in Adam Smith's assertion that the wealthy "in spite of their natural selfishness and rapacity . . . are led by an invisible hand to make nearly the same distribution of the necessaries of life which would have been made had the earth been divided into equal portions among all its inhabitants."[24] But the earth is not so divided, and

[19] Bernard Mandeville, *The Fable of the Bees*, 2 vols., ed. F. B. Kaye (1924; rpt. Indianapolis: Liberty Classics, 1988), Remark L, 1:116–17.

[20] R. S. Neale, "'The Bourgeoisie, Historically, Has Played a Most Revolutionary Part,'" in Kamenka and Neale, *Feudalism, Capitalism and Beyond*, p. 99.

[21] John Brown, *Estimate of the Manners and Principles of the Times*, 2 vols. (London, 1757), 1:22. Quoted in John Sekora, *Luxury: The Concept in Western Thought, Eden to Smollett* (Baltimore and London: Johns Hopkins University Press, 1977), p. 93.

[22] Commenting on Richard Baxter's condemnation of wealth, Weber observes that "[t]he real objection is to relaxation in the security of possession . . . [O]nly activity serves to increase the glory of God, according to the definite manifestations of His will." Max Weber, *The Protestant Ethic and the Spirit of Capitalism*, trans. Talcott Parsons (New York: Charles Scribner's Sons, 1958), p. 157.

[23] For a study of the role of the aesthetic in this project, see Terry Eagleton, *The Ideology of the Aesthetic* (Oxford: Basil Blackwell, 1990), esp. chs. 1–3.

[24] Adam Smith, *The Theory of Moral Sentiments*, eds. D. D. Raphael and A. L. Macfie (1976; rpt., Indianapolis: Liberty Classics, 1982), part IV, ch. 1, p. 184.

Smith's version of a natural distributive justice arising from a harmony of interests still needs arguing.

Argument, however, has little effect upon the feelings of alienation that are said to spring up with modern social relations. Those feelings are clearly visible in the isolation that Defoe's protagonists suffer. Means of producing identification, on the other hand can relieve feelings of alienation. Here, too, there is a coincidence between juridical and fictional discourses, for both the jurist and the novelist look for the general in the particular. Both, as it were, use reason in order to pattern multifarious experience. And yet, it is not just any reason or any one's individual reason which is responsible for the body of law that has arisen within English society. There is no single great legislator who spins the law from his own mind. Instead, for someone like Blackstone, "the great outlines of the law had been prescribed by Nature."[25] Nature makes itself known in the minds and feelings of its creatures, but it does so communally as well as individually. Henry Neville believed that the common law "is reason itself, written as well in the hearts of rational men as in the lawyers' books."[26] Charles M. Gray has argued that for a jurist like Sir Matthew Hale, the strength and the authority of the common law lay in its embodiment of "values shared by people who identify with each other across the barriers of individuality and class, values learned by imitation, confirmed by habit, transmitted through national history."[27] In short, the common law enjoys the same universal character and appeal that critics have found in realist literature. Both law and literature hearken to and help create social values to order their worlds.

Patterning, regulation, and order, then, appear as mere and unavoidable consequences of a natural reason. The peculiar continuity within English legal history, furthermore, helps explain how historians such as Alan Macfarlane and J. C. D. Clark can argue persuasively that England saw no revolutionary changes in its social structure until well after the eighteenth century. Macfarlane asserts that all the structures and institutions that produce modern individualism were in place by the thirteenth century; Clark that English society was "traditional, hierarchical, and deferential," a relatively peaceful and unanimous church state, until the First Reform Bill of 1832.[28] Order is a product of Burkeian custom, of the kind described by Sir John Davies in 1612:

---

[25] Boorstin, *Mysterious Science*, p. 50.

[26] Henry Neville, *Plato Redivivus* (c. 1681), quoted by Christopher Hill, "'Reason' and 'Reasonableness,'" *The British Journal of Sociology* 20.3 (1969), rpt. in his *Change and Continuity*, p. 118.

[27] Sir Matthew Hale, *The History of the Common Law of England*, ed. and intro. Charles M. Gray (Chicago and London: University of Chicago Press, 1971), p. xxxiv.

[28] Alan Macfarlane, *The Culture of Capitalism* (Oxford: Basil Blackwell, 1987), ch. 7, esp. pp. 161–66 for continuity in English law. See also his *The Origins of English Individualism: The*

*Common Law* . . . is nothing but *Common Custome* . . . For a custome taketh beginning and groweth to perfection in this manner: When a reasonable act once done is found to be good and beneficiall to the people, and agreeable to their nature and disposition, then do they use it and practise it again and again, and so by often iteration, and multiplication of the act it becometh a *Custome*; and being continued without interruption time out of mind, it obtaineth the force of a *Law*.[29]

This is legislation from the ground up, autochthonous law-making of a kind to which any Englishman can give allegiance. It provides a national identity that counterbalances particular experiences of alienation. And just as the general good embodies itself in a universal English custom and character, so too the particular good works itself out in the fictional plots that put character to the test, that suspend it between the familiar and the newly – but sometimes hardly – civil.

As Roy Porter has recently pointed out in his criticism of Clark's thesis, continuity and relative ideological consensus need not necessarily entail an absence of social conflict or the lived experience of alienation. In fact, Porter contends, conflict tempers the hegemonic sword responsible for maintaining social stability.[30] At the same time, other ideological powers are called upon to consolidate the gains and salve the losses of conflict and change. By narrativizing aspects of juridical discourse, that is, by incorporating into its representation of a dynamic and inherently risky social life some of the rules that have guided England from time immemorial "across the barriers of individuality and class," the novel performs an essential ideological function, especially in the eighteenth century. That function has been described by Rosalind Coward and John Ellis as putting the subject "in a position of coherence and responsibility for his own actions so that he is able to act."[31] That is to say, ideology – like law – imbues the subject with power.[32] Although Crusoe's power on his island increases as he accumulates more, it reaches a plateau until he formulates the explanations and laws that enable a more or less smooth transition from his individual "meer State of Nature" to a kingdom and finally to a civil

*Family, Property and Social Transition* (New York: Cambridge University Press, 1978), p. 196. Clark, *English Society 1688–1832*, p. 43.

[29] Sir John Davies, *Irish Reports* (1674). Quoted in Pocock, *Ancient Constitution*, pp. 32–33.

[30] Roy Porter, "English Society in the Eighteenth Century Revisited," in *British Politics and Society from Walpole to Pitt, 1742–1789*, ed. Jeremy Black (London: Macmillan, 1990), p. 32.

[31] Rosalind Coward and John Ellis, *Language and Materialism: Developments in Semiology and the Theory of the Subject* (London: Routledge & Kegan Paul, 1977), p. 75.

[32] For the linkage of law and power, see Christopher Hill, "The Inns of Court," *History of Education Quarterly*, 12.4 (1972), rpt. in his *Change and Continuity*, p. 152; Porter, "English Society," p. 35. For the role of law in policing eighteenth-century society, see E. P. Thompson, *Whigs and Hunters: The Origin of the Black Act* (New York: Pantheon Books, 1975); Douglas Hay, "Property, Authority, and the Criminal Law," in *Albion's Fatal Tree: Crime and Society in Eighteenth-Century England*, eds. Douglas Hay, et al. (New York: Pantheon Books, 1975); Frank McLynn, *Crime and Punishment in Eighteenth-Century England* (London and New York: Routledge, 1989), ch. 2.

society that he governs.[33] Before Crusoe can become governor of his island, he must realize his own juridical subjectivity. Such subjectivity arises from conflict and leads ultimately to a stable sense of self as well as a stable society. Crusoe tells the story of laws that direct free and intelligent agents to their proper interests.

How propriety is determined in such instances is the province and the function of ideology, that empowering system of explanation that enables a person to act according to his or her own lights and yet at not too great a variance from the lights of others. It is the function of hegemony to maintain relative harmony among the competing proper interests.[34] The purposive integration of all these forces has been described by Antonio Gramsci in the following way: "If every State tends to create and maintain a certain type of civilisation and of citizen (and hence of collective life and of individual relations), and to eliminate certain customs and attitudes and to disseminate others, then the Law will be its instrument for this purpose (together with the school system, and other institutions and activities)."[35] One such activity is narrative's plotting of legal principle and the characters that such plotting produces.

In *Tom Jones* there are good examples of the kind of subjects that Fielding hoped eighteenth-century England would not produce. Both Blifil and Black George have little or no respect for *meum* and *tuum*, nor do they govern their behavior by loyalty or sociability. Allworthy wishes to punish both in order to produce the kind of collective life and individual relations that will make Paradise Hall into a secure place for its new owner. And that new owner, as Homer Brown has shown, is indeed a departure from past customs, including those embodied in the law.[36] But his new attitudes, it should be noted, are formed in the jail cell where he (mistakenly) believes that he has committed incest with his mother. The law, in this instance, by supplying the stage for feelings of natural revulsion on behalf of the hero, provides the opportunity for the dissemination of a new, more continent system of values than the young Tom had practiced. In the words of Michel Foucault, it "reaches into the very grain of individuals, touches their bodies and inserts itself into their actions and attitudes, their discourses, learning processes and everyday lives."[37] This is not necessarily a conspiratorial view of juridical discourse, for it is impor-

---

[33] Daniel Defoe, *Robinson Crusoe*, ed. J. Donald Crowley (Oxford: Oxford University Press, 1972), p. 118.

[34] I have taken the distinction between ideology and hegemony from Eagleton, *Ideology of the Aesthetic*, p. 145.

[35] Antonio Gramsci, *Selections from the Prison Notebooks*, ed. and trans. Quintin Hoare and Geoffrey Nowell Smith (New York: International Publishers, 1971), p. 246.

[36] Homer O. Brown, "*Tom Jones*: The 'Bastard' of History," *Boundary 2* 7.2 (1979):201–33.

[37] Michel Foucault, "Prison Talk," in *Power/Knowledge: Selected Interviews and Other Writings, 1972–1977*, trans. Colin Gordon, Leo Marshall, John Mepham, Kate Soper, ed. Colin Gordon (New York: Pantheon Books, 1980), pp. 38–39.

tant to view this new regime of power in its productive capacity. Although positive law intervenes to punish social malefactors, it also enables its adherents and adepts to function successfully in a competitive market society; that is, it enables them to exert their wills over against the wills of others who oppose them. Social power – another phrase for the attainment of happiness – is predicated on the internalization of the juridical discourse. This is part of the law's cultural function, and the novels "imagine the real" by making an alignment between juridically induced and rational self-restraint.

The successful juridical subject's ultimate reward is a distanced mastery of hostile social forces and relations. No longer connected in any functional way to the collective, the individual receives ideological permission to withdraw to an internally ordered and externally shielded world of personal pleasures. In his study of natural law, Ernst Bloch writes that "Epicurus banished the polis as that which had turned out to be a burden for the private life," justifying this banishment on the "right to undisturbed, tranquil pleasure."[38] Natural law, in the guise of reason, directs us to maximize pleasure.[39] Of course, pleasure too is socially constructed. For the bourgeois juridical subject, pleasure is located within the self's private properties. Eighteenth-century juridical and fictional discourses produce a cognate subject: the private subject of ordered pleasures. Peter Brooks, in his psychoanalytic narrative model (a model predicated on the juridical subject in question), writes that narrative satisfies desire by giving it "a lucid repose, desire both come to rest and set in perspective."[40] One might say that narrative constructs a natural law of satisfaction of an eminently social desire. Together the law and the eighteenth-century novel displace the subject from a contentious civil society to the newly emergent nuclear family, which is in turn represented as the natural home of the rational, pleasure-seeking individual.

That subject, faced with the often contradictory demands of a refined domestic culture and a brutal civil one, has the opportunity of learning and using the law's instrumental powers in the *bellum omnium contra omnes.*

---

[38] Ernst Bloch, *Natural Law and Human Dignity*, trans. Dennis J. Schmidt (Cambridge, MA and London: MIT Press, 1986), pp. 10–11. Natural Law was a dominant tradition within English jurisprudence until Bentham attacked it in his zeal to reform English laws. See David Lieberman, *The Province of Legislation Determined: Legal Theory in Eighteenth-Century Britain*, Ideas In Context (Cambridge: Cambridge University Press, 1989), pp. 231–35. For a discussion of the suggestion that Hume's philosophy enabled the undermining of Natural Law jurisprudence, see Philip Milton, "David Hume and the Eighteenth-Century Conception of Natural Law," *Legal Studies* 2 (1982):14–33.

[39] See Hans Aarsleff, "The State of Nature and the Nature of Man in Locke," in *John Locke: Problems and Perspectives*, ed. John W. Yolton (Cambridge: Cambridge University Press, 1969), p. 126.

[40] Peter Brooks, *Reading for the Plot: Design and Intention in Narrative* (New York: A. A. Knopf, 1984), p. 61.

Most fiction, however, is to double business bound, mixing moments of criticism with moments of affirmation. Thus, the novels in this study often bear out Ernst Bloch's remark that "[w]here everything has been alienated, inalienable rights stand out in sharp relief. Yet because these rights had no real, enduring place for themselves, this provided little comfort for the obedient subject."[41] The criticism of abstract natural rights is the primary secular lesson of *Clarissa*, and it applies in all the narratives to a greater or lesser degree. The novels' criticisms of juridical practice can also be seen, however, as part of the law's strength as I have sketched it in the preceding pages. Native English narrative is one of the chthonic influences in the slow but steady course of cultural adaptation and social reform. That which it diagnoses as corrupt can be purged from the body politic, which is subsequently strengthened from this course of physic. Given the unlikelihood of a complete cure, the novels are ready to describe the public sphere as a universal lazaret. The plague of self-interest that afflicts society means that some houses will have to be shut for the general good. As compensation, others will be opened, aired, filled with the sweetness and light of innocent pleasures. This, of course, is the ideal domestic household, the private solution to public problems. It still survives today, as the fortunately mobile flee the cities for what they hope to be places of enduring comfort.

The rhythms of in and out migration, from city to country back to urbanized country and then again to gentrified city, suggest that there is nothing really new under the sun if one ignores the labels that we affix to such movements. Perhaps, as Fredric Jameson has suggested, narrative exists to help us escape the sense that the more things change the more they remain the same.[42] If, however, it serves the ideological function of empowering the subject to act in the present moment, if it provides the individual with a "yardstick ... [of] self-preservation, successful or unsuccessful approximation to the objectivity of his function and the models established for it," it also escapes the problem of Hobbesian individualism by supplementing the pragmatic or instrumental measure with a yardstick calibrated differently.[43] Although realism demands at times a reading that evaluates the accommodation of character to circumstance, of desire to the potential for fulfillment of that desire, a different reading can reveal the subject's resistance to fulfilling a "function" and her or his dreams for a cooperative communal life, a dream of a civil society that provides a "real, enduring place" for the individual subject as well as for all those like and unlike, who share in the desire for commodious living. In

[41] Bloch, *Natural Law*, p. xviii.

[42] Fredric Jameson, *The Political Unconscious: Narrative as a Socially Symbolic Act* (Ithaca: Cornell University Press, 1981), pp. 281–99.

[43] Adorno and Horkheimer, *Dialectic of Enlightenment*, p. 28.

the next section I want to describe briefly the juridical subject's spheres of experience.

## II Civil society's family and the family's civil society

In *An Essay on the History of Civil Society*, Scottish Enlightenment philosopher Adam Ferguson maintains that the individual can be truly known only as social being: "Mankind are to be taken in groupes [sic], as they have always subsisted. The history of the individual is but a detail of the sentiments and thoughts he has entertained in the view of his species: and every experiment relative to this subject should be made with entire societies, not with single men."[44] Karl Marx follows Ferguson almost a century later with the maxim that "[i]t is not the consciousness of men that determines their being, but, on the contrary, their social being that determines their consciousness."[45] In the one hundred and thirty-odd years since Marx wrote that sentence, it has become axiomatic for many thinkers that the individual, to be known, must be considered as both source and product of social life.[46] As source, human beings together make culture and history in their efforts to master necessity and provide themselves with a commodious existence. As product, they do not make it just as they would like, sometimes falling under the dominion of residual and emergent forces that operate independently of their wishes.

The eighteenth-century novel, by contrast, presents the individual in her or his heroic phase of development, at a time when sentiments, thoughts – the whole ensemble of consciousness – seem to owe a debt to society only in the negative sense that society makes it so difficult for the individual to differentiate him or herself, as Amelia and Evelina both learn at Vauxhall. At the same time, however, the history of the individual represented in novels – individualism's drama of autonomy and subjection – plays itself out in the family's domestic sphere, in the association of competing individuals that make up civil society, and finally in the shadow of institutions under the control of state power. Both the family and civil society, in contradistinction to the state, appear to be *relatively* free from state power.

One modern analyst writes that "[w]ithin the family, privatization created a limited 'state of nature,' in which the state refused to protect one

[44] Adam Ferguson, *An Essay on the History of Civil Society*, intro. Louis Schneider (New Brunswick and London: Transaction Books, 1980), p. 4.

[45] Karl Marx, Preface to *A Contribution to the Critique of Political Economy*, in Tucker, *Marx-Engels Reader*, p. 4.

[46] Jean L. Cohen, *Class and Civil Society: The Limits of Marxian Critical Theory* (Amherst: University of Massachusetts Press, 1982), p. 34.

family member from the harmful acts of any other family member."[47] The private quality of family life, as I will argue below, is both a threat to and a goal for the protagonists of the novels. It threatens them with dangers against which they have little or no defense, either because they are women or because of a sentimental discourse that hampers the unfettered exercise of will within the family. And yet the family also stands as goal for the protagonists, as protection against hostile forces in civil society and of the state. Just as it is important to recognize that the law performs a constitutive and regulative function in the absence of other developed discursive systems and in the face of weakening religious arguments, so too is it important to recognize that state power at this moment is caught between the old regime of excessive force and the new regime of discipline.[48] In such a moment of transition, the state still threatens the individual and the family with the disintegration that Fielding sketches in the initial prison scene in *Amelia*. For Fielding and the other eighteenth-century novelists, the law's invasion of the family signals its end. This is as true for *Roxana* and *Clarissa* as it is for *Amelia*. If the Vicar of Wakefield's family is finally rescued from the prison, it is because the Vicar has domesticated the prison instead of the prison savaging the family. The family stands as a goal for the protagonists, for it alone appears set off from civil society's competitive forces and the state's coercive forces.

The family, then, appears at once as the subject's source and telos, an instance of individual ontogeny recapitulating political phylogeny in the minds of the writers. It is in the family that the person in the state of nature first comes to realize the value of association. John Locke writes that the *"first Society* was between Man and Wife, which gave beginning to that between Parents and Children." And although "strong Obligations of Necessity, Convenience, and Inclination" work toward the creation of this first association, it is in essence free rather than an instance of necessity because *"Conjugal Society* is made by a voluntary Compact between Man and Woman."[49] David Hume's version of the origin of society is similar. He writes that "the first and original principle of human society ... is no other than that natural appetite betwixt the sexes, which unites them together, and preserves their union, till a new tye takes place in their concern for their common offspring. This new concern becomes also a principle of union betwixt the parents and offspring, and forms a more numerous society."[50] Although Hume makes no mention of a voluntary

---

[47] Frances E. Olsen, "The Family and the Market: A Study of Ideology and Legal Reform," *Harvard Law Review* 96 (1983): 1521.

[48] See Michel Foucault, *Discipline and Punish: The Birth of the Prison*, trans. Alan Sheridan (New York: Random House, 1979).

[49] John Locke, *Two Treatises of Government*, ed. and intro. Peter Laslett (New York: New American Library, 1963), 2.77–78.362.

[50] Hume, *Treatise*, 3.2.2.486.

compact between the sexes, his version of events nonetheless points to the fortunate outcome of human appetites, for they lead human beings to create larger and better structures for their comforts, thereby enlarging themselves from the "numberless wants and necessities, with which [nature] has loaded" them.[51] Thus, this first society is free and reasonable.

The freedom of the family, however, as liberalism's feminist critics have long pointed out, is an unequal freedom. John Locke may have characterized conjugal society as that "which draws with it mutual Support, and Assistance, and a Communion of Interest too," but it remains a hierarchical relation in which power – as Locke himself concedes – belongs to the male.[52] Carole Pateman has argued convincingly about the inequality – and thus the logical contradiction – within the sexual contract. The material development and theoretical articulation of the doctrines of "separate spheres" of experience, with relative equality within the different spheres, temporarily defused the explosive power of such contradictions between liberal theory and practice. Liberalism exempted the conjugal sphere from the formally equal relations that supposedly pertained within the rest of society.[53] Nancy Armstrong, in turn, has argued that these material and theoretical developments are essential moments in the ideological construction of modern subjectivity as such, especially the experience of freedom from domination by political and economic power.[54]

These analyses are salient and ever-useful reminders to modern readers of the necessity to resist the naturalizing powers of bourgeois society's domestic ideology. And yet it is important to hold in mind the dual function that the family – like the novel – plays in the ideological emplacement of the subject. On the one hand, it is an instrument for inscribing the individual with various norms, "an agency of society [that] served especially the task of the difficult mediation through which, in spite of the illusion of freedom, strict conformity with societally necessary requirements was brought about."[55] This is the family's ideological moment. On the other hand, the family looks back to a pre-social history

---

[51] Ibid., 3.2.2.484.

[52] Locke, *Two Treatises*, 2.78.362. Locke writes that when disagreements arise, authority belongs to the male, "as the abler and the stronger" (2.82.364).

[53] Carole Pateman, "Feminist Critiques of the Public/Private Dichotomy," in her *The Disorder of Women: Democracy, Feminism, and Political Theory* (Cambridge: Polity Press, 1989), pp. 120–21. See also her *The Sexual Contract* (Cambridge: Polity Press, 1988), pp. 3–4, 55–59; and Linda J. Nicholson, *Gender and History: The Limits of Social Theory in the Age of the Family* (New York: Columbia University Press, 1986), ch. 5.

[54] Nancy Armstrong, *Desire and Domestic Fiction: A Political History of the Novel* (New York: Oxford University Press, 1986), p. 48.

[55] Jürgen Habermas, *The Structural Transformation of the Public Sphere: An Origin into a Category of Bourgeois Society*, trans. Thomas Burger with Frederick Lawrence (1962; Cambridge, MA: MIT Press, 1989), p. 47.

in which associations were imagined to be natural, mutual *and* reasonable. The recuperations of masculine authority that succeed that originary moment are suspended if not cancelled. This ideal image of the family draws upon a memory or an illusion of the childhood of the species or, perhaps, of the individual liberated of the burden of dependency. This is its utopian moment. To understand the family's functions in the construction of juridical subjectivity in the eighteenth century, these two moments must be considered dialectically, for from them springs a third moment, the moment of potential liberation. Theodor Adorno has written that "[w]ith the family there passes away, while the system lasts, not only the most effective agency of the bourgeoisie, but also the resistance which, though repressing the individual, also strengthened, perhaps even produced him. The end of the family paralyses the forces of opposition."[56] In Adorno's view the dialectic of domination and resistance played out within the family produces progress toward a more egalitarian social life.

If the family offers protection from the hostile relations in civil society, civil society offers relief from hierarchical relations in the family. In its ideal form civil society is represented as "not only ... free from domination but ... free from any kind of coercion."[57] Just as necessity and affection lead to a conjugal union, which in retrospect seems reasonable to the male member, so for John Locke, Hans Aarsleff has argued, reason also leads "men" to the constitution of larger, public associations: "Men are 'urged to enter into society by a certain propensity of nature', they are sociable to the degree that they follow reason, 'according to the law of nature men alike are friends of one another and are bound together by common interests'."[58] Reason transforms necessity into freedom. And reason, as I have suggested in the preceding section, is the essence of law for the age. Even if, as Thomas Hobbes writes, the crucial question arises "whose Reason it is, that shall be received for Law," there is scant debate over the need for settled reason and thus law in civil society.[59] When David Hume argues that both reason and interests are served by the conventions that establish justice and private property, he claims that such rules are "only contrary to [the] heedless and impetuous movement" of our passions, and that they are "necessary to [our] well-being and subsistence."[60] Established by law and reason, civil society offers an advance in freedom over the family because all wills in civil society are *formally* equal.

In short, civil society embodies the ideal of freedom in market society.

---

[56] Theodor Adorno, *Minima Moralia: Reflections from a Damaged Life*, trans. E. F. N. Jephcott (London: Verso, 1974), p. 23.

[57] Habermas, *Structural Transformation*, p. 79.   [58] Aarsleff, "State of Nature," p. 108.

[59] Hobbes, *Leviathan*, 2.26.187. Hobbes' answer: "not that *Juris prudentia*, or wisedome of subordinate Judges; but the Reason of this our Artificiall Man the Common-wealth, and his Command, that maketh Law" (2.26.187).

[60] Hume, *Treatise*, 3.2.2.489.

But just as many critics have demonstrated that the relative autonomy of the family does not withstand scrutiny, so too civil society carries within it actual relations of domination based on gender, race, and class differences. According to Jean L. Cohen, Hegel recognized that civil society "constituted the basis on which the principle of free, self-determining individuality with a claim to satisfaction and autonomy emerged. But he also knew that this principle was concretized in the form of privatized individuals whose needs appear as conflicting self-interests that threaten ethical communal life in a war of each against all to attain satisfaction."[61] Cohen finds the same true in Marx, for whom "the emergence and development of civil society could appear simultaneously as the sine qua non for freedom, autonomy, individuality, and social justice and as the basis for new forms of domination, restriction, alienation, and inequality."[62] Civil society's dual nature as the embodiment of freedom and as the battlefield for social predominance guarantees its centrality in the narratives that seek to emplace the subject in a position of security and comfort.

The eighteenth-century novel also discovers civil society's positive and negative moments. The negative moment is best epitomized by the competition and alienation that drives the novels' protagonists from the public sphere to safer enclaves. Thus, the negative, Hobbesian moment of civil society demands positive laws to restrain persons from violating others' rights in using unacceptable force in their pursuit of happiness. "For the Lawes of Nature," Hobbes writes, "(as *Justice, Equity, Modesty, Mercy*, and (in summe) *doing to others, as wee would be done to,*) of themselves, without the terrour of some Power, to cause them to be observed, are contrary to our naturall Passions, that carry us to Partiality, Pride, Revenge, and the like."[63] Such a description fits both Clarissa's family and Lovelace.

If Richardson's *Clarissa* provides an illustration of civil society's negative moment in the Harlowes and Lovelace, it also provides us with representatives of the positive moment: Anna's Hickman or the reformed Jack Belford. These moderate men know the pleasures of association, which David Hume, writing in the tradition of *doux commerce*, observes accruing to individuals in the civil society of a commercial nation: "The more ... refined arts advance, the more sociable men become: nor is it possible, that, when enriched with science, and possessed of a fund of conversation, they should be contented to remain in solitude, or live with their fellow citizens in that distant manner, which is peculiar to ignorant

---

[61] Cohen, *Class and Civil Society*, p. 25. For Hegel's analysis of civil society, as well as the other two components of human culture – the family and the state – see G. W. F. Hegel, *Hegel's Philosophy of Right*, trans. T. M. Knox (London: Oxford University Press, 1967), The Third Part. Norberto Bobbio provides a helpful summary of the changes in meaning of the term. "Gramsci and the Conception of Civil Society," in *Gramsci and Marxist Theory*, ed. Chantal Mouffe (London: Routledge & Kegan Paul, 1979), pp. 25–30.

[62] Cohen, *Class and Civil Society*, p. 23.      [63] Hobbes, *Leviathan*, 2.17.117.

and barbarous nations."[64] Commerce helps human beings to move out of the "natural" state of brute solitude by developing the equally natural propensity toward social intercourse. In short, the refinement that the increase of productive forces brings makes human beings more inclined to respect the rights of others, a respect that such increased proximity demands.[65] That respect, ideally, enables civil society to function with a minimum of coercion, since all members consent to the obligations and advantages that such association entails. Hume's countryman Lord Kames describes the positive moment yet more fully:

Moral duties, originally weak and feeble, acquire great strength by refinement of manners in polished societies. This is peculiarly the case of the duties that are founded on consent. Promises and covenants have full authority among nations tamed and disciplined in a long course of regular government; but among Barbarians it is rare to find a promise or covenant of such authority as to counterbalance, in any considerable degree, the weight of appetite or passion.[66]

The more "advanced" a nation is, the less need there is for coercive means "to counterbalance ... the weight of appetite or passion." Endowed with refined manners and a fund of conversation, tamed and disciplined by the public conscience of government, "men" can construct a sociable, authoritative, and self-regulating public sphere. In such a society, the law appears as a hostile force only to those who are deaf to reason but still sensible to pain. For others, law is merely an expression of the opinions that they hold in common with their fellow members of the public sphere.[67] And just as the experience of the family can be conceived as the experience of the conflict between mutuality and domination, so too can civil society be conceived as the experience of the conflict between association and competition. Both conflicts, furthermore, have the potential of leading in a dialectical manner to the resolution of differences and the installation of something that approximates the ideal upon which the positive moment rests.

[64] Hume, "Of Refinement in the Arts," in *Essays Moral, Political and Literary* (Oxford: Oxford University Press, 1963), p. 278. For the history of *doux commerce*, see Albert O. Hirschman, *The Passions and the Interests: Political Arguments for Capitalism before its Triumph* (Princeton: Princeton University Press, 1977), pp. 56–63.

[65] It is well, however, to recall an appropriate observation by Adam Smith, just as a reminder that Hume's remarks did not apply universally: "The man whose whole life is spent in performing a few simple operations, of which the effects too are, perhaps, always the same, ... generally becomes as stupid and ignorant as it is possible for a human creature to become. The torpor of his mind renders him, not only incapable of relishing or bearing a part in any rational conversation, but of conceiving any generous, noble, or tender sentiment, and consequently of forming any just judgment concerning many even of the ordinary duties of private life." *An Inquiry into the Nature and Causes of the Wealth of Nations*, 2 vols., eds. R. H. Campbell and A. S. Skinner (1976; rpt., Indianapolis: Liberty Classics, 1981), 2: 782.

[66] Henry Home, Lord Kames, *Historical Law Tracts*, 2 vols. (Edinburgh, 1753), 1:91–92.

[67] For the ideological development of the public sphere, see Habermas, *Structural Transformation*, ch. 2, esp. pp. 36–38, 53–56.

The dialectical relations of experience within the family and within civil society, between the longing for freedom and love on the one hand and the effects of domination and competition on the other, also are at work in a dialectical relation between family and civil society. The more competitive and hostile the public sphere, the greater chance for pain for the individual forced to perform in it. In order to avoid this pain, the person seeks an exit from the war of all against all. Or, perhaps better said, the subject seeks the profits that will enable a dignified and secure retirement. The kind of retirement that the novels most often feature – a retreat to the idyll of the family – identifies their ideological commitment to the constitution of a private life and the abandonment of a hopelessly conflicted public sphere. The ideological solution to the various dialectical conundrums thrown up by the consideration of the individual within these social spheres is central to my understanding of the construction of the juridical subject within the eighteenth-century novel. But in retreating to the domestic space of the family, the protagonists do not simply leave the public sphere behind; rather, they carry with them the principles which have enabled both survival and profit in that sphere. On the one hand, a patriarchal hero like Roderick Random bears the scars of the actual experience that has transformed him from a marginal picaro into a solid landowner. On the other hand, a hero like Captain Booth (through the intercession of Dr. Harrison) has learned to derive a personal code from a tardy realization that, in the words of Peter Stallybrass and Allon White, "[t]he emergence of the public sphere required that its spaces of discourse be *de-libidinized* in the interests of serious, productive and *rational* intercourse. Not least of course because sobriety and profit hang together."[68] If the public sphere is not quite ready for the universal accession of the new regime, domestic life can benefit from its principles, for sobriety can secure the household from external dangers.

The *rational* public sphere, however, provides neither good material for extended novelistic representation nor an enduring place of comfort for the subject. The *unreformed* (irrational) public sphere, which exists beneath its bourgeois counterpart as the urban underworld, provides good material but transitory and devalued comforts. Representation is threatened with an impasse, for rationalizing public intercourse requires social and psychical repression, which in turn produces pain contrary to natural law. If the rational pleasures of the bourgeois public sphere are "de-libidinized" and if the libidinal pleasures of the unreformed public sphere threaten to overwhelm the subject in the way that the vapors from the assembly at Bath overcome Smollett's Matthew Bramble, then only the family remains as a possible site of sanctioned and enduring comfort as

[68] Peter Stallybrass and Allon White, *The Politics and Poetics of Transgression* (Ithaca: Cornell University Press, 1986), pp. 96–97.

well as an anodyne for the pain of civic repression. Furthermore, if exchange relations can potentially reduce human life to the relative equivalency of a commodity (except for the possessor of that life, for whom it almost always has an absolute value), then a place where human life will be appreciated as an absolute good is an ideological necessity given individualism's celebration of the unique person. A heartless world requires a haven, and a "de-libidinized" public sphere requires an eroticized private one. The family holds out the promise of both as it rises to ideological prominence.

In *The Family, Sex and Marriage* Lawrence Stone describes the emergence of a "new family type," one "serving rather fewer practical functions, but carrying a much greater load of emotional and sexual commitment ... more bound by affection or habit ... more sexually liberated, preferably within marriage, and less sexually repressed ..."[69] Despite the criticisms of Stone's thesis, the very fact that he presents a coherent picture of this type is *prima facie* evidence of its ideological power.[70] The affective individual and member of an eroticized domestic unit, whose essence is cooperation, stands heroically over against the possessive individual – "the proprietor of his own person or capacities, ... [whose] human essence is freedom from dependence on the wills of others."[71] The possessive individual of civil society's market relations (and again it is necessary to recall the gendered nature of that subject), endowed with a dream of autonomy and a need for comfort, finds fulfillment in the ideal of the nuclear family. This is the family that all the protagonists long for. This remains the normative version of home, modified by the elimination of patriarchal oppression. The family must be viewed as a response to the objective conditions produced by and producing the subject's quest for self-realization. If it appears as the only rational choice, it owes that eminence to the relative poverty of the other associational forms to hand. In short, the novel transforms this pragmatic choice into an ideal even as it preserves many of the ideal's features.

Because the eroticized family is partly a consequence of unpleasurable social relations, its ideological sufficiency depends upon a continuing perception of the superiority of its pleasures. Thus, in a somewhat perverse way, the family benefits from the continuing perception of the inferiority of pleasures available outside the domestic sphere. By commodifying sexuality and parodying the family in Mrs. Sinclair's public brothel, Richardson's *Clarissa* makes its contribution to the ranking of the pleas-

---

[69] Lawrence Stone, *The Family, Sex and Marriage in England, 1500–1800* (New York: Harper and Row, 1977), p. 657.

[70] For a survey of the criticism, see Ellen Pollak, *The Poetics of Sexual Myth: Gender and Ideology in the Verse of Swift and Pope* (Chicago: University of Chicago Press, 1985), pp. 23–25.

[71] C. B. Macpherson, *The Political Theory of Possessive Individualism, Hobbes to Locke* (Oxford: The Clarendon Press, 1962), p. 3.

ures. At the same time, the Harlowe family, as I shall discuss at some length below, stands as an instance of the destruction that results when public relations penetrate domestic life. In most instances the family derives strength from the rigors of competition not unlike the way that Antaeus derives strength from the earth. The greater the war of all against all in civil society, the greater attraction its own non-competitive pleasures enjoy. Meanwhile, the novels also work to repress the realization that the bourgeois family owes part of its strength to the market place, whether through trade in commodities, land, or women. In all the novels, happiness hinges upon securing one's libidinal investment – one not subject to the fluctuations of the market – rather than upon successful material exchanges.

The eighteenth-century novel plays a significant role in orienting the subject to different social spheres. It is a much needed function, for as the political anthropologist Louis Dumont remarks, "[w]ith the dominance of individualism, as opposed to holism, the social as we understand it was replaced by the juridical, the political, and, later, the economic."[72] With the disappearance of *"universitas* in the sense of a whole in which man is born and to which he belongs willy-nilly," with the disappearance of the totality that Georg Lukács considered to be characteristic of epic culture, authority is fragmented into competing discourses, each driven by a particular aim.[73] In this brave new world, the individual is measured against the standards that such discourses provide. In eighteenth-century English novels – where representations of imprisonment for debt, for example, are quite common – juridical discourse provides a functional standard of measurement for the narrative and often for the protagonists themselves. Those protagonists who bring their behavior in line with juridical discourse without sacrificing a self-regarding freedom can look forward to familiar satisfactions. Those who fail to make the law their reason are deprived of domestic happiness through exile, death, or transcendence. In the final section of this introduction, I want to consider – again briefly – the function of juridical discourse in English society.

## III Law, regulation, and freedom

In the first part of this introduction I argued that as England becomes distinctly more modern, law acts the part of an enduring reasonable form to the developing content of its socioeconomic forces. Social life may change, but law remains reassuringly predictable, providing its adherents

[72] Louis Dumont, *Essays on Individualism: Modern Ideology in Anthropological Perspective* (Chicago and London: University of Chicago Press, 1986), p. 75.
[73] Dumont, *Essays*, p. 75. Georg Lukács, *The Theory of the Novel*, trans. Anna Bostock (Cambridge, MA: MIT Press, 1971).

with the fiction that the wisdom of the ages still shapes contemporary events even as it preserves ancient rights and liberties. In the words of Sir Matthew Hale, writing in the second half of the seventeenth century,

> tho ... particular Variations and Accessions have happened in the Laws, yet they being only partial and successive, we may with just Reason say, They are the same English Laws now, that they were 600 Years since in the general. As the Argonauts Ship was the same when it returned home, as it was when it went out, tho' in that long Voyage it had successive Amendments, and scarce came back with any of its former Materials ...[74]

The common law's fabled immutability enables it to adapt to changing circumstances without loss of its essential identity. Variations and amendments are absorbed by the law's purpose, which is to carry its passengers safely on their journeys and back again to the comfort of home, materially changed and yet somehow fully the same. In law, this end is often reached through the *legal fiction*, defined by Sir Henry Sumner Maine as "any assumption which conceals, or affects to conceal, the fact that a rule of law has undergone alteration, its letter remaining unchanged, its operation being modified."[75] In Greek culture, Kathy Eden has argued, legal fictions share characteristics with poetic ones, relating particulars to the general rule and adapting the general rule to the particular instance in the interest of understanding motive and serving equity.[76] They humanize a Procrustean law by accommodating it to changing circumstances without new legislation. In like manner, eighteenth-century novelistic fictions rely on the premise that the essence of human nature remains unchanged even though changing social conditions modify its "operation," especially with regard to social relations. *Roxana*, a significant exception to this rule, reveals clearly and decisively the effects of operation upon essence in debarring its heroine from returning to the home port for the "crime" of accepting the law's freedoms without its regulations. On the whole, however, legal and novelistic fictions create continuity that makes change acceptable.[77]

Predictability alone, however, is insufficient to guarantee that law will provide freedom through regulation; it must also be universal in its effects. In eighteenth-century England, Roy Porter writes, the law "commanded the assent of the vast majority of the nation ... Practically everyone owned something which the law protected."[78] The kind of universality that Porter describes might be termed "objective universality," in that law is

---

[74] Hale, *History of the Common Law*, p. 40.
[75] Sir Henry Sumner Maine, *Ancient Law* (London: J. M. Dent, 1917), p. 16.
[76] Eden, *Poetic and Legal Fiction*, pp. 43–47.
[77] For a different approach to fiction and identity, see Bender, *Imagining the Penitentiary*, pp. 35–40.
[78] Porter, "English Society," p. 35.

materialized in the objects that it protects. And whether that object is the possessive individual's property in the self or more traditional forms of property, law affords a universal yet socially immanent standard of rights by which such property can be described and defended. It creates a point of identity without requiring that the individual sacrifice the particular objective quality of that very individualism.

Yet for identity to reside in an alienable and often alienated objectivity would be scandalous. Liberalism demands a subjective component that will allow for the free operation of the will without sacrificing the kind of identification provided by objective universality. According to Thomas Hobbes's version of the state, law provides just such a standard by supporting or displacing the individual conscience that is one's sole guide only in "the condition of meer Nature ... [Y]et it is not so with him that lives in a Common-wealth," Hobbes continues, "because the Law is the publique Conscience, by which he hath already undertaken to be guided."[79] In the congruence between promulgated law and private conscience lies the law's ideological efficacy and the key to political hegemony. As the conscience of that artificial person the commonwealth, the law subsumes all individuals, thereby completing the appearance of universality. In guiding, protecting, and punishing transgressors, it produces a subject congruent with itself and with all other juridical subjects. It reinforces and creates social norms as well as instances of deviance. In short, the law produces a formal harmony that is missing from the adversarial transactions – the content – of civil society.

That which is everywhere, the structure of objective and subjective relations, and which is also ready at hand to aid a person in accomplishing aims and defending against unwarrantable interference, soon becomes second nature. The law's social prominence leads E. P. Thompson to call it eighteenth-century Britain's "central legitimizing ideology, displacing religious authority and sanctions of previous centuries."[80] This gradual displacement of other socially authoritative discourses by the law is the beginning of legalism, in which, "[t]he legal rule (in so far as it is publicly announced and positively articulated) will subsume existing customs leaving them redundant as guides to correct behaviour."[81] Social actors govern their behavior according to law because they believe – and are often correct in assuming – that the law sets the standard for others'

[79] Hobbes, *Leviathan*, 2.29.223. In this regard it is interesting to consult the sermon in *Tristram Shandy*, 2.17. Sterne calls law and religion to the aid of the individual conscience. He preached it "on July 29, 1750, at the close of the summer assizes in York." *The Life and Opinions of Tristram Shandy, Gentleman*, 3 vols., eds. Melvyn New and Joan New (Gainesville: University Presses of Florida, 1978, 1984), 2:946.

[80] Thompson, *Whigs and Hunters*, p. 263.

[81] Hugh Collins, *Marxism and Law* (Oxford and New York: Oxford University Press, 1984), pp. 87–88. See also ch. 5, n. 22, below.

behavior. In her study of the justices of the peace in England, Norma Landau has discovered an important change in the handbooks that local justices relied upon to help them administer their parishes and towns. Whereas popular seventeenth-century manuals had used moral exhortation on the justices, for Richard Burn's *The Justice of the Peace and the Parish Officer* (1755) "law and law alone provided sufficient definition, counsel, and dignity for the English justice."[82] Moral suasion is displaced by the explication and indication of known law. In theory the subjective and the objective become one, and society is freed from the tyrannous reign of strong individual wills.

Predictability without loss of adaptability on the one hand, and "law and law alone" on the other indicate the dialectical role played by law within society. It is the unmoved mover of individual and social progress, that which guides the nation and its subjects through the chaos of change. Its ideological strength lies in part in appearing responsive to and regulating the contingencies that beset human nature. At the end of his study of the Black Act, E. P. Thompson summarizes the attributes that make the law such a powerful instrument: "the rules and categories of law penetrate every level of society, effect vertical as well as horizontal definitions of men's rights and status, and contribute to men's self-definition or sense of identity. As such law has not only been imposed *upon* men from above: it has also been a medium within which other social conflicts have been fought out."[83] Law saturates, nourishes, and defines a culture. By making claim to the general practices of a culture as they are embodied in law, a person can plot a regular scheme of relations: what is owed to social superiors, inferiors, and equals (for I do not mean to suggest that objective and subjective universality plays a levelling function). Regularity within the parameters of law is the essence of reason, and reason authorizes and legitimizes self and the actions stemming from that self.

The role played by law in the constitutional and political crises of the seventeenth century is the paradigm case for its function within English society. According to Howard Nenner, from the Restoration to the Glorious Revolution both Whig and Tory, Jacobite and Williamite used legal arguments and tactics in the struggle for political authority. In this regard, law acts the role of midwife of the great bourgeois revolution in politics, "declaring the rights and liberties of the subject and settling the succession of the crown."[84] The prominence of legal argument during the last part of the seventeenth century leads Nenner to draw a conclusion similar to that

---

[82] Norma Landau, *The Justices of the Peace, 1679–1760* (Berkeley: University of California Press, 1984), p. 340.

[83] Thompson, *Whigs and Hunters*, p. 267.

[84] 1 Will & Mar., sess. ii, c. 2., Bill of Rights, 1689, in E. Neville Williams, *The Eighteenth-Century Constitution, 1688–1815: Documents and Commentary* (Cambridge: Cambridge University Press, 1960), p. 26.

drawn by Porter, Thompson, and Geertz: "Law had become so much a part of the educated Englishman's culture and of his assumptions about society that in every area of discourse and thought he drew automatically upon its vocabulary and relied instinctively upon its forms."[85] The discourse of law and the intuitive conviction of rights make the political actor into a juridical subject, endowing that subject with the means to prevail in the struggle between subjugation and freedom.

No matter what its actual impact upon English politics of the eighteenth century, the Glorious Revolution is a decisive moment in the ideological emergence of modern liberalism, epitomized in the codification of the subject's ancient rights and liberties.[86] One element within this moment of ideological emergence, I maintain, is the coeval appearance of the juridical subject as an object of representation in novelistic narrative. Over the course of the eighteenth century, this ideological subject – which can also be conceptualized as a provisional solution to a crisis of social authority – is itself subjected to yet newer discursive forces that further modify it. I will not pursue that modification here, but suffice it to say that it involves a change from a more or less pristine form of *homo juridicus* to an ever more complex form of *homo economicus*, a "great transformation," when – according to Karl Polanyi – politics is subsumed by economics.[87] The period during which the change is occurring stands as liberalism's classic moment, when the subject is self-conceived as inhabiting a public sphere in which political equality (for the bourgeoisie) remains unaffected by economic inequality.[88] Over the course of the century, however, both the culture at large (for example, in the great explosion of penal legislation) and the novel (in its representation of the theory of equality before the law and the reality of social and gender hierarchies) expose an adulteration in the pure political subject. In fact, the interdependence of rights and needs was being prepared in the seventeenth century when, as J. G. A. Pocock has shown, the concepts "ancient constitution," immemorial custom, and the common law – all genealogically related – were "constantly asserted to be in some way immune from the king's prerogative action," thereby carving out a space within which the subject could follow dictates of economic self-interest free from the interference of the crown.[89] In short, the separation of economics and politics – of attaining a commodious living and protecting that achievement – was always partly illusory. That illusion, nonetheless, is one that drives the plots of many eighteenth-century novels.

[85] Nenner, *By Colour of Law*, pp. 81, 3–4; W. S. Holdsworth, *A History of English Law*, 12 vols. (Boston: Little, Brown, and Company, 1924), 5:352.
[86] See Clark, *English Society, 1688–1832*, pp. 46, 132.
[87] See Karl Polanyi, *The Great Transformation: The Political and Economic Origins of Our Time* (Boston: Beacon Press, 1957), ch. 10.
[88] Habermas, *Structural Transformation*, pp. 79–87.      [89] Pocock, *Ancient Constitution*, p. 46.

The interrelation of needs and rights that the novels consider so obsess-
ively is also apparent in the common law itself, both in a formal and
historical sense. Christopher Hill has argued that Edward Coke "systema-
tized English law and in the process continued and extended the process of
liberalizing it, of adapting it to the needs of a commercial society."[90] In
favoring "economic liberalism," Coke pitted the common law against the
prerogative of the crown, thus enlarging civil freedoms and modernizing
the law itself. Although Coke's innovations might be viewed as having
consequences only for the struggles between Parliament and Crown, they
in fact have important ramifications for the individual subject. Through
the interrelation of law and economics, the subject is conceived not only as
a carrier of rights but also as an economic agent. In fact, as David Little
argues, rights and economic agency go hand-in-hand, contributing to a
new "sense of identity" for human nature: "The minute and direct
restrictions which had been imposed and sanctioned by the law of the land
were now at various points dismissed. Individuals acting economically
possess, it was thought, the capacity for a high degree of self-regulation
and self-determination. The place and function of the law was to provide
the broad framework within which men would be both encouraged and
enabled to develop economic self-control."[91] Little is describing an
ongoing process within sixteenth and seventeenth-century England, where
lawyers "helped to introduce a set of economic and social patterns that
undermined the ancient realm and paved the way for rational capitalism."[92] The growth of new productive forces demanded an individual who
could be represented as capable of self-restraint and for whom paternalist
intervention in *his* pursuit of property was unwarranted and counter-
productive. In the rhetoric of the time that A. O. Hirschman has studied
so profitably, self-interest was represented as a sufficiently effective
countervailing force to the irrational passions that threatened social
order.[93] A society so described – a market society – requires minimal
interference in private business transactions; at most, the state intervenes
only to enforce voluntary contracts.[94]

According to W. S. Holdsworth, by the end of the seventeenth century

---

[90] Hill, "Sir Edward Coke," p. 256.

[91] David Little, *Religion, Order, and Law: A Study in Pre-Revolutionary England* (New York: Harper
and Row, 1969), p. 204.

[92] Little, *Religion, Order, and Law*, p. 172; P. S. Atiyah, *The Rise and Fall of Freedom of Contract*
(Oxford: Clarendon Press, 1979), p. 113.

[93] Hirschman, *Passions and Interests*, pp. 43–44, 48–56.

[94] Olsen, "The Family and the Market," p. 1521. In eighteenth-century England the newly
emergent economic forces are not uniformly victorious. Economic liberalism, for example, did
not entirely supplant older theories about economic restraint and social obligation. Joyce
Appleby has shown how by 1713 a modified mercantilism was in place as national policy, in
part because its supporters doubted that individuals would be able to restrain their self-
interests when those interests conflicted with the national good (*Economic Thought* 263–65).

the common law assumed its modern character when "new rules and machinery are introduced ... to regulate new political, social and commercial needs and activities."[95] In this regard it is also possible to see how the juridical and economic discourses working in concert produce new objective forms of subjectivity. These new forms of subjectivity have a discursive and institutional history. Joyce Appleby has noted, for example, how sixteenth-century legislation produced new forms of character, both individual and collective. "Thus, at the end of the sixteenth century," Appleby writes, "the word people covered not only the normal transmitters of a rural tradition but also a new group of men and women who had been displaced by the irreversible forces of social change." It was this latter group that was given a social character by the Elizabethan Poor Law of 1601, which Appleby notes was described by a Restoration author as "'work for those that will Labour, Punishment for those that will not, and Bread for those that cannot.' "[96] In short, this law both reflects the dislocations effected by economic and political change as well as constitutes a group as an administrative category. The poor are those defined, enabled, and constrained by the statute; transformed from an aspect of village life to a social or national problem. It can be argued that law shapes perception. In this instance it creates a new way of seeing in response to threats from masterless men displaced by economic changes in the English countryside.

New ways of seeing bring about and are brought about by new ways of formulating social relations. An important – if not the most important – framework for the development of new forms of social intercourse is the idea of contract in English law and society. This is the formal interrelation of needs and rights. With its promise of gain and possibility of loss, the contract epitomizes the freedoms granted the self-regulating individual and the dangers of competition in civil society. At the same time, it establishes a paradigm for social relations in the public sphere. The importance of the contract is attested to by Holdsworth, who writes that "the theory of contract, evolved in the sphere of common law jurisdiction, became the theory of English law."[97] P. S. Atiyah, another historian of contract, writes that in the seventeenth and eighteenth centuries, the "still emerging idea ... of contract was, in short, replacing custom as a source of law – that is, as the regulator of social and political duties – and as the source of individual rights and obligations – that is, as the regulator of private obligations."[98] Under ideal conditions, contract provides the

---

[95] Holdsworth, *History of English Law*, 6:624.     [96] Appleby, *Economic Thought*, pp. 129, 131.
[97] Holdsworth, *History of English Law*, 8:5; see also 5:296.
[98] Atiyah, *Rise and Fall*, p. 37. For the thesis that contract law remained "equitable" until the very end of the eighteenth century, see Morton J. Horwitz, *The Transformation of American Law, 1780–1860* (Cambridge, MA and London: Harvard University Press, 1977), pp. 160–61; Roger Cotterrell, "The Development of Capitalism and the Formalisation of Contract Law," in *Law,*

framework for the subject to engage in advantageous agreements without considering the good of anyone else. This also means, however, that the other bargainers will be equally oblivious to the good of anyone other than themselves.[99] And yet, despite the contract's implicit egoism, it accords the individual both a sense of freedom and a means of establishing relations with others. According to Henry Sumner Maine, contract distinguishes progressive from traditional societies.[100] According to more recent critics of contract ideology, it "express[es] elements of people's authentic yearning for personal autonomy and social solidarity."[101] Its essence lying in an agreement or a meeting of equal wills, the contract represents ideally the socialization of fear, avarice, and all the other strong passions with which Hobbes (among others) invests human nature. In one sense, the contract can be a way back to that original harmony that supposedly reigned in the family before pride and self-love corroded those relations.

The ideological importance of contract is found in its economic, political, and psychological ramifications, creating those subjective effects described above by Little and Appleby. Enforcing adherence to private agreements "made seriously or with some recompense" becomes a necessity to preserve the ideological coherence of a society of self-restraining subjects.[102] For one "Tradesman of the City" writing during the South Sea troubles to urge the honoring of contracts made before the crash, there was no distinction between the bad subject and one who failed to adhere to a contract: "those who endeavour to bring Dishonour in Bargains into Fashion ... will even venture to take Methods which tend to create Riots in this City, in order to accomplish their monstrous Designs."[103] To preserve the contract is to preserve the order of society because no one makes contracts that are demonstrably to his or her harm. Likewise, the ideal subject is one who submits herself to the liberating discipline of the law. The law becomes the objective realization of the individual's own desires.

As the law changed in the eighteenth century, however, it did not always change in the direction of greater coherence or ideal rationality. In his study of eighteenth-century law and law-making, David Lieberman

State and Society, eds. Bob Fryer, et al. (London: Croom Helm, 1981), pp. 62–63. For a criticism of Horwitz's argument see A. W. B. Simpson, "The Horwitz Thesis and the History of Contracts," in his Legal Theory and Legal History: Essays on the Common Law (London and Ronceverte: Hambledon Press, 1987), pp. 203–71.

99 For the doctrine caveat emptor, see J. H. Baker, An Introduction to English Legal History (London: Butterworths, 1971), p. 199.

100 Maine, Ancient Law, p. 99.

101 Jay M. Feinman and Peter Gabel, "Contract Law as Ideology," in The Politics of Law: A Progressive Critique, 2nd edn., ed. David Kairys (New York: Pantheon Books, 1990), p. 374.

102 Baker, Introduction to English Legal History, p. 188.

103 [Tradesman of the City], The nature of contracts consider'd, as they relate to the third and fourth subscriptions, taken in by the South Sea Company (London, 1720), p. 23.

writes that Blackstone believed that "the more general ethical bases of human law ensured that nothing 'contrary to reason' would be allowed as law."[104] By the mid-eighteenth century, however, Lord Hardwicke complained that "'our statute books are increased to such an enormous size, that they confound every man who is obliged to look into them.'"[105] Lieberman provides evidence that the theorists of the time explained the growth in statute law as a necessary consequence of an expanding and free commercial nation.[106] Rapid commercial expansion, Lord Hardwicke's complaint, periodic criminality, and social disorders: all these suggest a need for re-ordering the house of the law and its subjects. Blackstone is the first to attempt a systematic ordering of English law in his *Commentaries*. He aims to rationalize the mainstay of the commercial nation (though without undercutting the majesty and authority of the law[107]), and to polish the glass in which all were to find their reflection. As an ideologue for the eighteenth-century ruling class, Blackstone was doing his bit to aid the law's construction of new forms of social life in a moment of change driven by economic forces. So too the novelists seek to bring order into the conflicting urges of the self by plotting their characters on the matrix of the law.

The discipline of the law, then, seems to guarantee that those who study it – and to recall Nenner this means most gentlemen – will have a better chance of realizing their goals because their powers of judgment will be predictable, universal, and free from unwarranted interference. David Hume makes this point in his commentary on the discovery of the Justinian pandects: "It is easy to see what advantages Europe must have reaped by its inheriting at once from the ancients, so complete an art, which was also so necessary for giving security to all other arts, and which, by refining, and still more, by bestowing solidity of the judgment, served as a model to farther improvements."[108] In Hume's view, law has a salutary effect upon judgments that were ostensibly once crude and unstable.[109] In justifying the introduction of law into the universities in the middle of the eighteenth century, William Blackstone echoes Hume's sentiment:

But that a science, which distinguishes the criterions of right and wrong; which teaches to establish the one, and prevent, punish, or redress the other; which employs in it's [sic] theory the noblest faculties of the soul, and exerts in its

---

[104] Lieberman, *Province of Legislation*, p. 45.     [105] Quoted in ibid., p. 28.
[106] Ibid., pp. 15–16.
[107] See Boorstin, *Mysterious Science*, pp. 25–30.
[108] David Hume, *The History of England from the Invasion of Julius Caesar to the Revolution in 1688*, 6 vols. (Indianapolis: Liberty Classics, 1983), 2:521.
[109] Leo Braudy, writing on Hume, makes the following observation: "Generalizations about character imply only a psychological coherence. But a study of the growth of law in government and its effects in society can discover a more purely historical coherence. In addition, such a study illustrates that stability can be achieved only when men support the

practice the cardinal virtues of the heart; a science, which is universal in its use
and extent, accommodated to each individual, yet comprehending the whole
community; that a science like this should have ever been deemed unnecessary to
be studied in a university, is matter of astonishment and concern.[110]

In Blackstone's formulation, law is both personal and social. Involving
both reason and sentiment in its deliberations, it becomes in effect the
master science, at once a design for living and the ultimate hermeneutic
tool. Such a version of the law appears in most of the novels in this study.
Its ideological function is to fix the individual in a settled pattern of
behavior and fit the subject for the enjoyment of rational happiness.

Without collapsing law and ideology into a single conceptual unit, I want
to suggest that the law – both as it is represented in and as its principles
inform the following eighteenth-century novels – provides the content and
the form for what Mikhail Bakhtin calls an internally persuasive speech
that enables a subject to constitute herself as an ethically sound and
coherent individual.[111] There are two main reasons for this claim. First,
Michel Foucault (among others) has made the reasonable observation
that "power is tolerable only on condition that it mask a substantial part of
itself ... Power as a pure limit set on freedom is, at least in our society, the
general form of its acceptability."[112] In a liberal society, the public
conscience merely sets limits to the exercise of individual choice. Those
limits, far from being arbitrary, appear as natural negations of the human
drive to engross as much as possible even at the cost of injury to others.
Thus, law appears to take away only so much freedom as is necessary to
insure the harmony of human society, as David Hume writes in "Of the
Original Contract": "Were all men possessed of so inflexible a regard to
justice, that of themselves they would totally abstain from the properties of
others; they had for ever remained in a state of absolute liberty, without
subjection to any magistrate or political society: but this is a state of
perfection of which human nature is justly deemed incapable."[113] Law is
the natural adjunct to human nature; power, rather than being arbitrary,
emanates from an internally persuasive speech that forwards the interests
of the subject of market society.

Second, the subject constitutes her own internally persuasive discourse
in order to represent to herself an imaginary form of the real relations of

system of law." *Narrative Form in History and Fiction: Hume, Fielding, and Gibbon* (Princeton: Princeton University Press, 1970), p. 68.

[110] William Blackstone, *Commentaries on the Laws of England*, "A Facsimile of the First Edition," 4 vols. (Chicago and London: University of Chicago Press, 1979), 1:27.

[111] See Preface, note 9.

[112] Michel Foucault, *The History of Sexuality. Volume 1: An Introduction*, trans. Robert Hurley (New York: Random House, 1978), p. 86.

[113] David Hume, "Of the Original Contract," in *Essays*, p. 460.

production.[114] That is, since ideology (in Althusser's definition) functions
to reconcile contradictions and to create unity from heterogeneity, the
subject must ultimately achieve some kind of détente between her or his
own needs and the limits to these needs set in part by the law. Civil society
may entail compulsive competition upon its inhabitants, but it needs to be
seen in some sense as free and equal. The internalization of juridical discourse collapses the distance between power and personal choice. Instead
of being governed by the will of another, the individual appears self-
governing. In the words of Edmund Arwaker, internalization of the law
"will make us blush as much to do evil, by ourselves, as in the presence of
the most grave, authoritative Person."[115]

Arwaker's description of the external censor could very easily represent
a magistrate clothed in the solemnity of his function. Whether a magistrate
or some other grave person, the figure represents the possibility of punishment or domination by the will of an other, neither of which is desirable for
the novels' protagonists. It is the threat of domination that will come to
pose the greatest danger because, like Godwin's "domestic tyranny," it
insinuates itself into the texture of everyday life and destroys the essence of
individualism. To make juridical discourse into one's own governing principles is to accept changing social conditions and the dominant way of
adapting to and profiting from those conditions. And adaptation and
profit can provide one with feelings of autonomy, thus rendering material
life and personal identity more secure.[116] I shall argue in the pages ahead
that by predicating certain revisions within juridical discourse upon the
notion of an individual capable of self-discipline, the reformulated discourse helps to bring that individual about. *Roderick Random*, *Amelia*, and
*The Vicar of Wakefield* all involve their heroes in legal difficulties that ultimately result in their fulfilling the expectations for individual self-restraint.
Despite their satires on legal corruption, these works affirm the juridical
discourse's conception of human nature by empowering the protagonists
who govern themselves by the discourse's economic principles.

Modern historiographical arguments over the political character of
eighteenth-century English society point to a conjuncture in which residual and emergent ideologies in the forms of custom and commerce are in
uneasy relation.[117] This uneasy relation produces disturbing conflicts and

---

[114] Louis Althusser, *Lenin and Philosophy and Other Essays*, trans. Ben Brewster (New York and
London: Monthly Review Press, 1971), pp. 162–65.

[115] Edmund Arwaker, *Thought Well Employ'd; or, the Duty of Self Observation in the Care and
Regulation of Life according to the Royal Pattern* (London, 1695), p. 14.

[116] Dominick LaCapra describes these dangers as "[i]nternal dialogization [that] introduces
alterity or otherness into the self. It renders personal identity problematic ..." *Rethinking
Intellectual History: Texts, Contexts, Language* (Ithaca and London: Cornell University Press,
1983), p. 312.

[117] For a recent review of J. C. D. Clark's arguments see Jeremy Black, "Introduction" in *British
Politics and Society*, pp. 1–28.

unsettling contradictions. Narrative appropriates juridical ideology as one means of settling conflicts and reconciling contradictions as it attempts to make culture whole, intelligible, and finally commodious. If the effects of juridical discourse upon character are not always manifest, they nonetheless make their presence known in the ways that the protagonists respond to their opportunities and limitations. In the readings that follow I shall examine the way narrative entails fortunes and misfortunes on particular kinds of social behavior and constructs the juridical subject, whose destiny it is to negotiate the demands and satisfactions of civil society and family, searching for an often elusive compromise between necessity and freedom.

# 2

# Roxana's contractual affiliations

In Trade, as in Gaming, Men know neither Father nor Mother, Friend or Relation; ... And if I can get Money by Trade, with getting it fairly, I am to do it against any Body's Interest or Advantage.

Daniel Defoe, Review

## I Introduction

Roxana, the heroine of Daniel Defoe's last novel of the same name, is a precursor of the novel's normative subject: a character who bases a claim to freedom on natural law and its enactment in the positive laws of civil society.[1] It is not as wife, or "widow," or mistress that Roxana gains freedom; rather, it is as one who makes bargains.[2] Her emergence as juridical subject is incomplete, however, because she remains split between affective needs and possessive aspirations. Defoe's narrative fails to integrate the various positions occupied by the heroine, and Roxana never attains the status of full-fledged juridical subject. His final novel – which some have seen as a major step toward the kind of consequentialist plotting that will come to characterize the novel's "great tradition" – presents a clear picture of potential contradictions inherent in the liberal market society that Roxana and her partners inhabit.[3] Roxana may

---

[1] The epigraph from the chapter is taken from *Defoe's Review*, 22 vols., ed. Arthur W. Secord (1938; rpt. New York: AMS Press, 1965), 19:38b (17 Apr. 1711). For the role of natural law in Defoe's fiction, see Maximillian E. Novak, *Defoe and the Nature of Man* (Oxford: Oxford University Press, 1963), pp. 65–88.

[2] Bram Dijkstra reads the novel as an allegory of early capitalist accumulation, a fictionalized rendering of Defoe's business principles found in *The Complete English Tradesman. Defoe and Economics: The Fortunes of "Roxana" in the History of Interpretation* (London: Macmillan Press, 1987), pp. 67–69.

[3] See, for example, David Blewett, *Defoe's Art of Fiction: "Robinson Crusoe," "Moll Flanders," "Colonel Jack" & "Roxana"* (Toronto: University of Toronto Press, 1979), p. 145; Michael Boardman, *Defoe and the Uses of Narrative* (New Brunswick: Rutgers University Press, 1983), pp. 139–41; and John Richetti, *Daniel Defoe* (Boston: Twayne, 1987), p. 118. For the similarity between the *chronique scandaleuse* and *Roxana*, see John Richetti, *Defoe's Narratives: Situations and Structures* (Oxford: Clarendon Press, 1975), 192–95; between "women's fiction" of the 1720s and *Roxana*, see Paula R. Backscheider, *Daniel Defoe: Ambition and Innovation* (Lexington: University Press of Kentucky, 1986), pp. 182–91.

choose to know neither friend nor relation, but she cannot prevent them from making claims upon her.

In his study of Defoe's novels, to which my reading is indebted, John Richetti has argued that the novels' heroes and heroines search for "a comprehensive autonomy of the self." About *Roxana* in particular, Richetti makes the following observation: "Roxana's story as a whole exemplifies the free individual who is somehow free precisely to the extent that he understands social necessity."[4] The precise nature of Roxana's freedom is the issue that I shall address in the following discussion. I will argue that the heroine's freedom is qualified by the very social necessity that she appears to master. If Roxana's story seeks to depict the emergence of the free *juridical* subject, self-conceived as subjected only to its own desires and society's positive laws, it also adumbrates the dialectic of enlightenment as described by Theodor Adorno and Max Horkheimer:

Enlightenment dissolves the injustice of the old inequality – unmediated lordship and mastery – but at the same time perpetuates it in universal mediation, in the relation of any one existent to any other ... The blessing that the market does not enquire after one's birth is paid for by the barterer, in that he models the potentialities that are his by birth on the production of the commodities that can be bought in the market.[5]

Over the course of her adventures, Roxana discovers that the subject is not constituted solely by "commodities that can be bought in the market." In the storm that overtakes her as she and her servant Amy return to England, for example, Roxana's money – or the realization of her potential as commodity – cannot buy safety. Only the combined efforts of the seamen save her from the forces of nature. In this allegory of civil society as ship, the individual alone cannot master nature. Social cohesion in the form of common effort is a necessary response to necessity itself, belying the imagined autonomy of the individual.

Necessity alone, however, cannot represent the cohesive force that binds society because civil society cannot be represented as a social formation in perpetual crisis. In addition to necessity, Defoe's text offers apparently voluntary relations of sympathy and gratitude as cohesive forces joining civil society's subjects. Although there are many examples of the cohesive function served by sympathy in *Roxana*, the paradigmatic instance involves the heroine and the Quaker, with whom Roxana lodges in her final quest for propriety. Roxana is moved to an act of gratuitous charity toward her landlady because Roxana sees in the Quaker a version of her younger self. The identification turns sympathy in the direction of egoism (self-interest), and civil society coheres because Roxana (the proto-

---

[4] Richetti, *Defoe's Narratives*, p. 14, n. 23; p. 225.
[5] Adorno and Horkheimer, *Dialectic of Enlightenment*, pp. 12–13.

juridical subject) recalls her own earlier necessitous condition. The role of identity and difference in the dynamic relation between giver and receiver, victim and savior is made clear in the following analogy used by Roxana to explain her concern for the Quaker: "When a poor Debtor, having lain long in the *Compter*, or *Ludgate*, or the *Kings-Bench*, for Debt, afterwards gets out, rises again in the World, and grows rich; such an one is a certain Benefactor to the Prisoners there, and perhaps to every Prison he passes by, as long as he lives; for he remembers the dark Days of his own Sorrow ..."[6] In the protagonist's imagination, it is only the once-victimized subject of civil society who comes to the aid of successive victims. Rather than being an innate attractive force, sympathy reveals itself as a by-product of victimization, a mechanism by which modern civil society effects its own cohesion. That which appears to be a spontaneous expression of the subject – and thus a mark of the subject's freedom – is actually an effect of the structures of civil society. Sympathy is not only the *necessary* psychological response to the juridical subject's vulnerable and anxious position, but it is also the memory of an originary violence that endows the person with subjectivity. Sympathy provides the proof of cohesion because all juridical selves share a common subjectivity by virtue of their liability to the workings of a market economy.

*Roxana* represents civil society as a social relation defined by both necessity and sympathy, which in turn correspond to conditions of dependence and autonomy. The narrator attempts to fashion herself as autonomous subject by rejecting "necessary" or compulsory filiations and choosing "sympathetic" or voluntary affiliations.[7] In her early career, having suffered victimization at the hands of her profligate male relations (necessary filiations), Roxana seeks contractual relations that will free her from future distresses. Her early actions are influenced by civil society's failure to provide the kind of voluntary charity that she later describes. She seeks freedom from unconditional dependence through the contract, and her actions suggest that this voluntary instrument will enable her to escape the material side-effects of the process of accumulation. Roxana discovers, however, that the contracting subject occupies various "positions" within society, and that the dreams of the pure subject of accumulation turn into a nightmare return of repressed and rejected relation. But before repressed relation erupts into the fantasy of juridically regulated

---

[6] Daniel Defoe, *Roxana*, ed. Jane Jack (Oxford: Oxford University Press, 1981), p. 253. All subsequent references are to this edition and are noted parenthetically in the text.

[7] I have taken the terms *filiation* and *affiliation* from Edward Said, "Introduction: Secular Criticism," in his *The World, the Text, and the Critic* (Cambridge, Mass: Harvard University Press, 1983), pp. 16–24. Writing about nineteenth and twentieth-century authors, Said states that "few things are as problematic and as universally fraught as what we might have supposed to be the mere natural continuity between one generation and the next" (16).

intercourse, Roxana creates a self that appears to have no obligations beyond those of the "mutual Compact [that] is mutually obliging."[8]

## II Naturalization of the subject

Roxana begins the "History of [her] Life and Vast Variety of Fortunes" with the following account of her origins: "I WAS BORN, *as my Friends told me,* at the City of POICTIERS, in the Province, or County of POICTOU, in *France,* from whence I was brought to *England* by my Parents, who fled for their Religion about the Year 1683, when the Protestants were Banish'd from *France* by the Cruelty of their Persecutors" (5). The phrase "*as my Friends told me*" indicates that the speaking subject – its autonomy boldly announced by the opening I – simultaneously reveals its dependence in its formulation as an object in the memory of "Friends," who recount her being brought to England. Thus, the first challenge to the subject's autonomy lies in its natural or filiative ties. France and Poictiers of 1683 fade into the abstractions of "Religion" and "Cruelty." These abstractions, revealing the subject's fantasy that all experience can be mastered through manipulating representation, denote her will to power over her origins.

From the very beginning of her narrative, then, Roxana strives to represent herself as she sees fit. This is more than a self-evident statement about what is after all confessional speech in which, as G. A. Starr has argued convincingly, the narrator intends to win the sympathy of her audience by emphasizing her victimization.[9] Nor is it only the rhetorical strategy demanded by Roxana's narrational conscience, the "*Constant wakeing Centinel,*" "The Rule of Life to a Man," supported by Reason and "Divine Law," that underwrites the truth of her observation, although this too is important.[10] Rather, Roxana's narrative can be read as the objective correlative of her juridical autonomy: the right to speak for herself without subjection to another's will. Gordon Schochet has noted that in Stuart England "[i]t was only as a member of a family that one acquired any meaning or status in society, for it was *through* the family that an individual came into contact with the outside world."[11] Rather than being "spoken

---

[8] Daniel Defoe, *Conjugal Lewdness; or, Matrimonial Whoredom* (1727; rpt. Gainesville: Scholars' Facsimiles and Reprints, 1967), p. 126. All works by Defoe cited in this chapter have been definitely ascribed to him. For a discussion of the Defoe canon, see P. N. Furbank and W. R. Owens, *The Canonisation of Daniel Defoe* (New Haven and London: Yale University Press, 1988).

[9] G. A. Starr, "Sympathy v. Judgement in Roxana's First Liaison" in *The Augustan Milieu: Essays presented to Louis A. Landa,* eds. Henry Knight Miller, Eric Rothstein, G. S. Rousseau (Oxford: Clarendon Press, 1970), pp. 59–76.

[10] *More Reformation,* l. 489, discussed in Backschieder, *Defoe: Ambition and Innovation,* p. 23; and *Conjugal Lewdness,* p. 125. On Defoe's attitudes toward conscience, see G. A. Starr, *Defoe and Casuistry* (Princeton: Princeton University Press, 1971), p. 3 and *passim.*

[11] Gordon Schochet, *Patriarchalism in Political Thought: The Authoritarian Family and Political Speculation and Attitudes Especially in Seventeenth-Century England* (New York: Basic Books, 1975), p. 65.

by" her friends, Roxana will speak herself. Michel Foucault has described this mode of address – confessional speech – as an indication of changing relations between the individual and the "order of civil and religious powers" in the early-modern period: "For a long time, the individual was vouched for by the reference of others and the demonstration of his ties to the commonweal (family, allegiance, protection); then he was authenticated by the discourse of truth he was able or obliged to pronounce concerning himself. The truthful confession was inscribed at the heart of the procedures of individualization by power."[12] In Roxana's fictional "authentication," civil and religious powers work at cross purposes. The contract's infinite potential is in contradiction with religion's limiting codes (at least as those codes are received by the narrator). Thus, in order to confess the truth, she must simultaneously represent her quest for a happy living (produced by the civil power) and condemn it (produced by the religious power). This discursive contradiction overlays the material contradictions that it seeks to reformulate, for the civil culture that remains independent of claims to kinship falls into conflict with the traditional (religious) culture that includes the patriarchal filiations that Roxana seeks to escape. The novel can be read as an heroic attempt to bring these conflicting powers to some kind of subjective understanding. But by the end of the narrative Roxana has produced the truth that she is unable to "represent" herself. In fact, in the famous conclusion to the novel, representation collapses beneath the weight of unresolved contradictions.

As she begins her story, however, Roxana sets out to solve the complex problems of filiation and affiliation. Describing herself as the child of "People of better Fashion, than ordinarily the People call'd REFUGEES at that Time were," Roxana chooses fashion and wealth over against religious, national, or political affiliations. Neither the language of France nor the Huguenots' confessional practices make up her self; rather, she is the product of material conditions, an important part of which involves the activities of truck, barter, or exchange. In her living memory (*"as I remember"* replaces the earlier *"as my Friends told me"*) she is distinguished from others by "a considerable Value in *French* Brandy, Paper, and other Goods." Or as Marx writes in *Capital*, she is in the process of becoming of that order of persons who "exist for one another merely as representatives of, and therefore, as owners of, commodities."[13] Home, community, nation signify only to the extent that in an international market specific national commodities have a high relative value. Roxana's preference for a materially fashioned self over determination by national or religious allegiances

---

[12] Foucault, *History of Sexuality, Volume 1*, pp. 58–59.

[13] Karl Marx, *Capital: A Critique of Political Economy. Volume 1*, trans. Samuel Moore and Edward Aveling, ed. Frederick Engels (New York: International Publishers, 1967), p. 85.

also indicates her wish to be exempt from the historical forces that enmesh the individual's destiny with that of a larger social unit.[14] In this regard she is exercising the mandate described by John Locke in his *Second Treatise*: "For *Every Man's Children* being by Nature as *free* as himself, or any of his Ancestors ever were, may, whilst they are in that Freedom, choose what Society they will join themselves to, what Common-wealth they will put themselves under."[15] Rather than being an entity determined by national or political powers, Roxana chooses to naturalize herself as an English subject.

Johnson's *Dictionary* defines *naturalize* as a process by which an alien is given the rights accorded to subjects of the adoptive country, and as a process by which the strange is made familiar.[16] As an implicit trope at the beginning of Defoe's novel, *naturalization* familiarizes the self-generating fantasies of civil society's juridical subject. First, it moves the heroine from an absolutist to a quasi-contractarian state, endowing her with universal rights and displacing the myth of chthonic identity. Second, it operates according to the rationale of exchange. Naturalization maximizes individual potential. In an ideal global capitalist market national identity would be displaced by commodity representation. In less abstract terms, the "naturalized" subject brings national enrichment, strictly speaking. In the England of 1709 the Whigs supported a General Naturalization Bill aimed at all resident Protestant aliens. According to historian Geoffrey Holmes, the Whigs were "eagerly welcoming the injection of foreign capital and enterprise into the English economy which Protestant refugees had already provided." A Tory MP on the other hand, feared that naturalized subjects might "go a great way to blot out and extinguish the English race." The bill was enacted and then repealed two years later.[17] Writing a half century after the repeal, William Blackstone claims that all persons are presumed to bear an allegiance to their natal land "'written by the finger of the law in their hearts.'"[18] Moreover, the allegiance due to a king from his natural-born subject is "a principle of universal law ... intrinsic, and primitive, and antecedent to the other [subsequently

---

[14] In the *Review* for 4 June 1706 Defoe writes that the Huguenots "receive Protection and Assistance from the protestant Powers as a People, *but are under no Form or Character as a Body*; and this I think, they are *short in*, tho' it is not too late to retrieve it" (7:271a). Clearly Defoe saw some advantage to collective action based on a communal identity, whether national or confessional. As a body, Defoe goes on to say, the Huguenots may be able one day to force the French King to "recognize that Sovereignty of Conscience over his and over all human Authority" (271b).

[15] Locke, *Two Treatises*, 2:73:358. See also Schochet, *Patriarchalism*, pp. 247–54.

[16] Samuel Johnson, *A Dictionary of the English Language* (1755; facs. rpt., London: Times Books, 1979), s.v. *naturalize*.

[17] Geoffrey Holmes, *British Politics in the Age of Ann* (London: Macmillan, 1967), p. 69. The MP's name was Henry Campion.

[18] Blackstone is quoting Coke in *Commentaries*, 1:357.

sworn]; and cannot be devested without the concurrent act of that prince to whom it was first due."[19] By virtue of Roxana's choice of national affiliation, the author of *The True Born Englishman* enters a discursive struggle between patriarchal and liberal theories of political obligation on the side of the latter.[20]

Roxana's naturalization proceeds, predictably enough, through her reconstruction of traditional familial patterns. She mentions her mother only twice, both times in passing and the last to note her death. The mother's insignificance emphasizes Roxana's identification with the good sense of her father, an astute businessman, who refuses to be cheated by the misrepresentations of his co-sectarians and fellow refugees. That this good business sense is passed from father to daughter (Roxana's brother is a bankrupt, something that the father and Roxana avoid) plays an important role in the heroine's plot. Whereas she acts wisely with her money, she does not always do so with her men. In other words, her father's good sense is not complemented by what we might assume was her mother's prudent spousal choice. Granted that this argument is speculative, it nonetheless brings into relief the discursive disjuncture between money and family that rends the heroine and her text. The brief mention of the mother registers an unrecognized loss that attends the naturalizing process in a text that yearns to masculinize its heroine.

The reconstruction of the family is necessary because of its potential for oppression. Both money and family are dangerous, but the dangers of family are the subject of the novel's opening. As her brother's bankruptcy and her subsequent marriage to the Brewer demonstrate, the family has the power to render each of its members helpless by making one member's obsession the grounds of misery for all others. Blood relations check the juridical subject's freedom by tying her to costly obligations. In Roxana's narrative the old pull of the blood and the desire for gain are in contradiction, for accumulation means at best the sublimation of relation and at worst its negation when relation is seen as a potential threat to the main stock. In *Roxana* the alienating effects of market society are not meliorated by *familiarity*: family and civil society cannot be harmonized. Rather than being conceived of as a haven from marketplace competition in the public sphere, the family appears as yet another institution that fixes identity, depletes resources, and limits opportunity.

If the family hinders the subject's quest for a naturalized, individuated self, neither does civil society allow her to do just as she wishes. Although

[19] Blackstone, *Commentaries*, 1:358. Schochet argues that the consent theorists made "[p]olitical obligation ... something artificial" (*Patriarchalism* 55).

[20] For the argument that Defoe's politics were more conservative than my statement suggests, see Manuel Schonhorn, *Defoe's Politics: Parliament, Power, Kingship, and "Robinson Crusoe"* (Cambridge: Cambridge University Press, 1991), pp. 4, 70–71.

Roxana is naturalized in the strict sense of the word – she later writes that she "esteem'd [herself] an *English-Woman*, tho' [she] was born in *France*" (111) – she does not attain the radical autonomy she seeks. As naturalized English-Woman she still accumulates lived experience through contact with other contracting and non-contracting social agents, even though she acts only as the representative of successive and determinate moments in commodity exchange. That such relations are not circumscribed spatially and temporally is made clearest in Roxana's relation to her servant Amy, a relation that is at once juridical and familial. As servant, Amy occupies a juridical position that Defoe proposed elsewhere to regulate by a formal, standardized contract.[21] At the same time Amy's devotion exceeds that belonging to her "place" and takes on a filiative, obsessive character. Although Roxana praises Amy's devotion, she also declares her status as servant: "tho' I acknowledg'd her Kindness and Fidelity, yet it was but a bad Coin that she was paid in at last ..." (16). To be sure Roxana speaks metaphorically here, but the metonymic structure which links servant to coin reminds us that Amy occupies two unharmonized positions. The disjunction between these two positions and the peculiar relationship that emerges therefrom enable Amy to accumulate "all the Secret History of [Roxana's] Life" (317), and thus power over her. The resulting conflict between the familial and juridical positions expresses itself in misunderstanding, aggression, rage, and finally in an extra-juridical act that reduces the narrative to incoherence.

In this brief discussion of the stakes underlying Roxana's opening rhetorical strategy, I have introduced Amy to indicate that other agents ultimately contest in a particularly intractable manner Roxana's desire for civil indemnity from all demands on her person and resources. The desire for indemnity, expressed in Roxana's naturalized self, emerges in the initial pages of her confession as a civil abstraction distinct from her natal origins and as a rhetorical construct representing the internally persuasive discourse of the authoritative speaking subject. Just as the heroine seeks to control "natural" events by selective representation of her entry into the world, so too she aims for civil mastery through contractually regulated affiliations. Thus the history that she begins to write with such deft assurance seems to promise to confirm her as the "Fortunate Mistress" of the book's title page. But as her contracts become ever more lucrative and enabling, the experience of striking these contracts accumulates in surprising and unforeseen ways, ultimately embodied in other agents, who

---

[21] Daniel Defoe, "Everybody's Business is Nobody's Business" (1725), in *The Novels and Miscellaneous Works of Daniel De Foe*, 7 vols. (London, 1854), 2:509–10. Through formal contract Defoe hopes to end the tyranny of the servant class, empowered by market forces of supply and demand. In the same pamphlet Defoe complains about the ease with which a servant-maid moves from place to place in search of higher wages, occasionally taking up whoring when between jobs. See pp. 500, 506.

demand a kind of editorial right over Roxana's confession. Before Roxana's initial eloquence lapses into final incoherence, however, come a series of contractual affiliations that constitute the juridical subject's precarious position between necessity and freedom, experience and representation.

## III Contract and consort

Much of Roxana's narrative describes the bargains that lead toward her empowerment as a full juridical subject and the liaisons through which she accumulates a "character." The tension between the form (contract) and the content (sexual liaison) of Roxana's affiliations reveals an imbalance between material conditions and juridical principles. As a wife, she suffers the legal disablements of *feme covert*. As independent juridical subject she enjoys the opportunity for profit through expressed or implied contracts. As a woman she possesses value as a desirable commodity in the concupiscent marketplace. At the same time, like a tradesman she must be careful of her reputation, which can be ruined by a rumor originating at the tea table or the coffee house.[22] With its protagonist as both juridical subject and woman, the novel represents both the economization of sex and the sexualization of the economy. Publicity vies with privacy, gender-constraints with contractual freedoms, decorum with the drive to accumulate. *Roxana*, then, describes the moment before sexuality and economy are relegated to separate spheres; its transitional status makes it possible to bring into full relief the anatomy of the juridical subject in its infancy.[23]

The split between rational calculation and affective association is a symptom of civil society's ideological contradictions, produced by what one critic has called "the secularization of life [that] leads to a growth of means-end rationality, whereby there is 'the methodological attainment of a definitely given and practical end by the use of an increasingly precise calculation of . . . means.'"[24] This increasingly precise calculation of means results in the individual's alienation from the society that provides the place for the exercise of such means. An instrumental reason that objectifies the world in order to master it for its own ends produces a radically impoverished and reified world. Peter Dews, commenting on Theodor Adorno's version of instrumental reason, notes that the bourgeois ego

---

[22] See Daniel Defoe, *Complete English Tradesman in Familiar Letters*, 2nd edn. (London, 1727), p. 188. John Robert Moore notes that "[t]his manual was spoiled by revisions made not long after Defoe's death." For a brief summary of its early printing history, including this edition, see his *A Checklist of the Writings of Daniel Defoe*, 2nd edn. (Hamden: Archon Books, 1971), p. 199.

[23] See Armstrong, *Desire and Domestic Fiction*, esp. pp. 23–24.

[24] David Held, *Introduction to Critical Theory: Horkheimer to Habermas* (Berkeley and Los Angeles: University of California Press, 1980), p. 65. Held is quoting Max Weber.

as the form of organization of the drives, contains a moment of freedom, insofar as it is only through this process that human beings acquire the ability to foresee, calculate and withhold which frees them from the contingencies of inner and outer nature ... At the same time, however, ... the unconscious drives can be seen as embodying the demand for a happiness which, for Adorno, is inseparable from sensuous contentment, and which is crushed by the pressure of instrumental rationality.[25]

On the one hand, Roxana begins her vast variety of fortunes by testifying of her failure to internalize the publicly and domestically encouraged restraints upon appetite. Customary restraints that might have checked her appetites are weakened by libidinized spectacles such as London, which, Roxana informs us, is "a large and gay City, [that] took with me mighty well, who, from my being a Child, lov'd a Crowd, and to see a great-many fine Folks" (5); or her first husband, a "jolly, handsome Fellow," who "danc'd well" (7). At the early stages of her formation she is insufficiently rational. In the eroticized spectacle, moreover, desire is freed from the limit of exhaustion, and pleasure is a function of conspicuous luxury. Roxana never fully masters these early libidinal tendencies. In fact, it is part of the novel's ideological project to show that they cannot be mastered by making them into the heroine's inner necessity, a "psychological" weakness (rather than an existential condition) that ultimately defeats her attempts to foresee and calculate. On the other hand, as Roxana details her progress, she begins to operate under the guidance of a rationality that categorically excludes all libidinal investments except mastery. Even when Roxana, disgusted by the excesses of her contractual life, asks herself "*What was I a Whore for now?*" (201), and shows some consciousness of the irrationality that has diverted her quest for freedom, she continues to choose the contract's logic over other kinds of "sensuous contentment." How she comes to this choice will be the focus of the rest of this discussion.

Roxana's first contractual adventure in her marriage to the Brewer follows the pattern of companionate spousal choice described by historian Lawrence Stone.[26] Having freely chosen her profligate husband, who "had no Knowledge of his Accounts" (9), Roxana discovers that she is powerless to influence him. Although she "foresaw the Consequence of this [neglect], and attempted several times to perswade him to apply himself to his Business," her husband sells the brewery, squanders the profits from the sale, and flees England to escape his creditors (10). Roxana lacks executive power over her life because she is subject *de jure* to her husband's

[25] Peter Dews, *Logics of Disintegration: Post-Structuralist Thought and the Claims of Critical Theory* (London: Verso Books, 1987), p. 141.
[26] Stone, *Family, Sex and Marriage*, pp. 325–36.

will. In fact, the marriage contract robs her not only of a voice in household affairs but also of the power to better her circumstances. At this point in the narrative, Roxana is far from being the self-reliant juridical subject who pursues her own interests with willed determination: "What to do I knew not, nor to whom to have recourse; to keep in the House where I was, I could not, the Rent being too great; and to leave it without his Order, if my Husband should return, I could not think of that neither; so that I continued extremely perplex'd, melancholly, and discourag'd, to the last Degree" (13). The marriage contract disables Roxana even after her husband has fled England. It has put her in the position of the obedient *femme*, passively awaiting the return of her absent *baron*. Moreover, she has not had an opportunity to accumulate either the knowledge or the money that will free her from want until his return.[27] As Carole Pateman has argued, the marriage contract appears here less a mutual agreement than an instrument of force.[28] To be contractually joined to this man, who reappears appropriately enough in the service of the absolutist French monarch, is to lose autonomy rather than to gain it.

As abandoned wife, Roxana lives in distress amidst a heap of rags, her only recourse to tears and her only resource the invisibility acquired by "miserable Objects." She appears to have returned to an almost Hobbesian state of nature, where, as W. Austin Flanders has observed, "she is confronted by the indifference of Londoners to the welfare of others, even their relations . . ."[29] As the first natural law of self-preservation assumes primacy, Roxana thinks of consuming her children in order to survive. The fantasy describes this particular family as the site of necessity, the antithesis of civil society's promise of an autonomous and commodious living. But the ideal family need not be characterized by the necessity of natural filiation. Marriage begins as an affiliative choice. This conundrum (that which is freely chosen changing into "natural" bonds of blood) is temporarily resolved in the way that Roxana escapes her misery: through the charity of an "Uncle-in-Law," who takes her children and enables her eventual return to civil society. Roxana's next liaison with a man of business further suspends the dilemma by civilizing a potentially filiative relation through an equitable contract.

When Roxana fails to pay her rent, she tells us, the landlord "had gone

---

[27] Defoe's attitude toward this situation can be assessed in his belief that a wife should be able "to carry on some business without [her husband], if he is forc'd to fail, and fly; as many have been, when the creditors have encourag'd the wife to carry on the trade for the support of her family and children, when he perhaps may never shew his head again" (*Complete English Tradesman* 294).

[28] Pateman, *The Sexual Contract*, pp. 87, 100–1, 104–15.

[29] W. Austin Flanders, *Structures of Experience: History, Society, and Personal Life in the Eighteenth-Century British Novel* (Columbia: University of South Carolina Press, 1984), p. 289. For another Hobbesian reading of the novel see Virginia Ogden Birdsall, *Defoe's Perpetual Seekers: A Study of the Major Fiction* (Lewisburg: Bucknell University Press, 1985), pp. 143–70.

so far as to seize my Goods, and to carry some of them off too." Once he "came to know [Roxana's] circumstances" and once the children have been sent away, however, he "look'd kinder upon [her]" (25). His attraction to this woman in distress voids the contractual relation existing between landlord and tenant and substitutes an act of kindness for it.[30] Although the Landlord derives his power from his material advantages, he does not use force or fraud to get what he wants from Roxana. Instead, this civilized man respects the limits defined by Roxana's as yet dominant discourse of "Honesty and Good Manners" (34) and counters that with the language of contractual rights and duties. He chooses contract and rational argument as the surest means to secure both of them the "Prospect of happy Living" (7).

Despite the fact that G. A. Starr finds the Landlord's moral stature qualified by his use of *double entendre*, he stands as a figure for whom the public conscience – as embodied in the equitable principles of a natural law only imperfectly realized in positive law – provides the means for personal fulfillment and freedom.[31] The natural legality of his ends makes them moral, and no amount of jest (an indicator of concupiscence) can qualify that morality. He justifies his coupling with Roxana by arguing that when obligation ceases to be mutual it also ceases to be binding. Because their respective spouses no longer fulfill their obligations, he and Roxana become free to "take one another fairly." He even claims that such behavior would be sanctioned by "the Custom of the Place, in several Countries Abroad" (38). Comparative jurisprudence allows him to ignore the sacramental character of marriage. He has a secular mind, and he uses it to justify his actions.[32]

No matter what intentional turn is accorded the Landlord's rhetoric and despite his motives for helping Roxana, his words and actions reveal an implicit understanding of the value and efficacy of reciprocity and trust

---

[30] Hugo Grotius defines the contract as "all acts of benefit to others, except mere acts of kindness," *De Jure Belli ac Pacis*, 2 vols., trans. Francis W. Kelsey (Oxford: The Clarendon Press, 1925), 2:346.

[31] Starr, "Sympathy," p. 70.

[32] Novak discusses the Landlord's and Amy's arguments in *Nature* and concludes that those arguments may be justified according to natural law (101). Pufendorf writes the following about the marriage contract: "by mere natural law one of the two will be freed from the marriage bond when the other is guilty of malicious desertion, as well as of obstinate and voluntary refusal to perform the due rights of marriage" (*De Jure Naturae et Gentium*, 2 vols., trans. C. H. and W. A. Oldfather [Oxford: Clarendon Press, 1934], 1:877; quoted in part by Novak, *Nature*, p. 101). One handbook of the period explains the law in the following manner: "By Statute, it is Felony for a Man or Woman, of the Ages to consent to Matrimony, to marry a second Wife or Husband, the first being then living: But if either a Husband or Wife, shall be beyond the Seas, or be absent in *England*, the Space of Seven Years, and the one of them not know whether the other be living within that Time, it is not Felony to marry again" (*A Treatise of Feme Coverts: Or the Lady's Law*, intro. Lance E. Dickson [1732; facs. rpt., South Hackensack, New Jersey: Rothman Reprints, 1974], pp. 46–47).

in what is clearly a "market" transaction. Roxana tells us that he restored her impounded furniture "as a Satisfaction for the Cruelty he had us'd me with before" (32). Instead of *caveat emptor*, the Landlord exhibits a much more complex form of calculation that embodies his individualist moral economy. He represents his actions as being governed by an equitable conscience that recognizes the need to temper a procrustean "justice." However one judges the motives' effect upon the action, the Landlord presents the reader with a complex instance of the intermingling of contractual freedom and moral obligation. That his equitable language is more than mere casuistry can be seen in his remorse after bedding Amy. He regrets this action both because he has violated the contract and because he has injured the wife of his "Affection" (47). He does not mention transgressing a metaphysical law. That he returned to Amy's bed only at Roxana's urging emphasizes the juridical nature of the bond that ties him to Roxana: he is temporarily released from obligation by the person who made the contract with him. This episode adumbrates the complex relations between contractual freedom and other social codes, relations that the text continues to explore as one possible path toward a general and satisfying version of autonomy.

To make the formal equality of the contract convincing, the narrative works through the Landlord to lessen the material inequalities dividing him from Roxana. The establishment of the preconditions for formal equality involves a nominal transfer of power from landlord to tenant. After supplying Roxana with all she needs to furnish her house and to "Let it out to Lodgings, for the Summer Gentry," the Landlord suggests that "he would furnish one Chamber for himself, and would come and be one of [her] Lodgers, if [she] would give him Leave" (32). Although Roxana demurs at his *need* to ask leave, the Landlord's request gives her sovereignty over the household, and thereby adjusts slightly the power relation between the two parties.

The establishment of material equality, however, is effected by a concluding contract, which protects Roxana's interests by providing mutually acceptable sanctions for any breach of trust on the Landlord's part. Roxana writes that the Landlord drew up "a Contract in Writing, wherein he engag'd himself to me; to cohabit constantly with me; to provide for me in all Respects as a Wife; ... an Obligation in the Penalty of 7000 l. never to abandon me; and at last, shew'd me a Bond for 500 l. to be paid to me, or to my Assigns, within three Months after his Death" (42). Earnest money of "three-score Guineas" seals the bargain and transfers actual power from the man to the woman in the form of wealth and security. The difference in the liaisons between Roxana and the Brewer, on the one hand, and her and the Landlord, on the other, is similar to the difference in Roxana's French and English origins. The first appears natural, spontaneous, and affective while the second is calculated, pragmatic, and supported by material guarantees. Roxana is not a wife but is *like* one, fashioned by agreement and granted limited powers. That the Landlord's motive for striking this agreement is his desire for the woman's person further indicates the objective powers of the contract to redistribute wealth through apparently subjective processes. That is, the calculations appear to be in accord with "natural" market forces, thereby introducing another moment of naturalization. The Landlord's civil actions prefigure a utopian moment in which desire recognizes reason, and both move toward fulfillment under the sign of subjective reciprocity. His unembarrassed negotiations constitute a juridical – perhaps even a social – ideal.

The contract works as it is intended, providing Roxana with the resources to meet the contingency of "a dreadful Disaster." In addition to making her "very Rich," the contractual arrangement with the Landlord (who has changed into a Jeweler) has also empowered her (51). Her condition at the Landlord/Jeweler's death differs substantially from her condition when her husband deserted her. Helpless and friendless, Roxana was then more determined object than determining subject. Her state was spontaneous, resistant to fashioning by her will. After the Landlord/Jeweler's death, however, she represents herself as a widow. When the dead man's "Head Manager" comes to France to inquire into his master's affairs, Roxana confidently assumes a juridical mask, to which belong certain rights:

> I made no Scruple of calling myself Madam –, the Widow of Monsieur –, the *English* Jeweller; and as I spoke *French* naturally, I did not let him know but that I was his Wife, married in *France*, and that I had not heard that he had any Wife in *England*; ... and that I had good Friends in *Poictou* ... who would take Care to have Justice done me in *England*, out of his Estate.                                  (56)

Although Roxana knowingly misrepresents herself, her determination suggests that she believes herself entitled to her partner's money. She goes about the business of acquiring that money with a decisiveness in marked contrast to the tortured self-examination preceding the sexual exchange that is the source of her empowerment. This important difference effectively separates the means of accumulation from accumulation itself, thereby creating a space for the moral register of the text. This moral register will come to tyrannize over sexual behavior (the means of accumulation rather than the originating practice of filiation) by relegating it to the private sphere over which the juridical discourse has no apparent power. At the same time, acquisitive motives themselves are rationalized (in both senses of that word) and exempted from critical scrutiny.[33] Thus

---

[33] This view runs counter to Novak's assertion that Defoe condemns avarice in *Roxana*. See Novak's *Economics and the Fiction of Daniel Defoe* (Berkeley and Los Angeles: University of

the mature juridical subject – Roxana as widow who, upon advice from "an eminent Lawyer" makes a "Process of Dower upon the Estate"[34] – exists simultaneously with the guilty sexual subject, and each subject answers ultimately to different codes.

The sexual subject dominates her next liaison with the Prince who resides at the French Court. In what appears to be a regression for the newly and contractually enriched heroine, this relationship is shaped primarily by gender and status. Paradoxically, but in a way that reveals Defoe's acute understanding of the interplay of residual and emergent structures of experience, Roxana's desire for autonomy is supported by patriarchal power. As a still untried public offering, Roxana needs an underwriter. Just as the Landlord grew rich by selling jewels to the French aristocracy, so Roxana stands to profit from her business with the Prince. As the old order barters a birthright for a buckle, the new order gains more and more substance. And yet there is something troubling about this alliance, as if association with aristocratic decadence contaminates the suppliers. In order to escape that tainting association, Roxana figures her liaison as a natural compulsion, based partly on the patriarchal discourse from which she is emerging.

In her retrospective narration, of course, she sees the event somewhat differently, as near to seeing it under the aspect of eternity as she ever comes. The experiential voice records the power of the Prince's charisma:

the Devil had play'd a new Game with me, and prevail'd with me to satisfie myself with this Amour, as a lawful thing; that a Prince of such Grandeur, and Majesty; so infinitely superior to me; and one who had made such an Introduction by an unparallel'd Bounty, I could not resist; and therefore, that it was very Lawful for me to do it, being at that time perfectly single, and uningag'd to any other Man ...

(68)

In the description of her willing subjection to the majestic and bounteous person of the ruler can be heard the languages of self-interest and patriarchal non-resistance. "Bounty," status, and law justify her action. Roxana has also learned from the Landlord, in that she reasons that the lawfulness of the Amour depends as much upon her own previous "uningag'd" state as it does upon the Prince's person. Despite her sub-

California Press, 1962), pp. 132–39. Dijkstra criticizes Novak's reading and writes that "[f]or Defoe 'avarice' was one of the motive forces of the world of trade, a basic concomitant of self-interest ... the 'necessity' of the rich" (*Defoe and Economics* 168–69). See Novak's damning review of Dijkstra in *Modern Philology* 87.1 (1989): 89–92.

[34] According to *A Treatise of Feme Coverts*, the widow of a man who dies intestate is entitled to one-third of his personal possessions and "the Third Part of such Lands or Tenements as were her Husband's at any Time, during the Coverture, whether she have Issue by her Husband or not ..." (62). For a recent study of the complicated historical evolution of dower rights in English law, see Susan Staves, *Married Women's Separate Property in England, 1660–1833* (Cambridge, MA and London: Harvard University Press, 1990), chs. 2–3.

sequent confession of error, Roxana's experience shows the way in which the juridical subject acquires personal power.

During her liaison with the Prince, Roxana takes an aggressive role in managing the seduction that betters her position. In a clever and startling adumbration of the *quid pro quo* that ultimately results in another real transfer of power, Roxana describes a dialectic of freedom and demand working itself out through the exchange of sex and money: "he had all the Freedom with me, that it was possible for me to grant, so he gave me Leave to use as much Freedom with him, another Way, and that was, to have every thing of him, I thought fit to command; and yet I did not ask of him with an Air of Avarice, as if I was greedily making a Penny of him; but I manag'd him with such Art, that he generally anticipated my Demands ..." (66). In this libertine moment of mutual freedom Roxana makes her fantasies of wealth and power the object of the Prince's desire. As John Richetti has astutely noted, "[s]he can use her nature to move the Prince to a state of surprise where he is effectively as much out of control as she is in command."[35] In terms of the text's political allegory, the juridical subject emerges with the executive assistance of the Prince, whose insistent need for her cannot be repressed. To manage the executive, the subject practices the "Art" of self-control, tempering demands and checking avarice under the reasonable assumption that moderately acquisitive self-interest compounded daily over a fixed term makes best business sense. Any sacrifice of autonomy by the subject is recompensed by both her material gain and the protection that the executive affords. As Richard Tuck notes in an article on natural law theory, "[b]oth Pufendorf and Grotius believed that what was *right* (*honestum*), was so because it was fundamentally *profitable* (*utile*) to an individual in need of protection from his fellow men ..."[36] Roxana's apparent subjection is actually a steady process of accumulation.

The narrative's representation of this elaborate process and its dangers provides a sketch of the juridical subject's prehistory. The power relations obtaining between Roxana and the Prince are the crucial part of this prehistory:

He sat as one astonish'd, a good-while, looking at me, without speaking a Word, till I came quite up to him, kneel'd on one Knee to him, and almost whether he would or no, kiss'd his Hand; he took me up, and stood up himself, ... he perceiv'd Tears to run down my Cheeks; My Dear, *says he*, aloud, what mean these Tears? My Lord, *said I*, after some little Check, for I cou'd not speak presently ... they are not Tears of Sorrow, but Tears of Joy; it is impossible for me to see myself ... in the

35  Richetti, *Defoe's Narratives*, p. 218.
36  Richard Tuck, "The 'Modern' Theory of Natural Law," in *The Languages of Political Theory in Early-Modern Europe*, ed. Anthony Pagden, Ideas In Context (Cambridge: Cambridge University Press, 1987), p. 105.

Arms of a Prince of such Goodness, such immense Bounty, and be treated in such a Manner; 'tis not possible, my Lord, *said* I, to contain the Satisfaction of it; and it will break out in an Excess in some measure proportion'd to your immense Bounty, and to the Affection which your Highness treats me with, who am so infinitely below you.                                                    (71–72)

Roxana commands the scene with a combination of self-assertive gesture and self-abnegating rhetoric. After she has robbed the Prince of speech (no small larceny when his word is taken as law), she approaches him boldly. While kneeling to him she kisses his hand in an act of seeming deference, yet one that is without regard to his will. For a brief moment Roxana has complete control over the Prince, who finally regains power and speech in order to raise her up, a literalizing of the effect of the relationship (for Roxana seems to be elevated first).

The Prince, however, is no mere puppet; nor is executive authority without power, as the following scene demonstrates:

at last he leads me to the darkest Part of the Room, and standing behind me, bade me hold up my Head, when putting both his Hands round my Neck, as if he was spanning my Neck, to see how small it was, for it was long and small; he held my Neck so long, and so hard, in his Hand, that I complain'd he hurt me a little; what he did it for, I knew not, . . . but when I said he hurt me, he seem'd to let go, and in half a Minute more, led me to a Peir-Glass, and behold, I saw my Neck clasp'd with a fine Necklace of Diamonds . . .                               (73)

The scene reminds us and Roxana of the executive's power. In this instance that power is doubly threatening because its aim is inscrutable. Roxana's fearful response is a weak complaint, the efficacy of which is temporarily in doubt. When the Prince releases her, he leaves her yet more enriched; but he also leaves behind the trace of his power in the pressure of his grasp, now deposited in the diamonds. The scene warns the individual against complacency in the face of a still powerful executive. This warning is the means of introducing the public conscience into the juridical individual in so far as the conscience responds to a utilitarian calculus of how best to avoid pain. With the internalization of the public conscience – and a subsequent emancipation from the interference of the executive power – the juridical subject's prehistory comes to an end.

The subject's emergence into history, as much as it is a desired end, is not without attendant anxieties. Roxana's sense of security is weakened at this time by her recognition of the law of relative value. She writes that "Great Men . . . raise the Value of the Object which they pretend to pitch upon, by their Fancy; I say, raise the Value of it, at their own Expence" (74). This law of relative value affects Roxana's present and future positions. On the one hand, she cannot stay where she is, for her "Carcass" as desired object has already lost much of its particular appeal. She can hardly believe, as she puts it, "that I should be caress'd by a Prince, for the Honour of having the scandalous Use of my Prostituted Body, common before to his Inferiours" (74). The "Rage of [man's] vicious Appetite," moreover, makes Roxana a likely object of resentment when the appetite is sated and relative value falls. On the other hand, to venture outward unprotected is to be subject to the rage of the market place, where envy and competition are as dangerous as the residue of extinct desire.

This dilemma is not so much resolved as it is enacted. Roxana is cast off by a converted Prince, but she is left "richer than [she] knew how to think of" and "at Liberty to go to any Part of the World, and take Care of [her] Money [her]self" (110–11). In the exercise of her "Liberty," she immediately encounters a Jew, who has been summoned to change Roxana's jewelry into money, and who recognizes the jewels as those belonging to the Landlord/Jeweler, murdered eight years before. Her entry into civil society as an all but full-fledged juridical subject is marked by the appearance of deadly competition, for the Jew does not want justice for the Landlord/Jeweler's murder as much as he wants to profit from his discovery. His desire to profit necessarily entails eliminating the present holder of the jewels. Roxana writes that "he looks as if he would devour" her, thus recalling the moment early in the narrative when she fantasized devouring her own children and suggesting an identity between a ferocious appetite for possession in a state of nature and in civil society.

Bram Dijkstra allegorizes this episode as a stage in Roxana's economic education, during which she passes from "pre-capitalist systems of value, wealth and exchange" to the "latest forms of capital management and the international transfer of funds." Why diamonds are necessarily pre-capitalist Dijkstra fails to explain. More to the point is his remark that the jewels "had a history, and could therefore become a source of considerable embarrassment if their history were in any way tainted."[37] To imply that the "latest forms of capital" bear no history in them, however, is to fall prey to the illusion that sustains Roxana throughout her narrative. History, we learn, is subjective as well as objective, a producer as well as a product of "character." Roxana's illusion that she is "at Liberty" encounters a new social necessity. That she has been freed from the Prince's bounty and demands does not mean that she has realized her autonomy. Rather than essentialize this moment as a transition from one economic formation to another, it is better to view it as an indication of the further ineluctable emplotment of the juridical subject within social structures. For the possessive individual, that structure is essentially competitive.

The encounter between Roxana and her adversary marks a further strengthening of the subjective motive for internalizing the public con-

---

[37] Dijkstra, *Defoe and Economics*, p. 43.

science. Accumulation must not only be rationalized by the contract, but it must also be legitimized according to social norms. The Landlord/ Jeweler's equitable treatment of Roxana is liable to be interpreted by interested others as a grand fraud. "[U]pon Examination," Roxana writes, "I cou'd not have prov'd myself to be the Wife of the Jeweller, … and then I shou'd … have brought all his Relations in *England* upon me; who finding by the Proceedings, that I was not his Wife, but a Mistress, or in *English, a Whore*, wou'd immediately have laid Claim to the Jewels, as I had own'd them to be his" (115–16). Through these dangers the text links propriety and possession. Accumulation, as long as it is libidinized, taints character. To be a whore is to be a thief and perhaps even a murderer, liable to a system of justice where "the most innocent People in the World have been forc'd to confess themselves Guilty of what they never heard of, much less, had any hand in" (119).[38] In absolutist France, the state power fashions the subject's conscience according to its own will, speaking her confession and robbing her of her own truth-producing discourse. Of course, Roxana is enabled to escape France once again, but this experience has demonstrated to her the necessity of both securing her accumulated wealth and aligning it with the normative public conscience.

Roxana's road to security is made smoother by her "Deliverer" from the "Devil" Jew: a sympathetic Dutch Merchant who helps her escape France with her fortune. In order to preserve her autonomy from this "Deliverer," Roxana turns the Merchant's act of kindness into a contractual relation, which can be satisfied through a limited exchange. The Dutch Merchant begins negotiations over the settlement of the debt auspiciously by telling Roxana that he has a proposal that "wou'd more than ballance all Accounts between" them (138). But he soon shifts his address from the reasonable rhetoric of contractual negotiations to a metaphysical and alien register: he tells Roxana "it was that seeing Providence had (as it were for that Purpose) taken his Wife from him, I wou'd make up the Loss to him" (141). Although it might be argued that this metaphysical rhetoric merely overlays an economic mentality of compensation for personal loss, the consequences of that rhetoric will exceed the mere balancing of accounts. To make up his loss, Roxana is expected to give the self that she has privately and skillfully fashioned. That gift will bring all further self-fashioning to an end. To believe that someone else's version of your election is a true and accurate representation of an ineluctable destiny in a divinely ordained cosmos is to cede to that other the power of representation. There is, in fact, only a slight difference between the

---

[38] Unlike criminal procedure on the continent, the "systematic use of torture to investigate crime never established itself in English criminal procedure." John H. Langbein, *Torture and the Law of Proof: Europe and England in the Ancien Régime* (Chicago and London: University of Chicago Press, 1977), p. 73.

Dutch Merchant and the Jew: both cast Roxana in private dramas that they have authored for their own ends.

The Merchant supplements his metaphysical rhetoric with an appropriate gesture: "and with that, he held me fast in his Arms, and kissing me, would not give me Leave to say No, and hardly to Breathe" (141). The passionate kiss – like the argument from Providence – stifles Roxana, making her temporarily unable to reply to his proposals. In this regard, it prefigures the consequences of the unequal terms of the English marriage contract.[39] At the same time, it refigures Roxana's relation with the Prince. Whereas she had cleverly managed to deprive the Prince of speech or to make that speech anticipatory of her own desires, now she finds herself in the situation where she is desired to speak the will of another. The text reaches an impasse: completely to internalize the public conscience by accepting the mode of legitimacy available to a woman is to surrender juridical subjectivity.

Roxana resolves this dilemma by rejecting the Merchant's offer and redefining her self. In retrospect, she makes the following reflection: "tho' I cou'd give up my Virtue, ... yet I wou'd not give up my Money" (147). To preserve her autonomy Roxana identifies the self with something not only extrinsic to it but also alienable, fungible, and uniform. She is her money. In the words of Adorno and Horkheimer, she strives for a unique individuality "so that it might all the more surely be made the same as any other."[40] There is some comfort in this uniformity, for by identifying herself with her money, over which she has had complete control since her first husband, she attains psychological mastery over self and the social objectification of the self. At the same time, the self has no necessary content; rather, it is a vehicle of exchange, an object of circulation. In order to retain a sense of autonomy that could be destroyed by this transmutation into the object of money, Roxana corporealizes the equation so that money becomes identified with her body, while the will performs the directive function of alienating the body when an opportunity for profit makes that alienation reasonable.

Roxana is at the point of becoming a juridical subject who acts as a disembodied, calculating intelligence and who increases her capital by directing the body's labor toward profitable ends. This has the important effect of enabling the subject to avoid or defer the demands of the religious discourse. Correlative with the will's escape from objectification is the commodified body's preservation from the conscious practice of accumu-

---

[39] For Roxana's own understanding of these disablements, see the marriage debate with the Dutch Merchant, pp. 150–55. See also Spiro Peterson, "The Matrimonial Theme of Defoe's *Roxana,*" *PMLA* 70 (1955):166–91, for background information and a summary of Defoe's views on various aspects of the theme.

[40] Adorno and Horkheimer, *Dialectic of Enlightenment,* p. 13.

lation. An instrumental reason directs an idiot body. This also strengthens the juridical subject's illusion of having escaped history by entering a chain of perfectly abstract and ephemeral equations, the body worth now so many diamonds, now so much plate. But Roxana's body seems to have its own will. It rejects this dematerialization by making demands for the early pleasures of visibility and status that first made London an acceptable abode to her. Having rejected the Merchant's offer, Roxana returns to England to continue her accumulation. Sir Robert Clayton, her financial adviser, not only helps her realize substantial income from investments but also suggests that she marry a merchant because they "liv'd in more real Splendor, and spent more Money than most of the Noblemen in *England* cou'd singly expend, and that they still grew immensly rich" (170). Roxana rejects his advice for the same reasons that she rejected her Dutch Merchant, and because in coming again to England she has been aiming at "nothing less than ... being Mistress to the King himself" (161). If the King is the center of "a large and gay City," the finest of a "great-many fine Folks," then Roxana's ambitions are determined by the memory of those early bodily pleasures. That is, the ambition to be mistress to the King – when there are so many Merchants living in real splendor – marks the body's infringement upon the will. And as such, it is a serious misstep for the juridical subject, whose very autonomy depends upon the subordination of bodily pleasures to rational calculation.[41]

Roxana's body dominates in her courtly adventures. Its spectacle enriches her and helps her to achieve the aim that she has set herself.[42] Domination by her body, however, has a disturbing effect, which Roxana describes as "a Scene ... , which I must cover from humane Eyes or Ears; for three Years and about a Month, *Roxana* liv'd retir'd, ... with a Person, which Duty, and private Vows, obliges her not to reveal, at least, not yet" (181). The narrative's lapse into the third person indicates that she has ceded the precious right of intimate self-representation, something she has not done before. She keeps silence because of "Duty" owed a superior and the obligation of "private Vows." These are mixed motives, one belonging to an obedient body and the other to a resolved will. Roxana's liaison with this never-named person introduces confusion into her account. It remains an unassimilated moment in the confessional construction of this juridical subject, the sign of the mute body's mysterious demands, the negation of the confessional production of the truth. Its virtual repression suggests that Roxana's desires for a happy Living demand disciplining of the body. Her

---

[41] For a provocative Freudian reading of the repression of bodily pleasures, see Gary Hentzi, "Holes in the Heart: *Moll Flanders, Roxana*, and 'Agreeable Crime,'" *Boundary 2* 18.1 (1991):174–200.

[42] David Marshall reads the episode in court as an example of fear of exposure. *The Figure of Theater: Shaftesbury, Defoe, Adam Smith, and George Eliot* (New York: Columbia University Press, 1986), p. 142.

failure to do so in this instance, to make the body an invisible spectator rather than a visible spectacle, leads to her eventual undoing as juridical subject when her estranged daughter through a series of coincidences recognizes the "natural" and maternal filiative presence.

Because the body's rebellion runs counter to the narrative's tendency, it cannot stand. The fantasy of the body as consort of a kind of political transcendental signifier is dispelled, and the body returns to its commodity status with a vengeance. The narrative suggests that this return is in fact a result of the body's ambitions, which have injured the subject in a material way. Roxana describes this injury in telling terms: "After the End of what I call my *Retreat*, and out of which I brought a great deal of Money, I appear'd again, but I seem'd like an old Piece of Plate that had been hoarded up some Years, and comes out tarnish'd and discolour'd" (182). Realizing that she now "look'd like *a cast-off Mistress*," Roxana enters a new liaison with a perverse old Peer, whose particular sexual predilection might be anal intercourse.[43] This excremental liaison is purely economic in a way that none of Roxana's other relationships are. In effect, her will reasserts control over the body by degrading it to a mere instrument of profit. In this relationship with the Peer, however, she foregoes the preeminent instrument of rational calculation and freedom: the contract. Thus, the "mutual" relation between these partners rests on an implied understanding free from the contract's regulating law. Roxana's abandonment of this regulatory and protective instrument indicates an increased disgust for the body and scorn for the traces of the history that it bears. Her actions aim to eradicate those traces by reducing the body literally to excrement, the most debased and valueless material of all.

The association of excrement and the body spills over into another association. "I wallow'd in Wealth," writes Roxana, "and it flow'd upon me at such a Rate, having taken the frugal Measures that the Good Knight [Sir Robert Clayton] directed" (188). Confronted by a solitary existence in which accumulation is its own end, Roxana risks becoming a retentive monstrosity, a creature living upon its own wastes. To forestall the self's decomposition, Roxana clearly needs something else. To borrow a term from Freud, she needs a new "aim" for her affective life.[44] Or, as Defoe wrote elsewhere, she needs to complete her life by knowing the pleasures of relation.[45] The injury done the subject by the reduction of the

---

43 Maximillian E. Novak, "The Unmentionable and the Ineffable in Defoe's Fiction," *Studies in the Literary Imagination* 15.2 (1982):85–102.

44 For the association between money and feces, see Freud, "Character and Anal Erotism," in *The Freud Reader*, ed. Peter Gay (New York: Norton, 1989), pp. 296–97.

45 In *The Complete English Tradesman* Defoe writes that "the very sight of, and above all, his [the tradesman's] tender and affectionate care for his wife and children, is the spur of his diligence; this is it puts an edge upon his mind, and makes him hunt the world for business as eager as Hounds hunt the woods for their game ..." (125).

body to its gross materiality can be healed only by a gratuitous act of will that is other-directed.

Roxana seeks a supplement to the contractual processes of accumulation by bestowing some of her wealth on the children she has left behind. She proceeds cautiously, however, "resolv'd not to discover [her]self to [her children], in the least; or to let any of the People that had the breeding of them up, know that there was such a-body left in the World, as their Mother" (188). Still the canny businesswoman not willing to be charged with her past debts, Roxana works through her agent Amy, who protects her employer from excessive or irrational filiative demands. Thus, Roxana's return to filiative associations is mediated by the juridical imperative of control as the juridical subject limits her liability through a series of fictions enacted by her agent. These fictions allow her to experience a consoling filiation while seeming to remain immune to the family's non-juridical demands. In short, the body has no real role in this transaction.

The satisfactions available to the disembodied juridical subject, however, cannot entirely constitute a new aim. The body remains insistent, clamoring for its recuperation. In answer to its demands, Roxana sends Amy to inquire after the Dutch Merchant. Tired of waiting for Amy's news and made restless by self-imposed confinement, Roxana and her Quaker landlady go "Abroad to take the Air" in a "plain Coach, no gilding or painting, lin'd with a light-grey Cloath" (217, 213). The unornamented coach – like the plain Quaker habit Roxana has adopted – removes Roxana from the excremental signs of past excesses. Furthermore, it enables her to see without being seen, except by her companion. Thus ensconced and empowered, spectator rather than spectacle, she sees the Dutch Merchant ride by her coach. The Quaker notices a change and makes the following comment: "Well, *says she*, ... one of them is a Man-Friend of Thine, or somewhat is the Case; for tho' thy Tongue will not confess it, thy Face does" (218). The scene says that the body's longings cannot be hidden (indeed, this is the maxim that produces the novel's catastrophe). But the solipsistic bodily pleasures that the child had enjoyed upon her arrival in London no longer suffice for the adult. Encoded in Roxana's blushes is the body's eloquent plea for connection, a plea that the juridical subject has heretofore ruled out of order because it threatens its autonomy. A moment of potential synthesis between possessive and affective needs seems at hand.

Roxana marries the Dutch Merchant, thus ending for her the "intrieguing Part of ... a Life full of prosperous Wickedness" (243). In complex negotiations preceding the final contract, Roxana reveals a new awareness of the insufficiency of material pleasures and – by implication – a discomfort with a purely juridical identity. Her solution to this discomfort, however, is a failure. At her urging, the Dutch Merchant is naturalized as a British Subject; he purchases a "Patent for Baronet"; and he gives Roxana the gift of the title of Countess, also through purchase. The confident juridical subject, who has internalized the public conscience, cares nothing for such nominal distinctions, especially in a world where "Honour is become a Merchandize, Nobility grows cheap, and Dignity comes to Market upon easy Terms in the World ..."[46] Roxana hopes to erase the history of her past by acquiring this "Title of Honour," which will "assist to elevate the Soul, and to infuse generous Principles into the Mind" (240). After all, she had once told her Dutch Merchant that to marry him after they had lived as Man and Mistress would be "the most preposterous thing in Nature, and ... is to befoul one's-self, and live always in the Smell of it" (152). Roxana urges her husband-to-be to barter his diamonds for a birthright, hoping that his action will have the effect of scouring the smell that lingers on her own instrumentalized body.

At this point in her narrative, with the "Prospect of happy Living" in view, Roxana represents herself as a "Passenger coming back from the *Indies*, who having, after many Years Fatigues and Hurry in Business, gotten a good Estate, with innumerable Difficulties and Hazards, is arriv'd safe at *London* with all his Effects, and has the Pleasure of saying, he shall never venture upon the Seas any-more" (243). A contractual affiliation has brought her to the shores of the promised land. And yet she will be granted only a brief, temporary residence on those shores. In Roxana's simile, the merchant leaves the Indies behind the barrier of the wide seas. In her story, however, a life of "abstract" juridical practices has left indelible traces that not all nations' honorific titles can hide nor all earth's oceans wash away.

## IV History made flesh

Roxana enjoys spectacular success for most of her narrative. Having given little thought to the consequences of her desire to slip the chains of necessity once and for all, she has exploited sometimes tacit, sometimes explicit agreements in order to accumulate wealth and gain autonomy. As an abstract juridical subject she makes herself anew at every negotiation. Once possessed of wealth and independence, however, she turns back to find the filiative comforts that she has denied since experiencing desti-

---

[46] Daniel Defoe, *A Plan of the English Commerce*, 2nd edn. (1730; facs. rpt., New York: Augustus Kelley, 1967), p. 71.

tution with her first husband. She seeks to heal the split between will and body, between action and responsibility by a simple but powerful fiat. This is the ideal genealogy of the juridical subject. In actuality, the "Vast Variety of Fortunes" of the woman called Roxana proves to have a social force that exceeds personal mastery.

As John Richetti has noted, the "sense of the past as an encircling net or inescapable weight on the present dominates Roxana's narrative of the last phase of her life ..."[47] The past returns in the person of Roxana's daughter and namesake Susan. Like her mother, Susan pursues "the Prospect of happy Living" without much concern for the wishes of others. She feels an absolute need not only to discover her mother's identity but also to compel her mother to admit the relation that exists between them. And the obsessional way in which Susan pursues Roxana indicates that for her the "Affection of a Mother" is an inalienable right. In the daughter's pursuit of the mother, then, emerges the central, unresolved contradiction of this novel: the juridical subject's claim to the right of a property-based autonomy falls into conflict with inclinations to and claims of obligation created by kinship and natural rights.

In Defoe's work history refuses to be appropriated as the individual's private property. As abstract juridical subject, Roxana has lived a fantasy of immunity to history. Although the text does indulge frequently in the fantasy of both unlimited accumulation and obligation-free autonomy, the juridical subject's illusion of mastery over human desire is finally shattered by the accumulation of events. To borrow Fredric Jameson's formulation, history hurts because human beings never can make their histories exactly as they choose.[48] With Susan's appearance Roxana slides back into "History," and her past is restaged without her consent in a drama of contested filiative obligations (270). In her relentless pursuit of her mother, Susan reasserts the rights of a previously mute social collective, which the juridical subject has represented as a means or hindrance to accumulation. Roxana fears that if Susan were to "claim her Kindred," then the mother "must for-ever after have been this Girl's Vassal" (280). The heroine's self-representation as "Vassal" may be only a manner of speaking, but in the political metaphorics of the text the word represents an ominous negation of the juridical subject's defining essence. Susan's obsessional search for knowledge of the historical forces that have made her proves the contract's power limited, purely voluntary affiliations illusory, and an obligation-free autonomy unobtainable.

As a result of Susan's demands, Roxana is driven to fantasize the transgression of civil society's founding principle: the protection of human life. She "wish'd her [daughter] in Heaven ... but if she had been carried

---

[47] Richetti, *Daniel Defoe*, p. 116.    [48] Jameson, *The Political Unconscious*, p. 102.

t'other Way, it had been much at one" (284). And although she distances herself from the idea of murder ("I was not for killing the Girl *yet*, I cou'd not bear the Thoughts of that neither" [emphasis added, 298]), she effects it through her agent Amy. Various critics have identified Amy as Roxana's alter ego, but Amy also plays a material function: she is a "Woman of Business" (245) who – Roxana tells us – "gather'd in my Rents, *I mean my Interest-Money*, and kept my Accompts, and, *in a word*, did all my Business ..." (318).[49] Just as Amy blurs the boundary between filiative and affiliative obligations in her own obsessive attendance upon Roxana (thereby suggesting the weakness of such distinctions), so she shows the difficulty in maintaining a separation between will and instrument in her attempt to protect the body's commodious living without troubling the will. Roxana feels herself personally implicated in Susan's murder, suggesting finally the moral impossibility of repressing the body's lived experience. She fails to reach "juridical maturity" because she sees no way of harmonizing possessive and affective demands. Another "Body's Interest or Advantage" or someone else's longing for connection threatens the fantasy of the juridical subject, who wishes to put herself beyond the claims of filiation while enjoying their pleasures at a distance, who wishes to extinguish the faults of the past and control the contingencies of the future while all the time enjoying "happy Living" in a perfectly regulated present.

---

[49] See, for example, Richetti, *Defoe's Narratives*, p. 203; Terry J. Castle, who calls Amy "Roxana's surrogate in the social sphere" ("'Amy, Who Knew My Disease': A Psychosexual Pattern in Defoe's *Roxana*," *ELH* 46 [1979]:85); and Birdsall, *Defoe's Perpetual Seekers*, p. 158.

# 3

# Clarissa Harlowe: caught in the contract

The religious reflex of the real world can, in any case, only then finally vanish, when the practical relations of every-day life offer to man none but perfectly intelligible and reasonable relations with regard to his fellow men and to Nature.

Marx, *Capital* 1:79

## I Introduction

In Daniel Defoe's *Roxana* filiative relations represent the greatest threat to the subject's desire for the unconditional freedom to strike the most advantageous bargains regardless of others' needs. Freedom and family are also at the heart of Samuel Richardson's *Clarissa*, as a juridical discourse of rights, economic imperatives of accumulation, and patriarchal pieties fall into conflict. In both Defoe's and Richardson's novels the contract and its underlying rationale play a crucial role in the heroines' fortunes. Roxana avidly exploits the contract. Clarissa is forced to consider it as protection against other contracting agents. In both instances the interaction of family entanglements and contractual freedom produces the narratives' subjects. In *Clarissa*, however, the narrative seeks to produce a subject of rights still allied to traditional values and immune from the consequences of accumulation. But as this tragic novel discovers the present impossibility of creating "reasonable relations," it reverts for consolation to a "perfectly intelligible" – if solipsistic – "religious reflex," represented as a lover's dying embrace of absolute and imperturbable fidelity.

In this first of two chapters on Richardson's novel, I will examine the heroine's reconstitution as a juridical subject, effected by her grandfather's bequest; her family's reaction to her new "character," which displaces her from the affective position that she had previously occupied; and Clarissa's response to these events. Whereas Roxana naturalizes herself through voluntary self-representation, Clarissa finds herself unwillingly transformed by juridical effects and strives to reverse the transformation through love and law. These efforts have led many critics to argue that Clarissa refuses to recognize what Alasdair MacIntyre has called "the modern liberal distinction between law and morality."[1] Linda Kauffman, for example, claims that Clarissa's "discourse ... posits a logic based on the integrity of the body and the supremacy of the heart, which is antithetical to the logic enforced by men."[2] According to Carol Kay, "Clarissa uses the dignity and publicity rather than the power of the law in order to symbolize the noncoercive relationships of sympathy and generosity which she prefers to contractual relationships but which have been denied her."[3] Both critics privilege Clarissa's heart without emphasizing enough that it is the site of an ideological contradiction. In short, Clarissa's heart is riven by the same historical forces that are producing the modern conditions of individualism. In the words of MacIntyre once again, the heart becomes the final arbiter of virtue in the "modern liberal state['s] ... arena in which each individual seeks his or her own private good."[4] In order to keep this "heart" from becoming just another version of private good, Richardson grounds his heroine's desires in a natural law, derived from and generating the affective bonds of social intercourse.

Clarissa's sentiments work against the effects of market principles. In the early moments of her confinement, she implicitly condemns her family's efforts to better its social status at others' expense: "And yet in my opinion the World is but one great family. Originally it was so. What then is this narrow selfishness that reigns in us, but relationship remembred [sic] against relationship forgot?"[5] Relationship is the matrix of Clarissa's natural law, the ground that determines rights and duties. It is inclusive rather than exclusive.[6] The power that is derived from relationship has a social rather than an individual instrumentality, as Clarissa's description of her grandfather's will indicates: "This is certainly a very high and unusual devise to so young a creature. We should not aim at *all* we have power to do. To take all that good-nature, or indulgence, or good opinion confers, shews a want of moderation, and a graspingness that is unworthy of that indulgence; and are bad indications of the *use* that may be made of the power bequeathed" (1:134) [1:92]. For Clarissa power is limited by

---

[1] Alasdair MacIntyre, *After Virtue: A Study in Moral Theory* (London: Gerald Duckworth, 1981), p. 160.

[2] Linda S. Kauffman, *Discourses of Desire: Gender, Genre, and Epistolary Fictions* (Ithaca and London: Cornell University Press, 1986), p. 133. For a similar position, see Rita Goldberg, *Sex and Enlightenment: Women in Richardson and Diderot* (Cambridge: Cambridge University Press, 1984), p. 98.

[3] Carol Kay, *Political Constructions: Defoe, Richardson, and Sterne in Relation to Hobbes, Hume, and Burke* (Ithaca and London: Cornell University Press, 1988), p. 192.

[4] MacIntyre, *After Virtue*, p. 160.

[5] Samuel Richardson, *Clarissa, or the History of a Young Lady*, 8 vols. (Oxford: Shakespeare Head Press, 1930), 1:49; and 4 vols. (New York and London: Everyman's Library, 1932), 1:34. All further citations appear in the text. The Shakespeare Head edition appears first in parentheses, thus: (1:94). The corresponding pages in the Everyman edition follow in brackets, thus: [1:34].

[6] For the definition of inclusive rights, see James Tully, *A Discourse on Property: John Locke and his Adversaries* (Cambridge: Cambridge University Press, 1980), p. 62.

social and moral considerations, even if law allows it amplitude. When the Harlowe family confines their daughter to her room, the text shows the family's attempt to shrink the breadth of Clarissa's inclusive vision and teach her the true meaning of power.

At the beginning of her trials Clarissa discovers that "the one great family" has been changed by historical circumstances into "a 'formal' society, with no 'real' association at its base, no effective community of interest, but only unsociability and the competition of private interests."[7] A powerful economic imperative to expand has negated traditional familial relations. Clarissa's discovery follows upon her abstraction into a juridical subject of rights. Only from that vantage can she describe a world in which relationship was not determined by a calculus of profit and loss.[8] And so with that world lost to her, the scene is set for a new, protracted conflict between affective and possessive individualisms.[9] As both woman and abstract juridical subject, Clarissa is torn between the two versions of individualism, unable to occupy either fully. As a woman, she confronts the considerable legal and ideological powers of what Carole Pateman has called "fraternal patriarchy," which dominates both the public and private spheres.[10] As juridical subject, she is excluded from the comforts of the patriarchal order's new affective regime. In short, Clarissa is caught between the contract's enabling powers and her gender's real liabilities, between the cold freedom of an abstract individualism and the warm comforts of a genuine affective life. Simultaneously enabled and disabled by her new legal mask and by customary gender norms, Clarissa learns – as Christopher Hill pointed out long ago – that her actual freedom is an "illusion."[11]

As the family ties that Clarissa once found solid melt into air, she finds herself not in a vacuum but in a field of new and alien social forces. The Harlowes stand at the threshold of what Karl Polanyi has called the "great transformation," when society becomes "an adjunct to the market. Instead of economy being embedded in social relations, social relations

---

[7] Lucio Colletti, *From Rousseau to Lenin: Studies in Ideology and Society*, trans. John Merrington and Judith White (London: New Left Books, 1972), pp. 166–67.

[8] Christopher Hill writes that civil society promotes the "abstraction of the individual from society." "Clarissa Harlowe and her Times," *Essays in Criticism* 5 (1955):328.

[9] Lawrence Stone defines the family of "affective individualism" as "organized around the principle of personal autonomy, and bound together by strong affective ties. Husbands and wives personally selected each other rather than obeying parental wishes, and their prime motives were now long-term personal affection rather than economic or status advantage for the lineage as a whole" (*Family, Sex and Marriage* 7–8). C. B. Macpherson provides the definition for "possessive individualism": "the individual in market society *is* human as proprietor of his own person. However much he may wish it to be otherwise, his humanity does depend on his freedom from any but self-interested contractual relations with others" (*Possessive Individualism* 275).

[10] Pateman, *The Sexual Contract*, pp. 80–83, 16.    [11] Hill, "Clarissa Harlowe," p. 328.

are embedded in the economic system."[12] The Harlowes subordinate everything to their material interests, ruthlessly ignoring individual rights and needs. As they deny Clarissa her right to make the best deal (as she sees it), they reveal their disregard for the principles that enabled their own ascent. Even Lovelace blames them with language that will play an important part in the development of capitalism when he boasts that "the whole stupid family were in a combination to do [his] business for [him]" (3:1) [1:493]. The *Oxford English Dictionary* defines *combination* as "[t]he banding together or union of persons for the prosecution of a common object: formerly used almost always in a bad sense = conspiracy, self-interested or illegal confederacy; hence (later) the term applied to the unions (formerly illegal) of employers or workmen to further their interests ..." Clarissa's plight might be described as the "prosecution of a [disputed] common object," and combinations are incompatible with the laissez-faire doctrines of neoclassical political economy. Although the Harlowes can be dismissed as aberrations, Clarissa's painful alienation from all that matters makes virtually meaningless the theory of the natural harmony of interests upon which capitalist political economy is based. In the world of the novel, Francis Hutcheson's assertion that "no man can ever imagine he can have any possible interest in opposing the public good, or in checking or restraining his kind of [sic] affections" is thrown into doubt.[13] In the rest of this chapter, I shall examine how the family defines and furthers its interest over against that of its one-time daughter and present heiress.

## II Conflicts of will and right

Many commentators on the novel have laid the cause of the family strife to the grandfather's will. Christopher Hill notes that it "sets personal affection in conflict with family ambition." Theodore Albert claims that the novel is "about the legal documentation and accommodation of experience," and observes that the grandfather's action embodies a "modern, bourgeois attitude."[14] As an unassimilated historical effect, the will instigates the narrative by creating a problem to be solved. Ideologically progressive, it redistributes wealth to the deserving and thus redresses

---

[12] Polanyi, *The Great Transformation*, p. 57.
[13] Francis Hutcheson, *Illustrations on the Moral Sense*, ed. Bernard Peach (Cambridge, MA: Harvard University Press, 1971), p. 160.
[14] Hill, "Clarissa Harlowe," p. 318. Theodore G. Albert, "1. The Law vs. Clarissa Harlowe. 2. Pastoral Argument of *The Sound and the Fury*. 3. Melville's Savages," Diss. Rutgers University 1976, pp. 2, 8. Although I treat the same subject as Albert, our emphases differ. He devotes much of his chapter to elucidating the rights of women and the laws governing marriage and kidnapping.

what Michael McKeon has called the problem of status inconsistency.[15] In redressing this problem, however, it also creates resentment in those who have been passed over.

The ideological character of Clarissa's grandfather's "modern, bourgeois attitude" becomes clearer when examined against recent explanations of inheritance in England during the early-modern period. Lawrence Stone has shown that from 1480 to 1660 common-law attorneys had found ways to break entails, thereby enabling the estate holder to alienate his lands at will and resulting in the fragmentation of several large estates.[16] After 1660, however, the "strict settlement" replaced the entail as a means of preserving estate integrity. This legal form, drawn up "at the marriage of the eldest son," worked by "limiting the interest in the estate of the father of the husband and, after him, of the husband himself, to that of a life tenant, and entailing the estate of the eldest son to be born of the marriage."[17] Because the grandfather's devise to Clarissa does not effect the consolidation of real property (and thus power in the hands of a single magnate), it appears to go against the actual trends of the time. (This tendency explains the family's outraged reaction to their being deprived of what they certainly viewed as an entitlement.) Despite its opposition to this historical trend, however, the will is in accord with William Blackstone's belief that the freedom to alienate one's lands at will was conducive to economic growth. A commercial nation fared best, Blackstone writes, with "a number of moderate fortunes engaged in the extension of trade." Nor was Blackstone alone in this opinion. Another jurist, Lord Kames, associated entails with feudalism and found them contrary "to nature and reason."[18]

Viewed in this manner, the bequest supports a progressive version of possessive individualism by working against the concentration of wealth and power in the hands of an already empowered elite. The grandfather justifies the bequest, furthermore, by his affection for a deserving granddaughter. The motive for this historical event, then, embodies the two

[15] McKeon, *Origins of the English Novel*, pp. 171–74.
[16] Stone, *Family, Sex and Marriage*, pp. 156–57.
[17] H. J. Habakkuk, "Marriage Settlements in the Eighteenth Century," *Transactions of the Royal Historical Society*, 4th series, 32 (1950):15. Life-tenants could not alienate their estates. See note 1 in Habakkuk. The strict settlement has been used to explain the increase in large estate holdings during the eighteenth century because the agreement had the practical effect of reinforcing primogeniture (Habakkuk 19). For the influence of indebtedness and "secondary effects of marriage and inheritance" in the increase of large estates, see Christopher Clay, "Marriage, Inheritance, and the Rise of Large Estates in England, 1660–1815," *Economic History Review*, 2nd series, 21 (1968):503–18. Clay argues that small landholdings were no longer a very profitable investment in the eighteenth century (513). For recent criticism of Habakkuk's linkage of the strict settlement to the rise of great estates, see Lloyd Bonfield, *Marriage Settlements, 1601–1740: The Adoption of the Strict Settlement* (Cambridge: Cambridge University Press, 1983), pp. 93–102.
[18] Blackstone, *Commentaries*, 2:374. Kames is quoted in Lieberman, *Province of Legislation*, p. 158.

most important values of bourgeois society: familial affection and merito-rious labor. Clarissa's labor, which involves both care of the estate and care of the old man, has created a sensuous bond linking her to her grandfather and his property. Together this pair enacts the requirements for the "justification of individual ownership" according to John Locke, as that justification has been explained by James Tully: "Labour justifies neither the accumulation of nor rights over one's goods; it provides ... a means of identifying something as naturally one's own ... Justification of accumulation and use is derived from the prior duty and right to support and comfort God's workmanship."[19] It is Clarissa's support and comfort of another that justifies her possession of the estate, and it is a telling irony that this relation enmeshes Clarissa in the trammels of subsequent con-tractual negotiations.

In devising his estate "according as the Behaviour of this or that Child hath comported with his Will and Humour," the grandfather pleases himself and enacts sound liberal doctrine.[20] Although Leopold Damrosch has called the grandfather's will arbitrary, the text offers evidence to the contrary from three separate sources.[21] First, the grandfather describes Clarissa's dutiful care in the will's preamble:

because my dearest and beloved Granddaughter Clarissa hath been from her infancy a matchless young creature in her duty to me, and admired by all who knew her, as a very extraordinary child; I must therefore take the pleasure of considering her as my own peculiar child; ... who is the delight of my Old age: And, I verily think, has contributed, by her amiable duty and kind and tender regards, to prolong my life. (1:30–31) [1:21]

Second, Clarissa calls her grandfather's "too distinguishing goodness" a "mark of his affection" (1:51, 115) [1:35, 79]. Finally, Anna Howe writes to her friend that her grandfather "knew what a noble spirit [Clarissa] had to do good," and therefore devised the estate to her to atone for his own selfishness as well as that of the other family members (1:182) [1:124]. Clarissa inherits the estate because of her extraordinary sense of duty and generosity, because of her amiability, and because her grandfather acknowledges that property entails social responsibility on the owner. The will that turns Clarissa into a juridical subject is just, natural, and ultimately ideologically progressive by vesting property in the most deserving and capable person.

Clarissa's family, however, shares Damrosch's view of the bequest. In their eyes the patriarch has erred by allowing sentiment to injure the family interest and by acting without their advice or consent. The hero-ine's Uncle Antony expresses the family's sense of having been defrauded

---

[19] Tully, *Discourse on Property*, p. 131.   [20] Locke, *Two Treatises*, 2:72:357.
[21] Damrosch, *God's Plot*, p. 236.

and impugns the competence of the testator: "But pray, is not this Estate *our* Estate, as we may say? Have we not *all* an interest in it, and a prior right, if right were to have taken place? And was it more than a good old man's dotage, God rest his soul! that gave it you before us all?" (1:235) [1:161]. Faced with a check to its interests, the family spokesman renames individual right "dotage," thereby hinting that they might seek to regain control of the estate through equity. Uncle Antony's action validates an observation made by Ernst Bloch, who writes that "[t]he rising middle class often only idealized itself in its natural law, but once it had established its power, it cunningly protected itself with an antinatural law, clearly for its own profit and often out of cynicism."[22] In this instance antinatural law would deprive Clarissa of a just reward, and cynicism would ignore the grandfather's written plea that any flaws in the will be overlooked out of respect for his manifest intentions. According to Blackstone, "a devise [should] be most favourably expounded, to pursue if possible the will of the devisor, who for want of advice or learning may have omitted the legal or proper phrases."[23]

Just as the will exposes the family's authoritarian opposition to natural law, sets them against the naturalization of bourgeois property interests, and reveals the degree to which market motives have invaded their intimate relations; so too does it force Clarissa into an independence that is ultimately characterized by absolute alienation. The beginning of this process – of the involuntary construction of Clarissa as juridical subject – is noted by Anna Howe, who writes that the Harlowe family has suffered "disturbances."[24] Clarissa describes the nature of these disturbances:

No-body indeed was pleased: For altho' every-one loved me, yet being the youngest child, Father, Uncles, Brother, Sister, all thought themselves postponed, as to matter of right and power. [Who loves not power?]: And my Father himself could not bear that I should be made Sole, as I may call it, and Independent; for such the Will, as to that Estate and the powers it gave (unaccountably as they all said) made me.                                    (1:80) [1:54]

Because there are not enough estates to satisfy everyone's appetite for distinction, another's good fortune occasions anxiety and envy. When Clarissa tries to counter these effects with assurances supported by filial piety, she discovers that such assurances no longer signify. Her status as

[22] Bloch, *Natural Law*, p. xxvii.

[23] Blackstone, *Commentaries*, 2:381. For a discussion of the complex mid-century debates on the courts' power "to follow the testator's intention even in those cases where the legal instrument under dispute had been inaccurately or imprecisely drawn," see Lieberman, *Province of Legislation*, pp. 133–42.

[24] Tony Tanner has written eloquently about the disturbances and Clarissa's resulting alienation. There are many points of agreement between his and my discussion of the Harlowes' treatment of their daughter. *Adultery in the Novel: Contract and Transgression* (Baltimore and London: Johns Hopkins University Press, 1979), pp. 106–7.

daughter has been erased by the bequest. In the eyes of others, Clarissa is now an heiress, a *feme sole* rather than a daughter. And so she attempts to regain her family's trust and affection with juridical actions.

Her recourse to legal guarantees, however, has the paradoxical effect of reinforcing her new character in the eyes of her family. Aware of the protection that the law affords a minor *feme sole*, they view her piously intended and good-faith actions of placing the inheritance under her father's management as a mere postponement of her "right and power." Having demonstrated her piety by placing the estate in trust, Clarissa later offers to give it outright to Arabella: "With what chearfulness will I assign over this envied Estate! – What a much more valuable *consideration* shall I part with it for! – The Love and Favour of all my relations! That Love and Favour, which I used for Eighteen years together to rejoice in, and be distinguished by!" (2:100, emphasis added) [1:307]. Whether Clarissa means *consideration* in its legal signification, her family understands it that way. They counter her offer with the observation that "It was equally against Law and Equity: And a fine security Miss Bella would have, or Mr. Solmes, when I could resume it [the estate] when I would!" (2:102) [1:309]. Love and favor cannot fulfill the requirements of a contract.

Clarissa's offer is not accepted because the family fears that Clarissa could at some future time recover the estate by law. A legal handbook of the period describes the protections afforded her: "If any person take by force, or otherwise, any woman sole, having any substance of lands, tenements or moveable goods, and enforce her before she be sat at liberty to bind herself to him by statute or obligation, such a bond shall be void."[25] As a minor, Clarissa is not at liberty to alienate her lands.[26] A legal dictionary lists the "infant" female's gradual accrual of rights: "at *twelve* is at years of maturity, and therefore may consent or disagree to marriage, and if proved to have sufficient discretion, may bequeath her personal estate; at *fourteen* is at years of legal discretion, and may choose a guardian; at *seventeen* may be executrix; and at *twenty-one* may dispose of herself and her lands."[27] Clarissa is caught once again, for the paternalistic law that is intended to protect her works against her deepest wishes. In an ideal situation Clarissa's future independence as a subject of civil society and present dependence as an "infant" member of a family would not be contradictory, for the laws of England merely reproduce parental care: "The restraints that are laid upon infants by the laws of England are no

---

25 *The Laws Respecting Women* (London: J. Johnson, 1777; facs. rpt. New York: Oceana Publications, 1974), p. 117. *Feme sole* is the legal name of "an unmarried woman, whether spinster or widow."

26 "It is generally true, that an infant can neither aliene his lands nor do any legal act, nor make a deed, nor indeed any manner of contract, that will bind him" (Blackstone, *Commentaries* 1:453).

27 Giles Jacob, *The Law Dictionary* (London, 1809), n.p.; entry, "infant."

other than such as a kind parent would subject a child to whom he tenderly loved, to prevent his committing such acts of indiscretion as an infantile judgment and want of experience might lead him to."[28] William Blackstone describes parental power as that enabling the parent to perform the duties of maintenance, protection, and education.[29] But this is not the ideal situation. Tony Tanner has noted that other interests bring into focus the ambiguity in the duration and extent of parental power.[30] As both daughter under the age of twenty-one (according to Blackstone still under the "[t]he legal power of a father") and heiress with prospective rights, Clarissa finds herself in a dilemma.[31]

In her attempt to resolve this dilemma, to defend her own rights, and to reinstate the affective relations that existed before the bequest, Clarissa invokes the principles of a pre-capitalist if not a pre-civil ethos. In her view property is for use and for comfort, less a possession than a means of securing social harmony.[32] Economic calculation and personal aggrandizement are subordinated to the general good. Thus she opposes her match to Solmes in part on the grounds of her duty to others. She finds it unjust of Solmes "to settle all he is worth upon [her], and if [she] die without children, and he has none by any other Marriage, upon a family which already abounds" (1:87) [1:59]. Clarissa's position resembles a pre-civil "Law of Nature," as described by an anonymous treatise written in the 1720s: "Whilst the Law of Nature was the Rule of Man's Life, Men sought for no larger Territories, than they themselves could compass and manure; they erected no other magnificent Buildings, than sufficient to defend them from Cold and Tempest; they cared for no other Delicacy of Fare, or Curiosity of Diet, than to maintain Life."[33] Clarissa supplements this edenic – if somewhat spartan nature – with her strong sense of obligation to others. She must do so in order to defend herself against charges that she is acting out of self-interest.

Arguing from sufficiency is itself an insufficient defense. Clarissa also claims the natural right to exercise her will in matters essential to her own preservation. She writes to her Uncle John that an enforced marriage "will deprive [her] of [her] free-will"; she will become Solmes's "absolute

---

[28] *The Laws Respecting Women*, p. 426.    [29] Blackstone, *Commentaries*, 1:434–40.

[30] Tanner, *Adultery in the Novel*, p. 7.

[31] Blackstone, *Commentaries* 1:441.

[32] See Richard Tuck, *Natural Rights Theories: Their Origin and Development* (Cambridge: Cambridge University Press, 1979), pp. 160–73, for late seventeenth-century theories of property and natural law. For Matthew Hale, Richard Cumberland, and John Locke, there was a qualified right to property even in the state of nature, a right that did not exist for Thomas Hobbes. Tuck writes the following about Cumberland: "All men are under an obligation to maximise general utility [in order to advance the common good], and it is simply the case that the means to such an end are provided most plausibly by property" (167).

[33] *A Dissertation on the Law of Nature, the Law of Nations, and the Civil Law in General* (London, 1723), p. 38.

and dependent property (1:222–23) [1:152–53].[34] The dangers of having one's will negated by marriage are expressed nicely by her brother James in his encouragement of the "odious" suitor: "Persevere, however, Mr. Solmes ... I know no other method of being even with her, than, after she is yours, to make her as sensible of your power, as she now makes you of her insolence" (2:230) [1:396]. The only defense against James' treatment of women is the claim to a natural right that supersedes positive law. In this regard, Clarissa goes against conventions in a way similar to Roxana's Dutch Merchant.

By combining arguments of social responsibility and personal freedom Clarissa shows that she is split between traditional values and innovations. "Surely, my dear," she writes Anna, "I should not give up to my Brother's ambition the happiness of my future life. Surely I ought not to be the instrument of depriving Mr. Solmes's Relations of their natural rights and reversionary prospects, for the sake of further aggrandizing a family (altho' *that* I am of) which already lives in great affluence and splendor ..." (1:136–37) [1:93–94]. Because Clarissa speaks a hybrid discourse, the importance of her regarding the world as one great family becomes apparent. It enables her to resist her *brother's* designs without appearing to place her own well-being over her father or a larger social unit. In response to Clarissa's own rhetorical strategies, the family converts itself into a corporate structure and resorts to arguments based on its general good.[35] As the conflict mounts, Clarissa is forced to rely more and more on her natural right to liberty; that is, she is forced to become a juridical subject of civil society. Rather than being a choice, juridical individualism becomes a necessity brought on by her grandfather's devise.

### III A family policy

After the instrument that has made Clarissa an heiress has also "lopped off one branch of [her] Brother's expectations" (1:80) [1:54], and after Lovelace has wounded James in the arm, the Harlowe family becomes an "embattled phalanx" drawn up to protect its interests. Tony Tanner reads the phrase "embattled phalanx" as a sign of the "disintegration of the

[34] Blackstone's familiar description of the effect of marriage on a woman bears repeating: "By marriage, the husband and wife are one person in law; that is, the very being or legal existence of the woman is suspended during the marriage, or at least is incorporated or consolidated into that of the husband" (*Commentaries* 1:430).

[35] The "struggle for interpretation" or the mastery of the world as text is the focus of the critical studies that brought new attention to Richardson's novel at the beginning of the 1980s. See William Beatty Warner, *Reading "Clarissa": The Struggles of Interpretation* (New Haven and London: Yale University Press, 1979); Terry Castle, *Clarissa's Ciphers: Meaning and Disruption in Richardson's Clarissa* (Ithaca and London: Cornell University Press, 1982); and – more recently – Linda Kauffman, *Discourses of Desire*, who relies on Castle's earlier reading of the novel for some of her insights, pp. 134, 144–45.

family rather than its increasing consolidation and expansion."[36] By telescoping the development of the family's fortunes in the narrative, however, Tanner overlooks the familial consolidation so important for furthering Clarissa's transformation from daughter to juridical subject. As Clarissa's resistance to their plan grows, the family members enter a compact in order to effect their ends. Once this compact – or *combination*, as Lovelace names it – has been established, the family directs its combined power against the dissident. And in order to magnify the power of the compact, especially in Clarissa's eyes, her brother James dresses the newly formulated general will in the garb of patriarchal authority. Finally, when psychological pressures fail, the family resorts to confinement. Clarissa then imagines that a juridical spectacle enacted under patriarchal direction will compel her to accept the family will. Deprived of the power of self-determination by the patriarchal component, she appeals to Lovelace for rescue.

The first hints of change reveal a realignment of intrafamilial alliances. Clarissa learns that her "Brother and Sister, who used very often to jar, are now ... entirely one, and ... much together" (1:32) [1:22]. Arabella, who had once allied herself with Clarissa against their "Brother's *rapacious views*" (1:79) [1:54], shifts her allegiance after she has been disappointed by Lovelace. Thereafter, James and Arabella "behave ... to each other, as having but one interest" (1:85) [1:58]. Arabella's behavior, attributable in part to her injured vanity, also attests to the dynamic power of interest: family attachments shift under irrational motives (resentment) and yet are justified by rational calculation (interest). Six weeks after the first mention of the "cabal" between James and Arabella, their schemes have acquired the added legitimacy of a family compact:

Upon some fresh provocation, or new intelligence concerning Mr. Lovelace (I know not what it is) they have bound themselves, or are to bind themselves, by a signed paper, to one another [The Lord bless me, my dear, what shall I do!] to carry their point in favour of Mr. Solmes, in support of my *Father's Authority*, as it is called, and against Mr. Lovelace, as a Libertine, and an Enemy to the family: And if so, I am sure, I may say against *me*.                    (1:92) [1:63]

In Clarissa's mind, Solmes comes first as motive for the compact. The man whom Lovelace describes as "the most unpromising in his person and qualities, the most formidable in his offers," embodies the seemingly irresistible power of money (1:211) [1:144]. His appearance at Harlowe Place (Clarissa observes that "[t]he man lives here, I think" (1:47) [1:32]) also marks the displacement of paternal authority by economic interests. It is both cause and effect of the "disturbances" mentioned at the novel's

---

[36] Tanner, *Adultery in the Novel*, p. 106.

opening. The family sheds its organic character and transforms itself into an opportunistic association of economic interests.

The new general will to subjugate Clarissa is based on "honour and interest" and embodied in material "Settlements." What might be described as duality of motive marks the family as an ideological hybrid, part aristocratic and part commercial, and leads to a confusion of tactics.[37] Honor involves them in the contest with Lovelace, which in turn makes them adopt coercive measures against Clarissa. Interest leads them to the negotiation with Solmes, which has a similar result. For this family who have prospered in trade, material interests blind them to the consequences of their mixed motives and tactics. Their behavior resembles that which was criticized by the opponents of tradesmen of the time, as described by J. G. A. Pocock:

the individual engaged in exchange could discern only particular values – that of the commodity which was his, that of the commodity for which he exchanged it. His activity did not oblige or even permit him to contemplate the universal good as he acted upon it, and he consequently continued to lack classical rationality. It followed that he was not conscious master of himself, and that in the last analysis he must be thought of as activated by nonrational forces ...[38]

"Classical rationality," to adopt Pocock's phrase, has been displaced by a calculating, instrumental, but short-sighted reason, just as the brother displaces the father as the prime mover of the compact. Myopic interests prevent the brother James from contemplating anything but his own unmastered self.

Clarissa's predicament is not an unusual one, for parentally arranged marriages were not altogether rare in Richardson's day.[39] What I wish to emphasize here is the way in which Richardson's narrative fashions the family into a corporate unity supported by economic interests. So fashioned, all are called on to further the corporate project. For example, Mrs. Harlowe tells Clarissa "that the Settlements are actually drawn; and that you will be called down in a very few days to hear them read, and to sign them: For it is impossible, if your heart be free, that you can make the least objection to them; except it will be an objection with you, that they are so much in your favour, and in the favour of all our family" (1:142) [1:97]. Economic considerations countervail the affections of those – like Clarissa's mother – inclined to side with the dissident. In the same dialogue quoted above, Mrs. Harlowe, though pained at the treatment

---

[37] See McKeon, *Origins of the English Novel*, pp. 131–32 for *honor* in aristocratic ideology; and Clark, *English Society, 1688–1832*, pp. 109–16 for the survival of this concept in the duel. For *interest*, see Hirschman, *Passions and the Interests*, pp. 43–44.

[38] J. G. A. Pocock, *The Machiavellian Moment: Florentine Political Thought and the Atlantic Republican Tradition* (Princeton: Princeton University Press, 1975), p. 464.

[39] See Stone, *Family, Sex and Marriage*, pp. 271–81.

accorded her favorite child, explains her acquiescence to the general will: "I have been told, that I must be convinced of the fitness as well as the advantage to the whole (your Brother and Mr. Lovelace out of the question) of carrying the contract with Mr. Solmes, on which so *many* contracts depend, into execution" (1:144) [1:98–99]. Although Mrs. Harlowe's explanation indicates that hers is a reluctant acceptance of the contract's reasonableness, it reveals quite clearly that the corporate "whole" takes precedence over the individual part. Through the mother's reluctance, however, the novel signals the fatuousness of this corporate rationalization, which is little more than the force of the empowered inflicted upon the weak, little more than an irrational drive for evergreater accumulation.

The confluence of rational calculation and irrational drives in Richardson's narrative also reveals the limits to liberty for the variously empowered subjects of civil society. The self-determining agent of the contract appears to have all the brave new world before her. As one radical legal scholar has noted, "by 1600 the principles of bourgeois private law, that law regarding interpersonal dealings in contract, property, and so on, had in theory though not everywhere in practice replaced personal feudal relationships."[40] Richardson's narrative demonstrates, however, the persistence of feudal relations in the family in the person of the weakened patriarch (and her father's physical infirmities suggest weakness). At the same time, new freedoms are accompanied by the transformation of interpersonal relations into exchange relations.[41] If one is related through contract rather than consanguinity, then one *may* be related solely by economic ties. In fact, another modern legal scholar attributes the contract's essence to business transactions: "The Common Law has long stressed the commercial flavour of its contract. An Englishman is liable, not because he has made a promise, but because he has made a bargain."[42] William Blackstone's definition of *consideration*, the

[40] Michael E. Tigar, "with the assistance of Madeleine R. Levy," *Law and the Rise of Capitalism* (New York: Monthly Review Press, 1977), p. 183. For the treatment of contract by other radical historians, see for example, Tigar's discussion of Karl Renner's work, *The Institutions of Private Law and their Social Functions* (1949), pp. 303–9. For a criticism of the "crude materialist" view of law, see Collins, *Marxism and Law*, pp. 22–30.

[41] It is instructive to look at Richardson's reflections on his experience of negotiating the marriage settlement for his eldest daughter Mary in 1757. Richardson thought that his paternal authority had been circumvented by the clandestine courtship between his daughter and her suitor, undertaken with the collusion of Richardson's wife. As important was his distaste for the almost exclusively financial nature of his interactions with the son-in-law. Richardson was so disillusioned by the negotiations that he allowed his executors only to see his reflections on it. They were instructed to prevent his son-in-law from acquiring still more of Richardson's property at his death. See Joseph W. Reed, Jr., "A New Samuel Richardson Manuscript," *Yale University Library Gazette* 42 (1968):215–31.

[42] G. C. Cheshire and C. H. S. Fifoot, *The Law of Contract*, 7th edn (London: Butterworths, 1969), p. 22.

*sine qua non* of contract, also emphasizes the contract's economic nature: "The civilians hold, that in all contracts, either express or implied, there must be something given in exchange, something that is mutual or reciprocal. This thing, which is the price or the motive of the contract, we call the consideration: and it must be a thing lawful in itself, or else the contract is void."[43] On the one hand, Clarissa is limited by residual, "feudal" loyalties. On the other, she is the *consideration* that the family offers Solmes for the reversion of his estates. Yet if Clarissa is merely an object in an exchange relation that exists between the Harlowes and Solmes, she is also a necessary participant in the marriage contract. Just as Roxana occupied the unharmonized positions of juridical and patriarchal subjects, so too Clarissa is split between being a subject to an agreement and an object of exchange in the same agreement. Pushed in two directions, she wishes to return to her status as pre-juridical subject of affection even as she is compelled to assert her rights as a participant in the contract.

Her family allows Clarissa to move in neither direction. Her repeated asseverations of continued loyalty go unheeded; instead, Solmes becomes the ultimate test of that loyalty. "Now that you are grown up to marriageable years," Mrs. Harlowe tells her daughter, "is the test; especially as your Grandfather has made you independent, as we may say, in preference to those who had prior expectations upon that Estate" (1:115) [1:79]. The "test," involuntary in nature, is another example of the Harlowes' regressive authoritarian tactics. As such, it runs counter to the development of enlightenment criminal procedure of the time. According to John Langbein, eighteenth-century criminal procedure in the early part of the century was much closer to the inquisitorial style of Continental jurisprudence; but by the century's end it was more like what it has evolved into today in the Common Law countries.[44] The family's inquisitorial style reveals the interest that shapes their justice. As Roy Porter notes in his social history of eighteenth-century England, "the law was at bottom framed and enforced by those with power to cajole and coerce the rest ..."[45] The struggle at Harlowe Place represents just such a struggle between liberal theories of rights and actual practices of social power.

---

43 Blackstone, *Commentaries*, 2:444.

44 John Langbein, "The Criminal Trial before the Lawyers," *The University of Chicago Law Review* 45(1978):284–300, 314–16.

45 Roy Porter, *English Society in the Eighteenth Century*, (Harmondsworth: Penguin, 1982), p. 150. Another historian writes that "justice ... was in the hands of the gentry." Alan Harding, *A Social History of English Law* (Harmondsworth: Penguin Books, 1966), p. 244. See also Douglas Hay, "Property, Authority," p. 25: "The criminal law was critically important in maintaining bonds of obedience and deference, in legitimizing the status quo, in constantly recreating the structure of authority which arose from property and in turn protected its interests." E. P. Thompson maintains that the administration of law was often disinterested (*Whigs and Hunters* 258–69). John H. Langbein denies that "'a ruling-class conspiracy'" against the underclasses can be found in criminal law in the eighteenth century. Langbein argues that the discretionary

As cajoling becomes more and more like plain coercion, Clarissa is forced to consider various means of defending herself. One way – although to be sure not the only way – of explaining her attraction to Lovelace is to see it as a product of what she calls her brother's "strange politics," which "unite *that man* and *me* as joint-sufferers in one cause" (1:201) [1:137]. Earlier she had written more tellingly on this consequence of the family policy: "How impolitic in them all, to join two people in one interest, whom they wish for ever to keep asunder!" (1:92) [1:63]. By echoing the words of the marriage ceremony, Clarissa hints where her family is driving her: toward a countervailing contract made necessary by the threat to her will. And herein lie other painful ironies: not only does she consider a union to be joined in part for reasons of the same self-interest that she has condemned in others, but she also moves toward a state that will deprive her of the rights that she seeks to protect.

If the family compact and its ancillary contracts demand a countervailing contract from Clarissa, she is nonetheless forestalled if not entirely prevented from adopting this course of action by an internal resistance to using the rights of the juridical subject. That resistance is strengthened by her brother's exploitation of paternal authority. As mastermind of the family policy, James succeeds in making his own "grasping views" into his "*Father's will*" (1:118) [1:80]. Thus, Clarissa cannot resist her brother's interest without also resisting her father's prerogative. As she tells Anna Howe, she cannot think of exercising her rights by bringing suit against her father: "I would sooner beg my bread, than litigate for my right with my Father: Since I am convinced, that whether the Parent do his duty by the Child or not, the Child cannot be excused from doing hers to him. And to go to Law with my *Father*, what a sound has That?" (2:60) [1:280]. For Clarissa, the relationship between parent and child is not determined by the fulfillment of contractual obligation in the way that the Dutch Merchant argued the marriage contract is. I will return to this point in the final section of this chapter. Now, however, I wish to emphasize that once again the text shows how Clarissa is disabled by occupying two subject positions: in one she can consider going to law; in the other she cannot. When patriarchal power complements the family compact/contract, their combined effects secure order while preserving the appearance of liberty.

Order is further strengthened by concentrating authority in a single inaccessible figurehead and by simultaneously delegating it to numerous representatives. Shortly after the beginning of her troubles, Clarissa is beset by aunt, uncles, brother, sister, and mother. Like Kafka's petitioner before the door of the law, Clarissa is denied the chance to appeal to her father directly. Paternal authority is reproduced without being dim-

treatment of criminals – crucial to Hay's argument – was universally applied and within the reigning ethical norms. "Albion's Fatal Flaws," *Past and Present* 98 (1983):96–120.

inished, and its proliferation weakens her by dividing her attentions. It seems as if power is everywhere that Clarissa is. It is not yet the omniscient surveillance described by Michel Foucault, however, because it is still visible and works through reproduction of the father's body upon a variety of actors or emissaries.[46]

Mr. Harlowe's personal withdrawal and the magnification of his power through representatives is made obvious shortly before Clarissa leaves Harlowe place. Walking alone in the garden – or so she thinks until she is met by Betty, who tells her that "your Papa sends me to see where you are, for fear that he should meet you" – Clarissa writes to Anna that she "struck into an oblique Path," and then describes her reaction on seeing her father:

> You cannot imagine what my emotions were behind the yew-hedge, on seeing my Father so near me. I was glad to look at him thro' the hedge, as he passed by: But I trembled in every joint, when I heard him utter *these* words: Son James, To You, and to Bella, and to You, Brother, do I wholly commit this matter. That I was meant, I cannot doubt. And yet, why was I so affected; since I may be said to have been given up to the cruelty of my Brother and Sister for many days past? [1:411]

Clarissa's letter breaks off momentarily after her reflection on this incident, indicating the intensity of her response to the overheard conversation. In referring to his daughter as "this matter," the father objectifies her, turning her into that troublesome and costly burden, the chicken "brought up for the tables of other men" (1:79) [1:54]. That Clarissa assumes that she is the "matter" referred to suggests that she has already lived her objectification by and in the family. As a result she who was once used to treading the narrow way and strait is driven into an oblique path by a decentered power that treats her as a matter for exchange.

It is well to pause in this somewhat abstract argument in order to imagine Clarissa's "unimaginable" feelings. Somewhat later in the correspondence Clarissa characterizes parental obligation in the following way: "the wings of our parents are our most necessary and most effectual safeguard from the vulturs [sic], the hawks, the kites, and other villainous birds of prey ..." (3:216) [2:125]. The ambiguous shudder that passes through her while she spies on the family group expresses both fear of harm and rage at being handed over to her persecutors by the father who should have protected her from their raptorial intentions. In this lapsarian garden where sentence is pronounced (appropriately enough from behind a hedge whose leaves are poisonous and its name an emblem of death), Clarissa must feel like Eve being exiled to an alien earth, where law is

---

[46] "Disciplinary power ... is exercised through its invisibility; at the same time it imposes on those whom it subjects a principle of compulsory visibility." Foucault, *Discipline and Punish*, p. 187.

instituted to control the intemperate desires of men and always fails its purpose, and where she will remember the face of her maker in its wrath rather than in its benevolence. Clarissa responds so strongly to this overheard conversation because the deathly yew hedge, in marking the parturition of the juridical subject, fails to shield her from her father's delegated power even as it puts her out of the way of his mercy.

The scene in the garden stages Clarissa's growing realization of her fall from the family into juridical subjectivity and unprotected independence. To be enfranchised as juridical subject the heroine must undergo alienation from her natal surroundings. That which once had been familiar and a source of comfort now appears strange and threatening, as if Clarissa has entered a denatured world as an object. In such a world, women do not possess the subjectivity provided by the phallus. At best, they can bear its poisonous, juridical powers on behalf of the male.[47] So it seems at least when Clarissa describes a visit from her Aunt Hervey, who is bringing her the settlements to sign: "And then, to my great terror, out she drew some parchments from her handkerchief, which she had kept (unobserved by me) under her apron; and, rising, put them in the opposite window. Had she produced a serpent, I could not have been more frighted" (2:276) [1:428]. The serpent and the parchment are one in the young woman's imagination, both signifying the fall from the sensuous connections that she had known while she tended to her grandfather's Dairy House.

In the fallen world, however, one person's sensuous connection means disconnection and disempowerment for others. Responding to this disempowerment and hoping to get her to change her plea from the single life to a life with Solmes and his settlements, the Harlowes subject Clarissa to a kind of psychological *peine forte et dure* by denying her the pleasures of correspondence and association. Mrs. Harlowe, once again fulfilling her duty as the instrument of ambitious male power, brings the father's sentence to her daughter: "he declared he would break your heart, rather than you should break his. And I now assure you, that you will be confined, and prohibited making teazing appeals to any of us: And we shall see who is to submit, You to us, or Every-body to you" (1:156) [1:107]. The proscription of such "teazing appeals" to common nature underscores their power to move all who will not profit individually from the family policy. If the end of the compact is to be realized, then the daughter must remain an abstracted object to be exchanged for another good that furthers their scheme of aggrandizement.[48] The struggle becomes a classic battle of

---

[47] See Gayle Rubin, "The Traffic in Women: Notes on the 'Political Economy' of Sex," in *Toward an Anthropology of Women*, ed. Rayna R. Reiter (New York: Monthly Review Press, 1975), pp. 157–210.

[48] Carol Flynn maintains that the men's sadistic behavior toward Clarissa is a result of repressed incestuous desires. *Samuel Richardson: A Man of Letters* (Princeton: Princeton University Press, 1982), pp. 91–96.

nature against culture, spontaneity against calculation, affection against policy, similar to that which Roxana waged with her own impulses. Clarissa's physical body must be mortified and ultimately negated for the men of the family to sustain their resolve. Her Uncle John cannot even read her letters "without being unmanned": "how can we resolve to see you? There is no standing against your looks and language. It is our Love makes us decline to see you. How *can* we, when you are resolved *not* to do what we are resolved you *shall* do? ... Alas! Alas! my dear Kinswoman, how you fail in the trial" (2:95) [1:304].[49] Clarissa's very presence threatens the new order that has been established by the family contract in a way that Carole Pateman has noted in describing woman in civil society:

Women, their bodies and bodily passions, represent the 'nature' that must be controlled and transcended if social order is to be created and sustained ... Unlimited feminine desire must always be contained by patriarchal right. Women's relations to the social world must always be mediated through men's reason; women's bodies must always be subject to men's reason and judgments if order is not to be threatened.[50]

Clarissa's Uncle John expresses his dismay at his niece's failure "in the trial" because that failure calls into question the strength, adequacy, and justice of patriarchal right and reason. Just as Lovelace's schemes are undermined by Clarissa's "failure" to respond to his tests, so too the family disturbances grow ever more violent as the daughter seeks to reassert her nature against corporate ends. That nature *stands* in opposition to a disembodied juridical reason. Although Clarissa's "heart" is no less an ideological sign than the men's heads, it is a sign of resistance rather than a means of oppression. If her heart represents a natural threat to the bourgeoisie's rise to power, then that heart must be put in harness by having it internalize the rational calculation of the new juridical world.

And so the confinement that the family subjects her to is meant to break the heart of its wild liberty and condition the woman to accept the harness that the laws put into the hands of the husband. Clarissa has no doubt about her family's intentions, nor does she think them fit for preparing her for her "future" state: "to be confined, like a prisoner, to narrow and disgraceful limits, in order *avowedly* to mortify me, and to break my spirit; ... to be so put out of my course, that I have as little inclination as liberty to pursue any of my choice delights? – Are these steps necessary to reduce

---

[49] As Terry Eagleton and Judith Wilt have pointed out, Lovelace experiences similar difficulties. His first and last "stand" with Clarissa occurs when she is unconscious. Clarissa's "presence" is one way that Richardson's text criticizes an "abstract" juridical subjectivity. Eagleton, *The Rape of Clarissa: Writing, Sexuality, and Class Struggle in Samuel Richardson* (Minneapolis: University of Minnesota Press, 1982), p. 62. Wilt, "He Could Go No Farther: A Modest Proposal about Lovelace and Clarissa," *PMLA* 92 (1977):19–32.

[50] Pateman, *The Sexual Contract*, pp. 100–1.

me to a level so low, as to make me a fit Wife for this man?" (1:228–29) [1:156]. She recognizes that the policy's purpose is to accustom her to the death of her recently acquired juridical self, a death that will occur when that self is incorporated into Solmes's through marriage. Clarissa imagines this death in the vivid picture that she paints of the family assembling for her "trial": "oh! how my heart fluttered on hearing ... each person's stepping out," she writes Anna Howe, "to take his place on the awful bench which my fancy had formed for them and my other judges!" (1:327) [1:223]. The awful bench, which is supposed to protect the rights of the juridical subject, assembles to deny the woman those very rights by condemning her to juridical and spiritual death through an involuntary union. As a gesture of submission to the bench's awful majesty, Clarissa agrees to "have an instrument drawn to tie [her] up to [her] good behaviour" (1:327) [1:223]. Having already lived confinement at the hands of others, the neophyte juridical subject offers to internalize their methods if not their rationale and confine herself by restricting her freedom of choice. She is willing to let a written promise – a contract in which the consideration for her is freedom from an unwanted marriage – guarantee her word. At this point Clarissa believes that her family will accept her as an equal subject. They, on the other hand, willing to entertain only an expression of absolute submission, reject her offer.

When persuasion and pageantry, intimidation and authority fail to bend and break Clarissa's will, the family plans more draconian measures. They hope to coerce her into the marriage by bringing her and Solmes together in her uncle's private chapel. Clarissa discovers her brother's cruelty in this plot: "So here is the master-stroke of my Brother's policy! Called upon to consent to go to my Uncle Antony's, *avowedly* to receive Mr. Solmes visits! – A Chapel! – A Moated-house! – Deprived of the opportunity of corresponding with you! – or of any possibility of escape, should violence be used to compel me to be that odious man's!" (2:27) [1:257]. The Gothic element, the excess of cruelty, and the hint of legally sanctioned rape in the Harlowes' policy signify an ideological regression that allies them with another rapist in the novel. Clarissa's removal from Harlowe Place to her uncle's castle is a removal in time as well as in space. The castle, with its moat and its private chapel is an emblem of absolutism. Private violence – and thus the abandonment of the rule of law – is once again the last resort when quasi-juridical suasions fail.

James's sadistic fantasy is preempted by Lovelace, who threatens to attack the family on the way to Uncle Antony's estate. Violence counters violence in this instance, as the Harlowes find themselves not on juridical grounds but in a feral state of nature brought about by the abandonment of the rule of law. Forced by their real adversary to reconsider their plan, they return to the coercive power of the juridical spectacle. Clarissa's imagination has become the magic lantern that projects the scene of her ultimate trial:

Next Wednesday morning ... [w]hen this awful court is assembled, the poor prisoner is to be brought in, supported by Mrs. Norton ... it is not believed that I can be hardened enough to withstand the expostulations of so venerable a judicature, altho' I have withstood those of several of them separately ... my spirits will never bear up, I doubt, at such a tribunal – My Father presiding in it.
(2:291–92) [1:438–39]

The accused imagines that all the powers and policy of the reorganized family will be brought to bear on her: the group united in one will by the compact; herself regarded as a hardened offender; the group's "venerable" authority, reinforced by her father's presence; and the recalcitrant other expostulated into reason by the awesome juridical theater. Who could bear it? Surely not the poor prisoner, who has only a compassionate but power-less outsider to lean on. And the outsider, the good Mrs. Norton, who had taken "kind and truly-maternal pains ... with [Clarissa] from [her] cradle" (6:124) [3:327], has no influence. Power is monopolized by a venerable judicature presided over by a father. Juridical subjecthood for Clarissa means being nothing more than a "poor prisoner," expelled from the bosom of her family into the blind and unsympathetic precincts of reason.

Given this frightening situation, Clarissa's decision to apply to Lovelace for protection seems overdetermined rather than surprising. Since her family has removed her from their hearts in order to place her in the prisoner's dock, is it any wonder that her heart should seek a new, fitter habitation? Lovelace promises Clarissa a society to replace the one she has lost, a society characterized by the magnanimity of Lord M and the Ladies Betty and Sarah. He speaks the language of romance and relation, of obligation and of natural right: "Remember only, that I come at your appointment, to redeem you, at the hazard of my life, from your gaolers and persecutors, with a resolution, God is my witness, or may he for ever blast me! [that was his shocking imprecation] to be a Father, Uncle, Brother, and, as I humbly hoped, in your own good time, a *Husband* to you, all in one" (2:353) [1:480]. That Clarissa misreads Lovelace (even though she notes his violence) is as much a consequence of her family's policy as it is of her naivete. Even as she imagines a new home established by a voluntary contract, she will learn that in a calculating world it is dangerous to follow the heart's counsel.

## IV The heart's counsel

The chief contradiction in *Clarissa* emerges in the novel's endowing the heroine with traditional desires and modern necessities. Clarissa wishes to belong to a society governed by a benign patriarchal authority, but she finds herself in one in which commercial expansion has made a contract between putative equals the dominant mode of social relation. Even in the best of worlds, however, patriarchal authority sometimes does not look out for the good of its charges. Richardson himself acknowledges the potential for such a lapse in a letter to Frances Grainger: "In all reciprocal Duties the Non-Performance of the Duty on one part is not an excuse for the Failure of the other." Even when the parent is grossly negligent or unjust, the injured child has no right of redress: "Parents and Sovereigns must in general be left for God to Punish, and seldom do faulty ones escape their Share of Punishment in this Life, and that even Springing from the Seeds sown by themselves."[51] Poetic justice here or hereafter is the only legitimate recourse. For Richardson to have made his heroine a fully fledged juridical subject – to have made her fully modern by giving her a will to litigate – would have undermined his political and ethical beliefs.

If neither Clarissa nor her family can be considered the voice of modernity in this novel, that does not mean that the novel lacks such a voice. Leopold Damrosch has called the fatherless Anna Howe "far more 'modern' than Clarissa."[52] Her letters are filled with the language of rights and individual self-assertion. She is modern not only because she is fatherless and thus appears free from patriarchal power, but also because she is ready to use the juridical subject's chief instrument – litigation – to protect her self-described interests. In one of her letters she censures Clarissa for failing to do what Anna would do in her position: "I must begin by blaming you, my dear, for your resolution not to litigate for your right, if occasion were to be given you. Justice is due to ourselves, as well as to every-body else" (2:9) [1:245]. If we cannot condemn Anna for her modernity (though Richardson seems to by subjecting her to Lovelace's imaginary vengeance), it is because she is responding to Clarissa's description of life at Harlowe Place, where obligations are exacted through trials and deference secured by litigation: "And now, if I do not oblige them, my Grandfather's Estate is to be litigated with me; and I, who never designed to take advantage of the independency bequeathed me, *am to be as dependent upon my Father's Will, as a Daughter ought to be who knows not what is good for herself.* This is the language of the family now" (1:85) [1:58]. Even Clarissa is moved into a more modern position by such language. And yet, although Anna's attitudes may be modern, it is Clarissa's hybrid voice that utters a progressive call to resist the monological discourse of instrumental reason.

Throughout her confinement Clarissa never loses her faith in the

---

51 To Frances Grainger, 22 January 1749/50, *Selected Letters of Samuel Richardson*, ed. John Carroll (Oxford: Clarendon Press, 1964), pp. 144–45.
52 Damrosch, *God's Plot*, p. 222.

potentially transformative virtue of the human heart guided by natural law. Her heart, which she calls her conscience and which remains distinct from the public conscience, cannot be alienated from her reason. Clarissa stands in the text as an embodiment of "the Law of Nature ... which is evident of it self, and wants no Demonstration, flowing from the first Principles of the Law of Nature, *viz.* that which is Good ought to be embraced, and that which is Evil avoided."[53] In a letter to Anna, she quotes the following from Ecclesiasticus: "'Let the counsel of thine own heart stand; for there is no man more faithful to thee, than It: For a man's mind is sometimes wont to tell him more than seven watchmen, that sit above in a high tower'" (2:322) [1:460]. Clarissa's intuitive sense has resisted the damaging effects of the new-furbished "publique Conscience" borne by the Harlowes. In Clarissa's utopian world view, society employs astute watchmen to keep reason instrumental to the holiness of the heart's affections rather than to the profit of the mind's calculations. The novel finally shows, however, that Clarissa's society cannot give a home to her heart. Even her closest friend cannot understand it.

Like watchmen who cast a cold and reasonable eye on interest, Clarissa's family cannot see her heart. Terry Castle has noted that Clarissa's family "reads" her in accord with their own wishes.[54] They refuse to let anyone outside the family mediate the dispute, unless it be to mediate it in their favor. In the words of Samuel Johnson, they demonstrate how the "end of all civil regulations ... is apparently neglected, ... when the distinction between guilt and unhappiness, between casualty and design, is intrusted to eyes blind with interest, to understandings depraved by resentment."[55] Blinded by their policy, they share no common language with Clarissa: "O that my friends but knew my heart!" she writes, " – Would but think of it as they used to do! – For once more, I say, If it deceive me not, it is not altered, altho' theirs are!" (2:251) [1:411]. Interest has riven heart from tongue and faith from action. When they see Clarissa – and they see her unwillingly – they see art and subterfuge only. They see antisocial behavior. They see what they would find if they looked into their own hearts. These literalists have confined themselves to scrutinizing surfaces in order to search out opportunity for profit, and they have thereby impoverished social life.

If I have willingly run the risk of falling victim to what William Warner has described as Clarissa's will to power, it is because her will is joined to a social vision.[56] Throughout her ordeal she embodies the wish for a social being that is real and sensuous, that combines labor and leisure in the

---

[53] *A Dissertation on the Law of Nature*, p. 34.    [54] Castle, *Clarissa's Ciphers*, p. 71.
[55] Samuel Johnson, *Idler* 22, 16 September 1758, in *The Idler and Adventurer*, eds. W. J. Bate, John M. Bullitt, and L. F. Powell (New Haven and London: Yale University Press, 1963), p. 70.
[56] Warner, *Reading "Clarissa,"* pp. 24–27.

service of an end greater than individual enrichment. Stripped of every comfort she has known, the burden of life in a society that is a mere association of competing interests becomes so great for Clarissa that she has nowhere to turn but heavenward. Although this is a traditional consolation – the court of last resort when civil justice fails – it is no earthly solution to the heroine's dilemma. *Clarissa* tells us that a civil society without enduring forms of association, a civil society founded upon adventitious alliances, gives its members thin subsistence even if they can find a way to conform their consciences to the contract. So, in the end, Samuel Richardson resorts to a religious reflex to dispense justice to the deserving as he dispatches his heroine to the lonely peace where the wicked cease from troubling and the weary are at rest. But he leaves the reader the utopian hope that the heart's counsel may be more physical than metaphysical when it seeks its own good in the well-being of others who respond in kind.

# 4

# Tame spirits, brave fellows, and the web of law: Robert Lovelace's legalistic conscience

[T]he novelistic hybrid is not only double-voiced and double-accented (as in rhetoric) but it is also double-languaged; in it there are not only (and not even so much) two individual consciousnesses, two voices, two accents, as there are two socio-linguistic consciousnesses, two epochs, that, true, are not here unconsciously mixed (as in an organic hybrid), but that come together and consciously fight it out on the territory of the utterance.

M. M. Bakhtin, *The Dialogic Imagination*, p. 360

In the previous chapter I examined the forces that make Clarissa become an unwilling juridical subject. Because of her strong allegiance to patriarchal tradition, however, she remains a divided subject, a hybrid of juridical and patriarchal values, just as the family is a hybrid of absolutist tactics and liberal principles. In the following chapter I intend to show that Robert Lovelace is yet another hybrid character. Like Roxana and Clarissa, Lovelace bears a divided allegiance. The division in him, however, a privileged male in a hierarchical society, is not the consequence of a choice between alienation and juridical empowerment. Rather, Lovelace's character is the site of the deliquescence of aristocratic ideals and the emergence of an anarchic version of individualism. Thus, critics have allied Lovelace with both an heroic past and a transcendent future.[1] Other recent critics of Richardson's novel have also noted Lovelace's familiarity with and reliance on the law. Rita Goldberg sees him sharing the legally sanctioned power enjoyed by other males in the text. Linda Kauffman finds evidence of a legalistic mentality in Lovelace's reliance on contracts to provide for the women he has ruined.[2] Neither of these critics, however, examine the sources of these characteristics; nor do they notice the pervasive juridical cast to his imagination. Like the

[1] See, for example, Margaret Doody, *A Natural Passion: A Study of the Novels of Samuel Richardson* (Oxford: Clarendon Press, 1974), pp. 112–18; and Warner, *Reading "Clarissa,"* p. 52 and *passim*. See also Terry Castle and Sue Warrick Doederlein, who have attributed Lovelace's popularity with modern critics to prevailing sexism. Castle, *Clarissa's Ciphers*, esp. p. 194. Sue Warrick Doederlein, "Clarissa in the Hands of the Critics," *Eighteenth-Century Studies* 16 (1983):401–14. Finally, I owe a general debt to Terry Eagleton's reading of the text in terms of a class struggle cast as sexual drama in his *The Rape of Clarissa*.

[2] Goldberg, *Sex and Enlightenment*, p. 101. Kauffman, *Discourses of Desire*, p. 148.

Harlowes, Lovelace is enslaved to civil society's instrumental reason, a reason that is divorced from any consideration other than the attainment of its ends. Although he believes himself free from the debased commercial motives of the dung-hill-bred Harlowe family, his ways of regarding Clarissa, his plots, and his language are derived from a common juridical discourse. I will argue in the following pages that Lovelace's aristocratic values have been altered by a juridical fancy and sanctioned by a legalistic conscience.

## I Lovelace and virtue

*Clarissa* opens with the report of a duel between Lovelace and James Harlowe, which establishes James's pretensions and Lovelace's aristocratic character.[3] Although loaded with negative connotations, the event also serves to reveal Lovelace's noble characteristics. Having disarmed James Harlowe, he nonetheless graciously grants him his life. To be sure, this gracious gesture is a matter of strategy, a way of sweetening the triumph by humiliating the opponent. At the same time, it finds corollaries in such actions as Lovelace's particular beneficence to distressed persons who acknowledge his power. Rather than being an "infernal figure," as Anthony Winner makes him, Lovelace possesses "redeeming" virtues.[4] Samuel Richardson described such virtues in his *Hints of Prefaces*: "the Gentlemen, 'tho professed Libertines as to the Fair Sex, are not, however, Infidels or Scoffers; nor yet such as think themselves freed from the Observance of those other moral Obligations which bind Man to Man."[5] Other virtues include a quasi-republican freedom from pecuniary obligations, called by him "*Tenant-courtesy*, the vilest of all Tenures" (3:132) [2:67].

Lovelace's identity is founded upon these aristocratic traits, which also affect the way that he treats those who fail to acknowledge his power and those who presume to take advantage of him, especially if he considers them to be of lower social standing. He rationalizes his seduction of Miss Betterton by resorting to his strong sense of what is due him because of his social status: "Miss Betterton was but a Tradesman's daughter. The family indeed were grown rich, and aimed at a new Line of Gentry; and were unreasonable enough to expect that a man of my family would marry her" (3:249) [2:147]. His dismissal of the woman is as much an assault on her

---

[3] See Clark, *English Society, 1688–1832*, pp. 109–16 for the meaning and survival of dueling. See also below, ch.5, nn. 26–30.

[4] Anthony Winner, "Richardson's Lovelace: Character and Prediction," *Texas Studies in Literature and Language* 14 (1972):57.

[5] Samuel Richardson, *"Clarissa": Preface, Hints of Prefaces, and Postscript*, The Augustan Reprint Society, No. 103, intro. R. F. Brissenden (Los Angeles: William Andrews Clark Memorial Library, 1964), *Hints of Prefaces*, p. 4.

overreaching family as it is a trial of her virtue, just as James Harlowe is Lovelace's absent rival, whom he attacks through the body of his sister. Virtue, in these instances, carries the classical meaning of power. Lovelace does what his status has licensed him to do in order to maintain it. In so acting he remains distant from a more modern meaning of virtue, embodied in the continence of a character like Anna's suitor Hickman.

And yet Lovelace's character is not as unified as his aristocratic demeanor suggests. Despite his sense of obligation and his contempt for the social aspirations of arrivistes like the Bettertons and the Harlowes, Lovelace has no desire for a life of public service that distinguishes the tradition of civic humanism, a part of aristocratic ideology. J. G. A. Pocock has described this ideal in the following way: "[T]he ideal of virtue was political, and ... the polis [was] based on the *vita activa* ... [I]t included an elite, characterized by wisdom and experience, leisure and property, whose virtue was to lead ..."[6] If we assume that Pocock's republican ideology was at least one norm available to the traditional aristocracy, then it is reasonable to see in Lovelace a hybrid who wishes to preserve the forms of aristocratic privilege without preserving their social function. Instead of actively promoting his values, Lovelace attacks those who challenge his right to social preeminence. This mutation of aristocratic virtue from a productive to a negating power is also in accord with the ideological developments described by Michael McKeon. McKeon notes that "as the progressive critique [of aristocratic ideology] forces the detachment of 'honor as virtue' from male aristocratic honor, it simultaneously encourages its relocation within not only commoners but women, who increasingly come to be viewed not just as the conduit but as the repository of an honor that has been alienated from a corrupt male aristocracy."[7] In order to preserve his aristocratic identity, Lovelace attacks the conduits of the new honor. As long as he penetrates the repository of his enemy's power – the daughters they barter for status – he remains empowered in his own eyes.

In his attempt to distinguish himself from the climbers whom he despises, Lovelace ultimately privatizes aristocratic traditions, thereby furthering the very changes he combats. As he comes more and more to represent himself as the heroic resistance to new social developments, that resistance becomes individualized, producing heroic results for himself and in the eyes of his followers only. Without a productive social function, his personal desires ultimately overwhelm all other values: "To ME, one country is as good as another; and I shall soon, I suppose, chuse to quit this paltry Island; except the mistress of my fate will consent to cohabit at *home*" (4:269) [2:419]. In this boast Lovelace sounds suspiciously like

---

6 Pocock, *Machiavellian Moment*, p. 485.    7 McKeon, *Origins of the English Novel*, p. 158.

Roxana's Dutch Merchant, the deracinated man of trade who goes where business or pleasure takes him. But because Lovelace cares little for trade, it is more accurate to see him as the prefiguration of the "aesthetic" individual, described by Alasdair MacIntyre as "those who see in the social world nothing but a meeting place for individual wills, ... who understand that world solely as an arena for the achievement of their own satisfaction, who interpret reality as a series of opportunities for their enjoyment and for whom the last enemy is boredom."[8] Because he knows no greater good than his own satisfaction, because he has discarded the public virtues of the tradition he espouses, and because he has no concern that extends further than the moment just prior to the fruition of his evanescent games and plots (like Roxana in this regard), Lovelace might be called a serial subject. He is blind to consequence and blind to the accumulation of evidence that identifies him with the rising class. He resorts to the same juridical feints, financial incentives, and physical intimidations that the Harlowes adopt to force their daughter into submission. Tactic for tactic, the aristocrat matches his hated antagonists. Law provides the ground for his fantasies and facilitates his plots. The theatrical imagination that critics have discovered in him is preponderantly juridical and cryptically economic.[9]

Lovelace's blindness can be attributed to the same lack of "classical rationality" that characterizes the trading Harlowes. On the one hand, he cannot see how his behavior travesties the most noble aspects of aristocratic heritage. A penitent Jack Belford, his friend and chief correspondent, recognizes this blindness in Lovelace's obsessive pursuit of libertine pleasures. Libertines, Belford writes, "move round and round (like so many blind mill-horses) in one narrow circle" (6:439) [4:15]. Earlier, he berated Lovelace for abandoning the "good old ways" out of "vanity" and "ignorance" (4:148) [2:337]. On the other hand, Lovelace can only mock the principle of interest because it has been tainted by its association with his bourgeois opponents. When he finally manages to steal Anna Howe's letters from Clarissa's quarters, for example, he ridicules the notion that interest could ever figure into his deliberations: "But *it is my Interest to be honest*, Miss Howe tells her – *Interest*, fools! – I thought these girls knew, that my *Interest* was ever subservient to my *Pleasure*" (4:189) [2:364]. Lovelace's pleasure, however, gives him no sturdy sustenance and no fixed orientation. It separates him from both the good old ways and the powerful new ones. It sparkles and then vanishes: "More truly delightful

---

[8] MacIntyre, *After Virtue*, p. 24.

[9] Mark Kinkead-Weekes, *Samuel Richardson, Dramatic Novelist* (Ithaca: Cornell University Press, 1973), describes Lovelace as a "born playactor," one who is "vividly and enjoyably aware of the drama he is creating" (177, 215). Warner finds that Lovelace "is forever adjusting his masks and roles according to the exigencies of the moment" (*Reading "Clarissa"* 33). See also Doody, *Natural Passion*, n. 1 above.

to me the seduction-progress than the crowning act: For that's a vapor, a bubble!" (4:148) [2:337], he tells Belford. Lovelace lives a feverish dream of insatiable desire.

Like Adam Smith's frivolous great proprietors who barter their birth-rights for diamond buckles, Lovelace gratifies momentary passions and scorns enduring interests. The novel finally indicts this choice for its nearsightedness. From where else should the indictment arise but from the democratic choral voice of the common people ("numbers of people of all conditions"), who attend Clarissa to her grave? What better foreman to deliver the jury's verdict than Morden, who has embodied the promise of justice and order throughout the novel? Morden describes the *exodus* of the tragedy to Belford: "Several expressed their astonishment, as people do every hour, 'that a man could live whom such perfections could not engage to be just to her;' To be *humane*, I may say. – And who, her rank and fortune considered, could be so disregardful of his own *interest*, had he had no other motive to be just! –" (8:95, 96) [4:409]. Having violated a moral imperative to respect innocence and a bourgeois imperative to recognize "his own interest," Lovelace is finally categorized and contained as an instance of abnormal psychology, a fatal contagion produced by the death of the old order. In an age where aristocratic honor can only destroy, positive laws are necessary to protect the innocent female who carries legitimate bourgeois interests. And yet it is both an irony and an instance of the conflicts within juridical discourse that these necessary laws provide Lovelace with his motives and suggest to him the means to achieve his reactionary ends.

## II Lovelace and the law

After forging a letter from Lord M. to Clarissa and acknowledging his talent for "*Manual Imitation*," Lovelace apprises Belford of his double standard: "It has been said, on this occasion, that had I been a *bad* man in *meum* and *tuum* matters, I should not have been fit to live. As to the girls, we hold it no sin to cheat them" (4:341) [2:468]. Lovelace respects the rights of property owners. "Girls," because they do not own property, he need not respect. Such a principle governs his dealings with Clarissa. In his creative plottings, he casts her as something to be possessed rather than as a possessor. His view coincides with Blackstone's famous definition of a *feme covert*, whose "very being or legal existence ... is suspended during the marriage, or at least is incorporated and consolidated into that of the husband."[10] One legal digest writer even suggests that these rights are proleptically suspended when he remarks that "an ancient Author has

---

[10] Blackstone, *Commentaries*, 1:430.

assur'd us, that all Women, in the Eye of the Law, are either married or to be married ..."[11] And a married woman, Chief Justice Hale writes, cannot be raped by her spouse because she "hath given up herself in this kind unto her husband."[12]

I do not mean to suggest that Lovelace rationalizes his behavior in this manner; rather, the juridical construction of *feme covert* provides a structure that parallels, informs, and enables Lovelace's behavior toward all women. According to Blackstone's version of the *feme covert* in common law, wives have no legal being; they are not accountable for many of their actions. According to Lovelace "women have no Souls ... And if so, to whom shall I be accountable for what I do to them?" (4:350) [2:474]. The implicit answer, of course, is that he is accountable to himself, the potential husband of any or all. Before he rapes Clarissa, he writes Belford that "Marriage will be always in my power" (3:34) [1:516]; and "I can marry her when I will. And if I do, after prevailing (whether by *surprize*, or by *reluctant consent*) whom but myself shall I have injured?" (4:217) [2:383]. Lovelace's reasoning here takes another important turn. By making Clarissa his wife, he makes her his property. Injury to one's own property, in most cases, is not actionable. Paradoxically, however, Lovelace thinks in terms of injury only after according Clarissa the respect that he – and the law – accord to property. In short, Lovelace thinks of Clarissa as a subject liable to be injured only after he has objectified her.

The role played by juridical discourse in Lovelace's imagination is complex. As an heiress of the new class, Clarissa is the perfect object upon which Lovelace can prove his mastery. She has rights as an heiress, which Lovelace scorns, thus showing his contempt for the law.[13] As a woman, however, she has no natural rights in his eyes. Thus, he justifies his actions by asserting a property-claim over her. From the joyful moment when he frightens her into fleeing her father's house, he claims imaginary proprietary rights. He founds these rights upon the Harlowes' abandonment of their daughter, who is fair game once she has been driven from the protection of the family haven. He refuses to allow that any woman can or would want to be self-possessed. The former assumption is explicit, the latter implicit in a rhetorical question which Lovelace puts to Belford: "And whose property, I pray thee, shall I invade, if I pursue my schemes of Love and Vengeance? Have not those who have a right in her, renounced that right? Have they not willfully exposed her to dangers?" (4:377) [2:492]. Part of Clarissa's value to Lovelace is an effect of being

[11] *Treatise of Feme Coverts*, p. v.
[12] Sir Matthew Hale, *Historia Placitorum Coronae. The History of the Pleas of the Crown* (London, 1736), p. 629. See also Pateman, *The Sexual Contract*, pp. 123–24, for a discussion of rape and conjugal right.
[13] On stealing an heiress, see n. 20 below.

"property" – a thing of value without a soul – to others. Thus, in the face of Clarissa's assertion of her rights, Lovelace steadies his wavering resolution by reminding himself that she belongs to the Harlowes.

Clarissa's abandonment by her family allows Lovelace to maintain the distinctions between *meum* and *tuum* that he finds so important. The structural importance of this kind of reason for both the dramatic action involving Lovelace and the psychological disposition of all the characters is made evident in a comment by Clarissa after she has escaped to Hampstead from Mrs. Sinclair's brothel. She tells Anna about the special dangers awaiting unclaimed chattel in the perilous common: "be pleased to consider my unhappy situation ... the man, who has had the assurance to think me, and to endeavour to make me, his *property*, will hunt me from place to place, and search after me as a 'Stray'" (5:52–53) [3:17]. Clarissa's self-representation shows some awareness of Lovelace's juridico-economic assumptions, found also in the following definition of "Stray" in the *Oxford English Dictionary*: "*Law.* A domestic animal found wandering away from the custody of its owner, and liable to be impounded and (if not redeemed) forfeited = Estray." Clarissa registers her society's attempts to turn her into chattel, incapable of being self-possessed, even as she realizes that Lovelace accepts this common attitude.

Although Lovelace claims that his new acquisition makes him feel like an "Emperor" with absolute power after he tricks Clarissa into leaving Harlowe Place (3:30) [1:513], his actions reveal that his "natural" sovereignty must be supported by juridical tactics. He schemes to implicate Clarissa in a "marriage" validated by her tacit consent, thereby reserving the law as an aid to his plots, as he tells Jack Belford: "Should she *actually fly*, cannot I *bring her back* by authority civil or uncivil, if I have evidence upon evidence that she acknowledged, though but tacitly, her Marriage?" (3:354) [2:218].[14] As he draws up affidavits and forecasts the legal actions he will take, Lovelace proclaims himself a devout believer in his own juridical schemes. Clarissa's "tacit acknowledgment" leads him to consider her virtually bound to him by the silken cords of love and the iron fetters of the law. Thus, he is shocked by Clarissa's reaction when he

[14] See Albert, "1. The Law vs. Clarissa Harlowe," pp. 29–31; and Florian Stuber, "Clarissa and Her World: Form and Content in Richardson's *Clarissa*," Diss. Columbia University, 1980, pp. 190–99, for discussions of the laws governing tacit consent to marriage. Of course, Lovelace would not have a case in law, there having been no marriage, but he would have been able to act as if there were and threaten others with prosecution or bodily injury. According to Blackstone, a husband "may lawfully claim and retake [his wife] wherever he happens to find [her], so it be not in a riotous manner, or attended with a breach of the peace" (3:4). This redress is called *recaption*. If the wife goes by her own consent, another treatise says, still "the law always supposes compulsion and force to have been used, because the wife is not supposed to possess a power of consent." In this instance, a husband can sue at common law and recover damages for the loss of his wife (just as he may do for loss of property), although he cannot recover possession (*Laws Respecting Women* 53).

kisses her breast, and he asks Belford for an explanation: "But why makes she every inch of her person thus sacred? – So near the time too, that she must suppose, that all will be my own by deed of purchase and settlement?" (4:354) [2:476]. Only by borrowing a vocabulary of dominance from legal sanctions and from the vulgar world of contract and bartering can his imagination transform Clarissa into a tractable object of desire. After his imagination has done its work, his reason reappropriates the transformed thing in order to make it the object of his claim to proprietary rights.

Lovelace continues in this juridical mode of thought after the rape. He tries to extenuate his guilt and assuage his misgivings by turning his and Clarissa's relation into a matter of property rights. He admits to Belford that "if a person sets a high value upon any-thing, be it ever such a trifle in itself, or in the eye of others, the robbing of that person of it is *not* a trifle to *him*. Take the matter in this light, I own I have done wrong, great wrong, to this admirable creature" (5:318–19) [3:199]. By raping Clarissa, he has been a "thief to [his] own joys" (5:323) [3:202]. When he presents his final defense to Lord M after Clarissa's death, he uses the same analogy: "I insisted upon it to them, and so I do to you, Jack, that I ought to be acquitted of every-thing but a Common Theft, a Private Larceny, as the Lawyers call it ... " (8:162) [4:453]. Lovelace had prefaced his assertion of relative innocence by putting the case of a miser and a thief, the miser owning something that he did not need, but without which the thief could not survive. For miser, read Clarissa; for thief, read Lovelace; for thing, read hymen. In these remorseful moments when he is nonetheless called upon to defend himself, Lovelace grants Clarissa relative equality as a possessor of her own person. He makes Clarissa's self-possession a matter of property rights because it allows him to consider restitution for his actions. Even now, however, Lovelace fails to see the injury sustained by the person as person. And this failure, in turn, makes it impossible for him to understand why Clarissa refuses to consider his offers of marriage after the rape. Never can he free himself from the compulsion to treat a woman as a thing, not even after Clarissa's death, when he wishes to possess her stilled heart.

If Lovelace views Clarissa as an object in order to justify his possession of her and to accord her a relative value that women lack, Clarissa's strong-willed resistance compels him both to acknowledge her status as a bearer of rights and to appropriate for his private ends the state's coercive powers. At the outset of Clarissa's "incarceration," Lovelace informs Belford that he intends to "put her to trials as mortifying to her Niceness, as glorious to my Pride," adding that should she show any hint of a preference to another, he "would shew her no mercy" (3:2) [1:494]. By choosing the strategy of selective enforcement of his rake's creed and by holding out the promise of mercy to the resistant subject, Lovelace imitates early-modern England's policing strategies, as they have been described by Douglas Hay.[15] Just as the law stages juridical spectacles to recreate its social authority, so too Lovelace subjects Clarissa to his private juridical theatricals. She must be found guilty of being a woman if his entire psychological and political edifice built upon female bodies is not to collapse. Clarissa's failure in the trial means more than her weakness; it means an acknowledgment of his power.

Clarissa's will, however, as tenacious as any freeborn Englishman's, forces Lovelace to resort to ever-more arbitrary measures. At first, he scrutinizes her actions for the signs he wishes to find. He places her under surveillance, and his spies look through keyholes and rifle dressers. In all he imitates the Harlowes. Just as they watched for the least sign of guilt in the daughter who resisted their will, Lovelace watches for the guilty moment when Clarissa will allow him to "awaken the *woman* in her": "Let me begin then, as opportunity presents. – I will; and watch her every step to find one sliding one; her every moment, to find the moment critical. And the rather, as she spares not me, but takes every advantage that offers, to puzzle and plague me; nor expects nor thinks me to be a good man" (3:94–95) [2:42]. By finding Clarissa's weakness, exploiting it to her own disadvantage, and punishing her for allowing herself to be exploited, Lovelace hopes to subdue her. These practices further reveal Lovelace's hybrid character. He complements spectacle and force with the surveillance that, according to Michel Foucault, ushered in new and more sophisticated regimes of power in the late eighteenth century. This new mode of discipline, works "without recourse, in principle at least, to excess, force or violence."[16] It aims to neutralize possible sites of resistance (puzzlement, plague, rebelliousness) by producing a particular social, political, and economic regime in the body of the object under scrutiny. In Lovelace's case, the order is psychosexual.

Failing to find the "one sliding" step he and his spies watch for, Lovelace seeks to create the conditions that will produce the guilty person, thereby giving him license to discipline her will. When Clarissa's behavior fails to provide a purchase for his power, he subjects her to conditions where that power can act independently of her choice. Once again, he shows his affinity to the Harlowes. When Clarissa failed to respond to surveillance, isolation, and alienation, they decided to try her resistance by placing her against her will in her Uncle Antony's castle, where she would be compelled to accept the family compact. At that crucial moment, replete with all the emblems of paternal authority, the Harlowes expected the "daughter" to subdue the woman. Lovelace expects Clarissa's trial by ordeal to end in the woman conquering the "angel." Thus,

[15]Hay, "Property, Authority," p. 42.        [16]Foucault, *Discipline and Punish*, p. 177.

to prove his theorem on the body of Clarissa, he resolves to stop at nothing, as he tells his correspondent: "Night, *mid*-night, *is* necessary, Belford. Surprize, Terror, *must* be necessary to the ultimate Trial of this charming creature" (4:206) [2:376]. Having failed in his aims with new techniques, he resorts to those associated with arbitrary power, thereby revealing again that he has an allegiance neither to the future nor to the past. Torture never had been a part of English criminal procedure, except in the instance of pressing a person who refused to plead.[17]

When terror and surprise (the fire at Mrs. Sinclair's) also fail to produce the guilty subject that Lovelace seeks, he redefines the "ultimate trial" to mean rape. Although he concedes that Clarissa has defeated all his stratagems, he still maintains his credo of "once subdued, always subdued." Clarissa need only feel his weight to plead that she is Lovelace's sort of woman. Rape becomes the necessary last resort that will enable him to preserve his illusion of omnipotence, as he writes to Belford on the night of the rape: "Is not *this* the hour of her trial – And in *her*, of the trial of the virtue of her whole Sex, so long premeditated, so long threatened? ... Whether, if *once subdued, she will not be always subdued*? And will she not want the very crown of her glory, the proof of her till now all-surpassing excellence, if I stop short of the ultimate trial?" (5:305) [3:190]. Lovelace turns his necessity into a benefit for Clarissa and for all women. He has no other choice, in effect, because he admits that "*[t]here's no triumph over the Will in force!*" If it comes to force then he must have ready a rationale that will justify it. Unlike the Harlowes, who try to justify their actions by claiming a good for the entire family, Lovelace acknowledges first a good to the individual and only by abstract extension to others. Furthermore, the implication is that once her crowning glory and all-surpassing excellence has been proven genuine (and only he can provide such proof), then Lovelace need no longer try the subject. Order will be restored when the trial comes to an end.

Despite Lovelace's abuse of her natural and civil rights, and despite her confinement and rape, Clarissa continues to express her will in a libertarian rhetoric: "I have no patience, said she, to find myself a slave, a prisoner, in a vile house – Tell me, Sir, in so many words tell me, Whether it be, or be not, your intention to permit me to quit it? – To permit me the freedom which is my birthright as an English subject?" (6:36) [3:267]. But that is not Lovelace's intention, and so he violates her civil rights. When he fails to extract a promise from Clarissa that she will not leave the house while he attends Lord M, he violates her natural rights by assuming that her prior promise to "rest easy" entailed consent to an unjust

[17] Leon Radzinowicz, *A History of Criminal Law and its Administration from 1750*, 4 vols. (London: Stevens & Sons Limited, 1948), 1:26. *Peine forte et dure* – pressing a person who refused to plead – was permitted until 1772.

imprisonment.[18] Clarissa's rhetoric and Lovelace's absolutist excesses begin the textual recuperation of the law. The penknife scene advances this gradual recuperation.[19] The mere mention of legal redress coupled with Clarissa's power to harm herself immobilizes Lovelace's accomplices and prevents him from raping Clarissa again. When Clarissa declares that "[t]he Law shall be all my resource: The LAW" (6:67) [3:289], the people of the house have real reason to be frightened. According to Sir William Hawkins, "[a]ll who are present and actually assist a man to commit a rape, may be indicted as principal offenders, whether they be men or women."[20] It is important to note, however, the context of this partial rehabilitation of the law: it is linked to Clarissa's threatened self-annihilation.[21] Thus, the moment in which Clarissa's invocation of the law aids her also reveals law's relation to property. Lovelace explains to Belford that the women in Sinclair's house are terrified by Clarissa's threat because it endangers their "ease and plenty" – that is, their livelihood rather than their life – thus foregrounding the economic nature of the law's deterrent power. This dramatic moment has even more resonance when juxtaposed to a remark made by William Blackstone in his *Commentaries*: "the legislature of England has universally promoted the grand ends of civil society, the peace and security of individuals, by ... assigning to every thing capable of ownership a legal and determinate owner."[22] Clarissa may have no one to protect her natural rights, but the law will deliberate over her carcass. The law, like Lovelace, respects *meum* and *tuum*.

Lovelace's legalistic rationalizations, his imperial prerogatives, and his malice prepense constitute the ground of his identity and the basis for his participation in the larger community. That he recognizes the law's

18 According to Hobbes, no one was obliged to submit voluntarily to punishment or imprisonment. See *Leviathan*, 1.14.93.

19 For another reading of the penknife scene and the law, see Goldberg, *Sex and Enlightenment*, p. 97.

20 William Hawkins, *A Treatise of the Pleas of the Crown*, 2 vols. (1716; rpt., London, 1824), vol. 2, ch. 16, sect. 10, p. 123. Albert mentions a case of heiress stealing in his study of *Clarissa* (21). The accomplices of Haagen Swendsen, who was convicted and sentenced to hang for stealing away Pleasant Rawlins, were tried under the same statute. The Solicitor General read the jury the indictment, from which is taken the following sentence: "The law, to shew how odious such offences are, and to deter all persons whatsoever from committing them, has made no distinction between the principle and the accesories: the abettors, procurers, and contrivers, are declared and enacted to be, and to be judged as principal felons." Two of his accomplices were acquitted; one was convicted, reprieved upon pleading her belly, and finally pardoned ("The Trial of Haagen Swendsen, at the Queen's Bench, for forcibly taking away and marrying Mrs. Pleasant Rawlins, 1 Anne, A.D. 1702" in *A Complete Collection of State Trials*, ed. T. B. Howell [London, 1816–31], 14:559–96).

21 Cf. Clarissa's earlier response to her mother's assurance that the law will protect them from Lovelace's violence: "But, Madam, may not some dreadful mischief first happen? – The Law asserts not itself, till it *is* offended" (1:122) [1:83].

22 Blackstone, *Commentaries*, 2:15.

opposition to his premeditated violence against Clarissa and that such opposition fuels his sadistic fantasies reveal the social origins of those fantasies and his own alacrity to think in terms of legal and illegal rather than, say, beneficial and harmful. Furthermore, Clarissa's invocation of the law exhilarates rather than frightens him, for it provides him with yet another opportunity to demonstrate a universal mastery, as he tells Jack Belford: "For a Rape, thou knowest, to us Rakes, is far from being an undesirable thing. Nothing but the Law stands in our way, upon that account; and the opinion of what a modest woman will suffer rather than become a *viva voce* accuser, lessens much an honest fellow's apprehensions on that score" (5:340) [3:214]. Lovelace assumes that womanly modesty will keep his victim from risking the shame and terror of the juridical spectacle.[23] In his affair with Miss Betterton, "a modest woman" deterred from prosecuting, supposedly, by the added incentive of love for her seducer, he enjoyed total immunity from the law (3:249–50) [2:147]. Yet the immunity actually deprives Lovelace of his crowning glory, a glory that the law only can provide him. His treatment of Miss Betterton is just another commonplace seduction, no different from all that have gone before and all that will follow.

Lovelace does not fear prosecution, because he feels secure in his knowledge of the law and women. When he elaborates a rape fantasy involving Mrs. Howe and Anna, he comments that "there will be greater likelihood, that these women will *not* prosecute, than that they *will*. For my own part, I should wish they *may*." (4:273) [2:421]. A prosecution will give him the relish of attaining a victory over his opponents within their own institutions. In his fantasy, Lovelace exploits his peculiar and status-based charisma within the juridical theater. The courtroom witnesses both the grand entrance of the heroes, strutting through the crowd, and the shameful spectacle of the accusers, plodding slowly with heads bowed under the weight of shame. In his description of the scene, Lovelace glories in the power of his person: "Would not a brave fellow chuse to appear in court to such an arraignment, confronting women who would do credit to his attempt? The country is more merciful in *these* cases, than in *any others*: I should therefore like to put myself upon my country" (4:273) [2:421–22]. The chilling pun in the last sentence links the rapist's attitudes toward women to those toward the law. Neither will be able to resist his superior force, but neither will dare to call that force coercion. Lovelace imagines himself and his co-defendants "dressed-out each man, as if to his wedding-appearance," just prior to the moment when he shall assume dominion and possession, ratified by the very covenants that he scorns. Nor does he

[23] For a discussion of prosecutions for rape, see my article " 'A Penetration which Nothing Can Deceive': Gender and Juridical Discourse in Some Eighteenth-Century Narratives," *Studies in English Literature* 29 (1989):535–61, esp. nn. 33–34.

espouse merely the women; he wins the hearts of all: "Then we shall be praised – Even the Judges, and the whole crouded Bench, will acquit us in their hearts; and every single man wish he had been me!" (4:273–74) [2:422].

Lovelace's confident mastery arises from his quick wit and his sexual prowess. Just as he cannot imagine any woman strong enough to resist him, so too he cannot envision a court able to convict him. The conquest of the law poses no greater difficulties to his imagination than the conquest of a maidenhead, and he suffers no performance anxiety when the scene shifts from the sexual to the juridical stage. Even in the worst of all possible scenarios – being condemned to death – he has the priapic ace up his sleeve:

being a handsome fellow, I shall have a dozen or two of young maidens, all dressed in white, go to Court to beg my life – And what a pretty shew they will make, with their white hoods, white gowns, white petticoats, white scarves, white gloves, kneeling for me, with their white handkerchiefs at their eyes, in two pretty rows, as Majesty walks thro' them, and nods my pardon for their sakes!    (4:277) [2:424]

The suppliant virgins are Lovelace's private phantasms, but they indicate his compulsive need for domination. In this scene, the absent emperor of sex nominates his minions to manipulate the king and to circumvent the court's finding. Relying on neither reason nor force, Lovelace conquers by his sheer presence (or the profit of that presence). He considers himself a supreme lawgiver, just as he had when he devised the "scheme for annual marriages," in which the law enabled his display of phallic might (5:292) [3:181].[24]

At the end of the fantasy of the suppliant virgins, Lovelace makes a curious legal observation, characteristic of the lawyer rather than of the dreamer. Having just secured a pardon for himself, he makes the following confident boast: "And, if once pardoned, all is over: For, Jack, in a crime of this nature there lies no appeal, as in a murder" (4:277) [2:424]. Has Lovelace been at the Inns of Court? (Hickman has, and Lovelace's contempt for him needs no elaboration.) The "appeal" of which Lovelace speaks is a private criminal prosecution brought by the injured. Blackstone defines this method of prosecution in the following manner: "An appeal, therefore, when spoken of as a criminal prosecution, denotes an accusation by a private subject against another for some heinous crime, demanding punishment on account of the particular injury rather than for the offense against the public."[25] It could be brought for murder, larceny, and rape; moreover, it could be brought even if the accused had been tried on

---

[24] It is interesting to note that Pufendorf lists the tribes and nations where the duration of marriage is determined by contract. He finds these nations either degenerate or barbarian. *De Jure Naturae et Gentium*, 2:876.

[25] Blackstone, *Commentaries*, 4:312.

indictment and acquitted or convicted and subsequently pardoned.[26] Although Blackstone notes that the appeal was seldom used, it was nonetheless an available process at this time. The point here is a minor one: Lovelace is mistaken in his assertion. Did Richardson choose to make this another instance of Lovelace's bravado, or was the law obscure in this point?[27] Whatever the answer, Lovelace's claim reveals his imagination's reliance on the law and the way in which the law limits that imagination.

Finally, Lovelace's confidence in his forensic skills is again evident in his first meeting with Clarissa's cousin Morden, who has come to investigate Lovelace's treatment of her. In their first meeting, the two men waver between challenging each other to a duel and resolving their conflict in a dispassionate manner. Lovelace, however, distorts the facts of the case, declares himself a man of honor, and produces evidence that temporarily satisfies his antagonist: a letter from Charlotte Montague, in which she tells Clarissa that Lovelace is ready to make suitable amends for his actions. Lovelace exults in this victory through manipulation:

So thou seest, Belford, that it is but glossing over *one* part of a Story, and omitting *another*, that will make a bad cause a good one at any time. What an admirable Lawyer should I have made! And what a poor hand would this charming creature, with all her innocence, have made of it in a Court of Justice against a man who had so much to *say* and to *shew* for himself!     (7:298–99) [4:230–31]

Saying and showing, wit and presence remain the man's primary strengths. These strengths, however, draw their power and their forms from juridical discourse. Without the judge, jury, and spectators who inhabit his imagination; without the laws protecting heiresses and securing property; without negotiated marriages and financial settlements, Lovelace would dissolve into the crowded night of sexual incontinence, a mere slave to lust along with poor Belton, Mowbray, and the others. Although he professes to be either heedless of the law or observant of mutual obligation when it suits him {(6:53) [3:278] and (5:64) [3:24]}, his desires depend upon juridical discourse. Rather than a perfect Proteus,

---

[26] "[S]o neither will a pardon by the king be any bar to an appeal" (Hawkins, *Treatise of the Pleas of the Crown*, bk. I, ch. 25, sect. 35, p. 344). "[I]f he [the accused] has been tried by indictment, and acquitted; or found guilty and pardoned by the king, he is still liable to be prosecuted at the suit of the party by appeal, not having been punished for the crime of which he stands accused" (*Laws Respecting Women* 316).

[27] In *The History of the Pleas of the Crown*, Sir Matthew Hale gives the requirements for an appeal of rape (which is disallowed if the woman consent after the fact): "As to the appeal of the party ravished two things are necessary, 1. That she make fresh discovery and pursuit of the offence and the offender, otherwise it carries a presumption that her suit is but malicious and feigned; ... 2. That the appeal be speedily prosecuted, for it seems, that a year and a day is not allowed in this appeal, but some short time, tho' it be not defined in law what time, but lies much in the discretion of the court upon the circumstances of the fact, yet the statute of West. I. cap. 13 allowd [sic] but forty days: long delay of prosecution in such cases of rape always carries a presumption of malicious prosecution" (632).

Lovelace resembles a Procrustes whose conscience and imagination are plotted upon the law's iron matrix, the axes of which are a respect for property and a willful disregard of the rights of the potential wife.

## III Clarissa's virtue and the law

The rape of Clarissa is never disputed, even though at least one recent commentator has found it justifiable.[28] Before leaving Richardson's novel, however, I want to consider Clarissa's refusal to prosecute Lovelace for the light that it casts on the text's juridical ideology. Margaret Doody attributes the refusal to a religious motive: the renunciation of bourgeois society in favor of an "ascetic" and "other-worldly" religion.[29] Richardson himself noted that he did not wish to leave his "Heroine short of Heaven," but religious vision need not necessarily entail a renunciation of all social ties and duties.[30] In fact, given Clarissa's express concern for society and Protestant suspicion of religious asceticism, one is forced to look for additional motives. Other critics emphasize the psychological consequences of victimization as the reason for Clarissa's choosing not to prosecute. Rita Goldberg has called Clarissa "the perpetual victim, the unjustly accused political prisoner in a male world where rapist and rapacious alike go free."[31] And Leopold Damrosch uses the words of Georg Lukács to characterize her as one suffering " 'the torment of a creature condemned to solitude and devoured by a longing for community.' "[32] Carol Kay argues that Clarissa eschews prosecution because of "[m]asculine sexual cruelty" and the possibility that prosecution might "further injure the victim and harden the public."[33] Law has no place in Clarissa's irremediably altered world because she no longer has a place in any human community. Finally, most critics – including Kay and Goldberg – emphasize Clarissa's reasonable assumption that she cannot expect justice to be done. Terry Castle concurs, noting that Clarissa's "lack of faith in the power of judicial testimony is justified ... A legal brief is as much an arbitrary 'construction' as anything else; the 'facts' of a situation can be interpreted and presented any way one wants. Fearing

---

[28] "[R]ape is the most cogent response to Clarissa's fictional projection of her self as a whole unified body 'full of light.' [Lovelace] can subvert this fiction by introducing a small part of himself *into* Clarissa" (Warner, *Reading "Clarissa"* 49). Terry Eagleton responds to Warner's position by noting that "[i]t seems logical, then, that a contemporary deconstructionist should find Lovelace the hero and Clarissa the villain, without allowing a little matter like rape to modify his judgement" (*The Rape of Clarissa* 66).

[29] Doody, Natural Passion, p. 179. Flynn also follows this line of reasoning in part. See *Richardson: A Man of Letters*, pp. 26ff.

[30] Richardson, "To Lady Bradshaigh," 15 December 1748, *Selected Letters*, p. 108.

[31] Goldberg, *Sex and Enlightenment*, p. 101.

[32] Damrosch, *God's Plot*, p. 256.    [33] Kay, *Political Constructions*, p. 187.

such contamination of her 'Story,' Clarissa thus refuses to litigate."[34] Reasoning from Blackstone's dictum that "a jury will rarely give credit to a stale complaint" in the case of rape, Carol Flynn also concludes that, even had Clarissa prosecuted Lovelace, its success would have been doubtful.[35]

Behind both the religious and the psychological explanations for Clarissa's failure to prosecute Lovelace for rape lies the same principle applied differently. In each, Clarissa is read as withdrawing her aims or energies from the society that has shattered her hopes and ideals. Psychological explanations emphasize the (secular) withdrawal from an offending world; religious explanations the translation to a just and rewarding afterlife. Neither, however, except by implication, criticizes the law as strongly as the readings of feminist and feminist-influenced critics like Castle, Flynn, Goldberg, and Kay. In order to describe Clarissa's virtue more fully, especially with regard to the religious and psychological determinants that define her relation to the law, I shall examine the vexed issues of virtue and prosecution, self-interest and civic duty in this section. By doing so, I intend to bring into greater prominence the dramatically minor but ideologically central compromise formation that arises from the traumatic violation of innocence, which in turn generates the recuperation of an ordering rhetoric: Jack Belford as model juridical subject. That Belford lacks the intensity of the other major correspondents (Clarissa, Anna Howe, Lovelace), that he undergoes a religious conversion, and that he becomes the final textual authority on which all readers within and without the novel ultimately rely illustrate the means by which the text recuperates civic order. Through the progressive absorption and ramification of juridical principles within a pious and worldly man, the narrative restores the law. In short, it endows it with a masculinized version of Clarissa's equitable virtue.

To understand fully the relation between Clarissa's virtue and the law, it is well to begin with Carol Flynn's conclusion that Clarissa could not have prosecuted Lovelace successfully. Flynn bases her conclusions on an extended comparison of Clarissa's case and the trial of Lord Baltimore for the rape of Sarah Woodcock, a twenty-nine-year-old milliner working in her father's shop. During the trial, the judge instructed the jury to note the time elapsed between the supposed rape and the complaint. He then added the following admonition: "She [Sarah Woodcock] has owned the injury was received December 21st, and the complaint was not made till December 29th, but she has accounted for it in the manner you have heard [fear and coercion prevented her from making the complaint]."[36] The jury

---

[34] Castle, *Clarissa's Ciphers*, p. 128.
[35] Blackstone, *Commentaries*, 4:211; Flynn, *Richardson: A Man of Letters*, pp. 111–12.
[36] "The Trial of Frederick Calvert, Esq; Baron of *Baltimore* ... for a Rape on the Body of *Sarah Woodcock*," (London: Owen and Gurney, 1768), pp. 73–74.

acquitted Lord Baltimore after hearing testimony that Sarah Woodcock never showed a single sign of distress during the entire time that she resided with his lordship.[37] The burden of their testimony implied that Miss Woodcock had prostituted herself for money and comfort. And although according to Hawkins even a "common strumpet" falls under the protection of the rape statutes, it is unlikely that a jury would credit the testimony of a strumpet, notorious or not.[38] Lord Baltimore's acquittal may well may have borne out the plaintiff's initial belief that she could not prosecute "with safety." When asked in the trial what she meant by this remark, she explained: "I meant, that as he was a man of so much money and power, that there might be a great deal of bribery, and that justice might not be done."[39] Flynn reads this trial as the jury's preference for the defense's corroborated – if circumstantial – evidence against the plaintiff's word and against expert medical testimony stating that Sarah Woodcock's genitals showed signs of recent brutal force. Flynn infers that Clarissa would have fared no better. Sarah Woodcock's fears also support Castle's reading.

Might Clarissa have fared better if she had decided to prosecute? She is raped on the night of June 12; she escapes from Mrs. Sinclair's on the morning of June 28. Already more than a fortnight has passed, nor did she go directly upon escaping to the local magistrate. There is a precedent, however, for seeking an indictment even after some time has passed. In 1631 Mervin Lord Audley was tried for rape and sodomy. In that trial the question of law regarding the lapse of time between crime and complaint was put to the judges:

Whether it is adjudged a Rape, when the woman complaineth not presently? And whether there be a necessity of accusation within a convenient time, as within 24 hours? The Judges resolve, that inasmuch as she was forced against her will, and then shewed her dislike, she was not limited to any time for her complaint; and that in an Indictment, there is no limitation of time, but in an appeal there is.[40]

Although the lapse of time would not necessarily be a bar to prosecution, Clarissa's need to "show dislike" might be. For one thing, she failed to contradict Lovelace's public assertions that they were married, and Lovelace had drawn up an affidavit to that effect from "witnesses" who attended the dinner given for Miss Partington (3:355) [2:219]. Despite this omission, Clarissa's powerful presence might have vied with Lovelace's for the court's sympathy. (It is important to note that he does not include her in his rape-trial fantasy.) Furthermore, as Richardson wrote to Lady

---

[37] One digest writer declared the acquittal to be "contrary to the opinion of the judge who tried him" (*Laws Respecting Women* 314).

[38] Hawkins, *Treatise of the Pleas of the Crown*, bk. 2, ch. 16, sect. 7, p. 122. See also n. 23 above.

[39] "The Trial of Frederick Calvert, Esq; Baron of *Baltimore*," p. 23.

[40] Howell, *State Trials*, 3:415.

Bradshaigh, Clarissa is "of equal Degree with the Gentleman, and of superior, at least equal Talents."[41] Because Clarissa is a woman with property, a jury sitting on the case would not necessarily have entertained a suspicion of prostitution or of fortune-hunting. Finally, would the testimony of the likes of Mrs. Sinclair, a notorious brothel-keeper, convince a jury? Would it not be as likely that Joseph Leman, stung by remorse, should turn to the aid of his young lady by revealing "his Honner's" plot? Or that Belford, forced to make a difficult moral choice, might give a material sign of his conversion?

Given these hypothetical variations on the plot, Clarissa's refusal to prosecute Lovelace *can* be read as the text's critique of the way that juridical principles have penetrated social relations as well as a reflection on certain failings in the law itself. The critique includes both Lovelace's economically inflected legalistic conscience and the social relations that accord Clarissa value only as property to be held. As I noted in the discussion of the penknife scene, the law offers protection to Clarissa's valuable body because through it may pass the inheritance so eagerly sought by all. By the statute 3 Hen VII, c. 2, "stealing an heiress" was made a felony, and by 30 Eliz c. 9, benefit of clergy was denied to "principals, procurers, or accessories *before* the fact." Under the statute it had to be proven that a woman was taken against her will for "lucre" and subsequently "married or defiled," thus leaving women without property the recourse of a complaint for rape only, a situation which, by 1770, lessened "the social and ethical value of the statute."[42] Clarissa's case certainly falls within the statute since she has "substance, either real or personal"; but neither the particular matter of her substantial complaint (rape) nor Lovelace's breach of faith would be addressed by it. This law, aimed as it is at Clarissa's juridical character as heiress, is ignorant of her chief concerns, which are non-economic. If any one were to prosecute Lovelace under this statute, it would most likely be Clarissa's brother.

What then about swearing a complaint of rape against Lovelace before a magistrate? Many cogent arguments in favor of prosecution come from Clarissa's correspondents. Anna reasons that prosecution would protect her, Clarissa, and "innocents who otherwise may yet be deluded and

---

[41] "To Lady Bradshaigh," 15 December 1748, *Selected Letters*, p. 106.

[42] Blackstone, *Commentaries*, 4:208. Radzinowicz, *History of Criminal Law*, 1:441. For an account of a trial under this statute, see note 20 above. The compiler of a legal digest notes that the statute can be construed to allow for the possibility that the woman may have been tricked by her abductor:

> And though possibly the marriage or defilement after her forcible taking away, may be by her consent, she being wrought upon to give it by persuasion and management; yet such subsequent consent does not abate the felony, if the first taking away was against her will; and so *vice-versa*, if the woman be originally taken away with her own consent, yet if she afterwards refuse to continue with the offender, and if forced against her will, as properly as if she had never given any consent at all. For till force was put upon her, she was in her own power.                                          (*Laws Respecting Women* 294)

outraged by him" (6:196) [3:375]. Mrs. Howe invokes the "good of Society" and admonishes Clarissa "to overcome her scruples out of regard to her Family, her Acquaintance, and her Sex, which are all highly injured and scandalized by [Lovelace's] villainy to her" (6:201–2) [3:378–79]. Her spiritual advisor, Dr. Lewen, offers much the same advice as Mrs. Howe: "your Religion, your Duty to your Family, the Duty you owe to your Honour, and even Charity to your Sex, oblige you to give Public Evidence against this very wicked man" (7:225) [4:181]. Except for a concession made to Anna, for whom she would sacrifice her "scruples" in a prosecution if she thought her friend threatened by Lovelace's vengeance, Clarissa rejects this advice. She tells the Howes that she could not bear to "prosecute him and his accomplices in a Court of Justice," and to Anna she confesses that she "should not survive [her] first appearance at the Bar he should be arraigned at" (6:194, 211) [3:374, 385]. By the time she writes to Dr. Lewen, however, some five weeks later and two weeks before her death, she explains that the publication of her private papers, which will be warning enough to others, makes a trial unnecessary. Furthermore, the trial's outcome (and thus its didactic efficacy) would be "doubtful" by comparison. Even if the prosecution succeeded, she argues, Lovelace's influential friends would very likely secure him a pardon. And a pardoned Lovelace would seek vengeance. All these reasons support the modern critics' observations on Clarissa's decision not to prosecute. In the same letter to Dr. Lewen, however, she also calls the prosecution "the end so much wished for by my friends," those same friends who had tried to use Clarissa before to advance their own interests. "The evil," she continues, "(respecting *myself*, and not my *friends*), is merely personal" (7:230–32) [4:184–86]. In rejecting her friends' ends, she also rejects the value that they have accorded her "person" but not her "self."

Clarissa's refusal to prosecute can be seen, then, as a criticism of the way that juridical social structures have objectified her as much as a criticism of the law itself. Because she has found the marriage contract to be primarily an economic negotiation, and because the social contract is similar to it, she rejects the ties that bind and the words that guarantee such bonds.[43] Even Lovelace, who at first seemed different from her family, has turned out to be just the same. Clarissa's profoundest experiences with most of the characters in the novel have been Hobbesian; and she discovers that "the bonds of words are too weak to bridle mens [sic] ambition, avarice, anger, and other Passions, without the feare of some coërcive Power."[44] This discovery underlies her rejection of Lovelace's appeals after the rape:

[43] For the homology between the two kinds of contract, see M. L. Shanley, "Marriage Contract and Social Contract in Seventeenth Century English Political Thought," *The Western Political Quarterly* 32.1 (1979):79–91.

[44] Hobbes, *Leviathan*, 1.14.96.

bind every word with a solemn appeal to that God whom thou art accustomed to invoke to the truth of the vilest falshoods [sic], and all will still be short of what thou *hast* vowed and promised to me. And, were *not* my heart to abhor thee, for thy *perjuries*, as it *does*, I would not, I tell thee once more, I would not, bind my Soul in covenant with such a man, for a thousand worlds!          (5:376) [3:239]

Like the worlds on worlds that John Donne's lover rejects in "The Good-Morrow," the worlds of exchange and accumulation, of prostitution and bad faith are rejected categorically by Clarissa. Because law constitutes more than one of those worlds – if not all of them – it falls under her blanket condemnation of all perversions of word and deed to attain worldly, selfish ends. And yet to read the heroine's case as a general indictment of law is to miss the text's gradual interweaving of Clarissa's rhetoric and socially necessary juridical principles. Clarissa does not stand over against actually existing juridical discourse; rather, her particular virtue contributes to its equitable correction.

Throughout her ordeal Clarissa expresses the principles that enable this equitable correction, though perhaps never so clearly as when she rebukes Lovelace for claiming that he has been just and generous to her:

TRUE GENEROSITY is not confined to pecuniary instances: It is *more* than politeness: It is *more* than good faith: It is *more* than honour: It is *more* than *justice*: Since all these are but duties, and what a worthy mind cannot dispense with. But TRUE GENEROSITY is Greatness of Soul. It incites us to do more by a fellow-creature, than can be strictly required of us. It obliges us to hasten to the relief of an object that wants relief; anticipating even such a one's hope or expectation.          (4:100) [2:304]

Clarissa's definition of true generosity describes a virtue that countervails self-interest and exceeds both middle-class civility and patrician noblesse oblige. As an active virtue that hearkens to the heart's counsel, true generosity – when allowed to speak in its turn – erases distinctions between duty and sympathy. In other words, it is the antithesis to legalism, which has not only shaped Lovelace's perceptions and projections but has also informed almost all social relations in the novel. Seen in this light, true generosity is the text's secular utopian moment. It rings continuously as a challenging summons to the individual to attempt to forge non-exploitative social relations despite the likelihood of betrayal in a society where words are weak and coercive powers take the side of the betrayer. In short, it provides one dialectical element necessary for the recuperation of the law.

The utopian nature of these sentiments is foregrounded, however, by Clarissa's only direct encounter with society's coercive powers. Although she refuses to use the law for self-vindication, deterrence, or punishment, it momentarily claims her, not as victim but as violator, a wrongdoer in a pecuniary matter. Arrested for failing to pay Mrs. Sinclair's bill for lodgings (in effect failing to pay an accessory to her own rape), Clarissa tells Belford that "[t]he prison was a large DEATH-STRIDE upon me – I should have *suffered longer else!*" (7:400) [4:299]. It is a fitting irony that the law that failed to protect her serves as executioner for the hostile powers active within the family and within gender relations. The realistic representation of her imprisonment almost negates Clarissa's utopian rhetoric.[45] In actual civil society one is either with the law like the Harlowes or against it like Lovelace; or one is nothing. And to be nothing is finally what the Harlowes and Lovelace had sought to make Clarissa. But her antagonists' joint success in reducing the woman to nothing marks them finally as knowers of the law's letter and ignoramuses of its spirit. Even if the law does not return to take revenge fully on this partial local knowledge, it does provide a repudiation of their various claims to social authority by relocating that authority in Jack Belford, who stands apart from both as the other element necessary for juridical recuperation.

## IV Jack Belford's juridical individualism

When Lovelace demands that Belford deliver Clarissa's dead heart to him, or when he expects to possess her testament even though he could not possess her will, the persistence of his juridical principles even in the face of their disastrous consequences is startling. Clarissa's reflection on Lovelace *before the rape* is also a reflection on the kind of juridical reason that he embodies: "What a dreadful, what a judicial hardness of heart must thine be; who canst be capable of such emotions as sometimes thou hast shewn; and of such sentiments, as sometimes have flowed from thy lips; yet canst have so far overcome them all, as to be able to act as thou has acted, and that from settled purpose and premeditation ..." (5:250) [3:152]. Clarissa's indictment gives the lie to Lovelace's contention that his passions rule his interests. She speaks with an intense conviction from a heart that sought its fellow in Lovelace's breast but found instead a heart ruled by egoistic calculation and disregard for social ties. So she writes to Belford after reading his extracts from his friend's letters: "men of very contemptible parts and understanding may succeed in the vilest attempts, if they can once bring themselves to trample on the Sanctions which bind man to man; and sooner upon an innocent person than upon any other; because such an one is apt to judge the integrity of others [sic] hearts, by its own" (7:72) [4:77]. When Clarissa speaks of "the Sanctions which bind man to man," one can almost hear Lovelace's parrying enumeration of settlements proffered, licenses gotten, reparations offered, and promises

---

[45] For a description of prison conditions in eighteenth-century England, see below, ch. 7, n. 32.

made. Yet these are not the "Sanctions" Clarissa has in mind. Although they remain unspecified, one imagines them to be mutually determined and mutually beneficial, the products of active virtue and the producers of positive obligation.

And yet, the implied ideal of Clarissa's sanctions is damaged by a double irony. The first irony is simple: such sanctions that actually exist she refuses to acknowledge or defend. At her death Lovelace remains unpunished. The second irony also follows from Clarissa's decision not to prosecute, for it leads to further violation of civil sanctions. Her cousin Morden, who has promised not to seek revenge, carries the burdensome knowledge of Lovelace's "vile heart" (afforded him by Clarissa's letters) and the conviction that evil of that magnitude must not go unpunished. So Morden breaks his promise to Clarissa and kills Lovelace in a duel, thereby breaking the law as well. Morden returns to the pre-civil principle of blood-feud, which Clarissa sought to avoid. The novel ends with yet another instance of the trampling of the "Sanctions which bind man to man."

And so at the end of *Clarissa*, the reader must accept poetic justice in lieu of civil sanctions. In the two main characters of the novel, two responses to the law have been embodied: silence, on the one hand, corresponding to a solipsistic spiritual individualism; and repudiation, on the other, corresponding to an egoistic heroic individualism. Both responses stand as an immanent critique of the failure or perversion of society's juridical institutions. But institutions, no matter how imperfect, must serve as best they can, and the critique is softened by Jack Belford's execution of Clarissa's will. At the end of the novel, when the calm of tragic resignation has settled upon the survivors, the law that has more than failed Clarissa enables Belford to carry out his "sacred trust."

In Belford the novel offers a third response to the law, different from both Clarissa's agnosticism and Lovelace's defiance. Belford's recognition of the law's power and usefulness might be called true bourgeois individualism. In the course of becoming Clarissa's most devoted attendant, he undergoes a spiritual conversion and a moral regeneration. Along the way of this transformation, he has been shown to be a responsible man, a man of the law and for the law, acting as executor of his uncle's and Belton's estates. He becomes so exemplary a bearer of the public conscience that his fellow rake, Mowbray, describes him after Clarissa's final escape from Sinclair's house as the embodiment of judicial thoroughness and reason: "Here's the devill to pay. Nobody serene but Jack Belford, who is taking minnutes of examminations, accusations, and confessions, with the significant air of a Middlesex Justice; and intends to write at large all particulars, I suppose" (6:94–95) [3:307]. As Clarissa's health fails and Lovelace grows distracted, even the reader relies more and more on the "signifficant air" and magisterial authority in Belford's particulars. It is not amiss to see the novelist with his particulars standing behind Belford, relying on the law for order at last.

By means of Belford's development Richardson attempts to recuperate the law his novel has criticized. The success of this compromise, however, is qualified at best. Belford's prosaic – if judicious – reliability cannot compete with the attraction of Clarissa's virtue and Lovelace's invention, nor can it negate the representation that has preceded it. In his somber thoroughness, Belford serves only to clear the bodies from the stage. And even in this action he reminds one of the law's fondness for carcasses. Nonetheless, the return of law offers a modest sense of ideological security to the reader, even if it fails to erase the earlier abuses.

Clarissa inhabits a corrupt world, a world where women rot in brothels, rakes cough out their lives, debtors scar the walls of sponging houses with their despair, and determined plotters silence persons of principle with violent calculations. Oddly enough, a revealing epitome of this corrupted world is found when Lovelace boasts to Belford how easy his abduction of Clarissa has been:

> For well thou knowest, that *the tame Spirits* which value themselves upon Repu-tation, and are held within the skirts of the Law by political considerations only, may be compared to an infectious Spider; which will run into his hole the moment one of his threads is touched by a finger that can crush him ... While a silly Fly, that has neither courage nor strength to resist, no sooner gives notice, by its buz and its struggles, of its being intangled, but out steps the self-circumscribed tyrant, winds round and round the poor insect, till he covers it with his bowel-spun toils ...                                            (3:66–67) [2:22–23]

Lovelace's cynicism aside (revealing as it does the law's failure to protect the innocent as well as the political motives of those who choose to abide by it selectively), his extended simile shows that he too apprehends the world as a place of corruption. It is well to recall that Lovelace called Harlowe Place a "dung-heap"; now he places the proper inhabitants upon that heap. Yet this is his picture of bourgeois society, it might be objected, a scavenging society living by its "toils" and glutting itself "at leisure upon [the] vitals" of those it has bound and immobilized. The image of "self-circumscribed tyrant," poisonous and solitary, living in part on its own waste, suggests the limitations and the harm of the kind of acquisitive individualism Lovelace hates and that threatened Roxana. Surely, Lovelace does not include himself in this denunciation?

His next remark proves otherwise: "But now I think of it, will not this comparison do as well for the *entangled girls*, as for the *tame spirits*? – Better, o' my conscience! – 'Tis but comparing the Spider to us brave fellows; and it *quadrates*." Lovelace's "conscience" finds the indictment: he too is a spider, bowel-spun toils and all. Lovelace's telling figuration leaves the reader little place to turn for comfort. Looking around for a habitable society, we can see only Clarissa's Father's House, which is no society at all. The law that is meant to constitute society as a place for commodious sociability turns it into an arena where the likes of the Harlowes and the Lovelaces don a protective armor of self-interest to do dubious battle over things that turn to nothing in their hands. At best, and it is a faint best, the civil reader is left with the wish that generosity might find its place in an equitable house founded upon a sociable law.

# 5

# *Roderick Random*: suited by the law

Arbitrary power, in all cases, is somewhat oppressive and debasing; but it is altogether ruinous and intolerable, when contracted into a small compass ... A people, governed after such a manner, are slaves in the full and proper sense of the word.

David Hume, "Of the Rise and Progress of Arts and Sciences"[1]

## I Introduction

In theory England is free of the arbitrary power that David Hume describes in the epigraph to this chapter. Not only do publicly promulgated laws promise freedom from the arbitrary whims of a ruler, but the law itself is a familiar part of the lived experience of the people of eighteenth-century England, from what Alan Harding calls the "amateur justice and the courts of local communities," to "the macabre carnival of the public hanging," as Roy Porter notes.[2] As a part of culture, law – in its ideal state – constitutes the grounds upon which all can consent to the exercise of social authority. The very need for consent, however, illustrates that English society is still divided into the governed and the governing, those subject to power and the wielders of that power. Even though the local Justice of the Peace, swears to "do equal right to the poor and to the rich, after [his] cunning, wit, and power, and after the laws and customs of the realm, and statutes thereof made," his dispensation of justice depends upon how his cunning and wit apply the statutes and customs of the realm to those who fall within his jurisdiction.[3] Alan Harding finds some reason

---

[1] Hume, "Of the Rise and Progress of the Arts and Sciences," *Essays*, p. 117.

[2] Harding, *Social History of English Law*, p. 245. Porter, *English Society*, p. 150. The Tyrolese villain, accomplice to Ferdinand, Count Fathom, gives a different view of the Englishman's love of liberty: "I look upon this opulent kingdom, as a wide and fertile common, on which we adventurers may range for prey, without let or molestation: for so jealous are the natives of their liberty, that they will not bear the restraint of necessary *Police*, and an able artist may enrich himself with their spoils, without running any risque of attracting the notice of the magistrate, or incurring the least penalty of the law." For Smollett, civil freedom had its disadvantages. *The Adventures of Ferdinand Count Fathom*, ed. Jerry C. Beasley (Athens and London: University of Georgia Press, 1988), p. 145.

[3] Richard Burn, *The Justice of the Peace and Parish Officer*, 2 vols. (London, 1755), 2:82.

to doubt "whether the respect [of the common people for the law] was not a form of social subservience to justices who promoted nothing so much as the dominance of their class."[4] And E. P. Thompson argues that the law "expresses" the "hegemony of the eighteenth-century gentry and aristocracy," a consensus-based authority further strengthened by its occasional use of force.[5] The ideal and the real may in fact be split by the period's fear of the mob. Such fears are assuaged not only by coercive power but also by culture's ideological powers.

Culture, ideology, the novel – all accord the privilege of bearing the consensual use of force through the law to a particular subject defined and created by the processes that distinguish the arbitrary from the legitimate, the corrupt from the honest. I have been arguing the ways in which the novel constructs a juridical subject, one who embodies a public conscience and thereby internalizes or fails to internalize socially advantageous constraints upon economic and psychological patterns of accumulation and expenditure. In turning to Tobias Smollett's *The Adventures of Roderick Random*, I shall turn to examine the construction of the subject of power, understood in the double sense of being subject to and wielder of various kinds of social force. The novel, I will argue in the pages ahead, educates its hero in what might be called the etiquette of power. No matter how odd a concept such as etiquette might seem in Smollett's violent fictional world, its appropriateness becomes clear when one views the consequences of the protagonist's first unreflected and violent reactions to the distribution of social goods. As the narrative educates the hero in the etiquette of power, it also provides a satirical purgative for the law itself in its representation of various corrupt and arbitrary authorities, who seek to wield power merely for their own profit. Corrupt officials are satirized as carriers of a social disease that threatens the health of the body politic just as other social diseases threaten the individual's health and fortunes. Corruption, however, is not without its use in the narrative, for if it can be diagnosed, dosed, and purged, the patient can be restored to health. And with this restoration, the ideal juridical subject can exercise a legitimate authority over the tractable and the intractable alike.

In *Roderick Random*, arbitrary authority is a form of corruption, both in the hero and in the society through which he travels. And yet if corruption is present in both, the cure for both is not equally successful. The hero undergoes a restorative and prophylactic regimen based on juridical and sentimental principles. The interaction of these principles within a body that has suffered from arbitrary powers produces a new *man*. The narrative

---

[4] Harding, *Social History of English Law*, p. 245.
[5] Thompson, *Whigs and Hunters*, p. 262. By an act of parliament, 18 Geo. II, c. 20, to qualify for a commission of the peace, a man must possess a 100 £ freehold, copyhold, or customary estate for life. Burn, *Justice of the Peace*, 2:71.

transforms Random from a practitioner of what Francis Bacon calls "wild justice" to a sentimentally enfranchised and juridically legitimated *paterfamilias*.[6] Society, however, as a public body, does not respond to the same specifics that cure Random. Sentiment has little effect upon the competitive public sphere. And so the public sphere can never be purged fully of corruption, nor can the law ever successfully discipline its own administrators. The differential in the two cures effected in the novel is essential to its ideological project because it makes necessary the creation of a domestic space in which the private cure can be enjoyed and the happy body put to productive use.

The arbitrary authority that reforms the hero and resists reform itself can be seen as a necessary complement to the novel's violent society that, according to Paul-Gabriel Boucé, "culminates in a compulsive need for vengeance."[7] Underlying such a need, whether in author or character, individual or society, is the fear – perhaps at times becoming a certainty – that society will neither protect the individual from violence nor punish those who injure her or him. Alice Parker has noted Smollett's own ambivalence toward the law, which "instead of serving the ends of justice," she writes "... becomes a tool for the unscrupulous and criminal."[8] Some four years after the publication of *Roderick Random*, this ambivalence resulted in Smollett's seeking "wild justice" against Peter Gordon, a former employee who had gone to the "verge of King's Bench" to avoid paying a debt he owed Smollett. His employer followed him, and – according to the formulaic indictment – attacked him "with Swords Stave Stones Knives Clubbs fists Sticks and Whipps." Gordon brought suit for the assault, and Smollett had to pay damages. For Smollett, his debtor's ingratitude was bad enough; worse was the behavior of the debtor's attorney, Alexander Hume Campbell. Smollett wrote an indignant letter to Campbell, complaining of the lawyer's base tactics: "This low subterfuge may, for aught I know, screen you from a prosecution at Law, but can never acquit you in that Court which every man of honour holds in his breast."[9] This incident suggests that the didactic work of *Roderick Random* remained unfinished for the author himself, that he did

[6] Francis Bacon, "Of Revenge," in *Essays, Advancement of Learning, New Atlantis, and Other Pieces*, ed. Richard Foster Jones (New York: Odyssey Press, 1937), p. 13.

[7] Paul-Gabriel Boucé, *The Novels of Tobias Smollett*, trans. Antonia White (London and New York: Longmans, 1976), p. 106. See also Angus Ross, "The 'Show of Violence' in Smollett's Novels," *Yearbook of English Studies* 2 (1972):118–29; and Alice Green Fredman, "The Picaresque in Decline: Smollett's First Novel," in *English Writers of the Eighteenth Century*, ed. John H. Middendorf (New York and London: Columbia University Press, 1971), p. 199.

[8] Alice Parker, "Tobias Smollett and the Law," *Studies in Philology* 39 (1942):555.

[9] Lewis Knapp, *Tobias Smollett, Doctor of Men and Manners* (Princeton: Princeton University Press, 1949), pp. 151–52; H. P. Vincent, "Tobias Smollett's Assault on Gordon and Groom," *Review of English Studies* 16 (1940):183–88; "[To Alexander Hume Campbell]," 23 February 1753, in *The Letters of Tobias Smollett*, ed. Lewis M. Knapp (Oxford: Clarendon Press, 1970), Letter 15, p. 22.

not fully assimilate his own narrative lesson on the costs of wild justice. But to find this a failing in the author is to forget that narrative's ideological work is always to be done again. Personal ideals and social realities remain doggedly irreconcilable, and the latter are acceptable only when one creates a suitable private substitute for them.

*Roderick Random* is an ambivalent text that both criticizes and extols the law. Some of that ambivalence can be traced to Tobias Smollett's lived experience. His biographer Lewis Knapp writes that Smollett followed the "aristocratic code," that he "was a firm believer in decorum, social order and subordination," and that "[i]n appearance, [he] was the conventional gentleman." Michael Rosenblum, Robin Fabel, and John Sekora have pointed out socially and politically conservative themes and images in his writing.[10] And yet Smollett's conservative ideals are often at odds with his experience. Like his early heroes, he too struggled to survive in London's competitive literary world. Many of his letters concern money, as do the first letters in his *Travels through France and Italy*. And even if Lewis Knapp is correct in asserting that earlier biographers exaggerated Smollett's poverty, his first years in London were far different from the country idylls that close most of his narratives.[11] David Punter chooses to see Smollett as a man forced to earn a living from Grub Street tasks, as "distanced from the ethical norms of contemporaneous literature."[12] Even if he is not so distanced as Punter suggests, Smollett frequently represents the world as a place where "every man has a right to avail himself of his talents, even at the expense of his fellow creatures."[13]

In such a Hobbesian world, in which the existing structures of authority may work against one's fortunes, it is often necessary to act in ways that the law might not approve. Individual exigency or personal outrage excuses stepping over juridically defined boundaries. Violation measures freedom even as it brings upon the violator a strengthened sense of the law's majesty and power. Smollett also knew this from experience. In his "Letter of Appeal to Lord Mansfield," written after the Knowles libel case in 1760, Smollett asks that his silence before the Chief Justice might not be

interpreted into Contumacy or Want of Respect for the Authority of this Court which I ever did and always shall revere with the most profound Veneration and Submission. What might be imputed to me in this respect as a Crime was really my Misfortune. My being produced in the Character of a Delinquent before such an

[10] Knapp, *Tobias Smollett*, p. 305; Michael Rosenblum, "Smollett as Conservative Satirist," *ELH* 42 (1975):556–79; Robin Fabel, "The Patriotic Briton: Tobias Smollett and English Politics, 1756–1771," *Eighteenth-Century Studies* 8 (1974):100–14. Sekora, *Luxury*, Part 2, *passim*.

[11] Knapp, *Tobias Smollett*, p. 159.

[12] David Punter, "Smollett and the Logic of Domination," *Literature and History* 2 (October 1975):61.

[13] Tobias Smollett, *The Adventures of Sir Launcelot Greaves. Together with The History & Adventures of an Atom* (Oxford: The Shakespeare Head Press, 1926), p. 283.

awful Tribunal had such an Effect upon my Spirits that I was really deprived of the Power of Utterance.[14]

Smollett here sounds more than a little like Clarissa as she describes the "awful Tribunal" that will judge her. And just as Clarissa's awe arose from the strong patriarchal ideology that she carried, so too does Smollett's respect for social authority. And yet he never admits his guilt in the letter, an omission that hints at a dissociation between the residual veneration and an emergent sense of personal right and desert. This dissociation also appears as a split in the juridical subject constructed in *Roderick Random*.

*Roderick Random* starts with a dream that suggests that dissociations and ambivalences will be worked through in the narrative after a series of repetitions that bring the hero misfortune and unhappiness. What John Richetti calls "a linear progress toward moral and social order summed up in the career of the protagonist as he moves toward integration within society" is driven by adverse consequences of wild justice and the coercive interventions of arbitrary authority.[15] The "belief ... in the orderly society" that Michael Rosenblum also finds "typical" of Smollett's heroes, however, is not always strong enough to counterbalance actions arising from a sense of slighted self-worth.[16] Random must learn that the law punishes and protects. It can stop him, or it can further his interests. All depends upon his learning to use it to do unto others what they once did unto him even as he discovers that the best alternative to living in a competitive world is to make its laws one's own before withdrawing behind the ramparts of sentimental self-satisfaction.

## II The hero's origins and the law's rigor

The law's dualism finds its narrative complement in *Roderick Random*'s genteel birth and vagabond fortunes. For much of the narrative Random's "gentle birth" is suspended. He becomes a variant of the picaro.[17] This

[14] "Letter of Appeal to Lord Mansfield," Letter 74, 24 November 1760, *Letters*, pp. 92–94.
[15] John Richetti, "Representing an Under Class: Servants and Proletarians in Fielding and Smollett," in *The New Eighteenth Century: Theory, Politics, English Literature*, eds. Felicity Nussbaum and Laura Brown (New York and London: Methuen, 1987), p. 86. James H. Bunn makes a similar argument in "Signs of Randomness in *Roderick Random*," *Eighteenth-Century Studies* 14 (1981):452–69.
[16] Rosenblum, "Smollett as Conservative Satirist," p. 560.
[17] For a survey of the literature discussing *Random*'s relation to the picaresque up to 1971, see G. S. Rousseau, "Smollett and the Picaresque: Some Questions about a Label," *Studies in Burke and his Time* 12 (1971):1886–1904; rpt. in G. S. Rousseau, *Tobias Smollett: Essays of Two Decades* (Edinburgh: T. & T. Clark, 1982), pp. 53–73. See also Jerry Beasley, "*Roderick Random*: The Picaresque Transformed," *College Literature* 5 (Fall 1979):211–20, esp. p. 219; and Richard Bjornson, *The Picaresque Hero in European Fiction* (Madison: The University of Wisconsin Press, 1977), pp. 228–44, esp. p. 239.

division between expectations and actual conditions is forecast in his pregnant mother's dream:

> She dreamed, she was delivered of a tennis-ball, which the devil (who to her great surprise, acted the part of a midwife) struck so forcibly with a racket, that it disappeared in an instant; and she was for some time inconsolable for the loss of her off-spring; when all of a sudden, she beheld it return with equal violence, and earth itself beneath her feet, whence immediately sprung up a goodly tree covered with blossoms . . .[18]

The dream registers the conditions that drive Random from the paternal estate. Familial and ideological conflicts are here rendered as a mysterious evil, perpetrated by a devil acting without a readily ascertainable motive. Driven from his mother by this seemingly incomprehensible force, the child returns with "equal violence," thus predicting the ferocity of the hero's struggle to establish his claim to the parental ground. To disappear from this ground in an instant is to be deprived of status and signifying power, as the narrative soon will prove. The dream, however, includes the moment in which the narrative will fulfill all wishes by making this violence generative of a new order. The son returns to his rightful earth under his own power, and the bouncing ball becomes a stationary "goodly tree," significant for the blossoms that mark it as both feminized and fruitful. Once the peripatetic hero is rooted, sweetness will be grafted to strength, and the division between birth and fortune will be ended.

Random's mother's dream foregrounds an important ideological conflict that will be enacted and solved over the course of the narrative. The mother's authentic gentleness is opposed to the nominal gentility of Random's grandfather: patriarchal intransigence governed by a "judicial hardness of heart" (to quote Clarissa) acts to destroy the maternal hopes and affections that seek recognition for its infant issue. Such a conflict must be read not only as generational, but also as a class conflict, as the dramatization of the parturition of a new social order from the old. The devil/midwife who would deprive the infant of all chances to establish himself comfortably in society is none other than the grandfather/judge, who sends Random's mother to an early grave, Random's father to a rumored suicide, and Roderick himself upon his vicissitudinous wanderings. In the dream's logic, the devil is to the grandfather as the midwife is to the judge. The amalgamated function of midwife and judge establishes the importance of proper administration of justice; for just as the evil midwife drives the infant from the mother's care, so the evil judge drives the hero from his patrimonial expectations. The good midwife, on

---

[18] Tobias Smollett, *The Adventures of Roderick Random*, ed. Paul-Gabriel Boucé (Oxford: Oxford University Press, 1979), 1:1 All further references to the novel are to this edition and appear parenthetically in the text.

the other hand, serves the same function for the pregnant woman that the good judge performs for the historical class about to be born: both assist nature in order to give the infant the most auspicious beginning possible. In the dream's political allegory a utopian rule of law acts as the midwife assisting at the natural birth of the emergent order. That this law is initially absent indicates that the new order will be responsible for instantiating its rule.

The hero's account of the actual conditions of his birth dispels some of the mystery of the dream. Random writes that he is the offspring of the youngest son of a local Scottish judge and a poor relation who keeps house for the judge. Having married clandestinely, Random's father is disinherited for disappointing the judge, who had educated him for the marriage market. At first glance, the judge seems merely to be following the social condemnation of "low marriages," which James Boswell claims result in "the fair and comfortable order of improved life ... be[ing] miserably disturbed."[19] Rather than being concerned for the preservation of a comfortable order, however, the grandfather is represented as being concerned solely for his own interests. His calculating selfishness is set in opposition to the emergent class's valorization of marriage for love. Thus, the judge embodies an old order of law that is partial, intransigent, and productive of resentment. Random tells us that his grandfather – who "was remarkable for his abilities in the law, which he exercised with great success, in the station of a judge, particularly against beggars, for whom he had a singular aversion" (1:1) – has an "antipathy to everything in distress." Here too he seems to be in harmony with prevailing social attitudes. W. S. Holdsworth writes that "persons who sought relief by the agency of the poor law were regarded as persons who were to some extent to blame for their position ..."[20] William Blackstone says as much: "Idleness in any person is also a high offence against the public economy." He defines *public economy* as "the due regulation and domestic order of the kingdom, whereby the individuals ... are bound ... to be decent, industrious, and inoffensive in their respective stations."[21] And yet the judge's legalism – defined by Judith Shklar, as "following rules, pre-established, known, and accepted ... [that] may make people especially uncompromising"[22] – is at odds with paternalist obligation. That he is rule bound, and furthermore that by being so he defeats his long-term interests, is shown by his strict adherence to primogeniture. He devises his estate to his fox-hunting grandson, thereby germinating the bad seed that will

[19] Boswell, *The Life of Johnson*, ed. George B. Hill; rev. by L. F. Powell (Oxford: Clarendon Press, 1934), 2:329. Quoted in part and partially misattributed (to Johnson) in Stone, *Family, Sex and Marriage*, p. 394.

[20] Holdsworth, *History of English Law*, 10:173.     [21] Blackstone, *Commentaries*, 4:169, 162.

[22] Judith Shklar, *Legalism* (Cambridge, MA: Harvard University Press, 1964), pp. 104–5.

destroy his legacy. His chosen heir's imbecility results in the mortgaging of the estate and makes room for the very persons that he sought to exclude from its benefits. This ironic outcome of the grandfather's inflexible and short-sighted resolve makes the narrative into a deposition on the collapse of the old authority.

Just as these two accounts describe Random's fortunate genealogy and unfortunate birth, so will two codes inform his behavior: the genteel code of honor and the vagabond's code of survival at all costs. Like the *picaro*, whom Claudio Guillen has called the "half-outsider," Roderick is inside and outside the society to which he aspires.[23] This divided position causes him to act according to two different ethical codes. The first code appears timeless, belonging to immemorial usage and a prescriptive right to his patriarchal earth. The second code is suited to the constant struggle required to master a contingent world. In the narrative, the vagabond's code invigorates an increasingly effete patriarchal tradition, while the residual value of that tradition in turn ennobles the vagabond with the proper heritage. In the dialectical relation between tradition and experience Random's new nature is forged. At the same time tradition and law are sentimentalized by being reinscribed in a hero whose feeling heart promises to soften his grandfather's "resolves . . . invariable like the laws of the Medes and the Persians" (1:2). Before that softening occurs, however, the hero's passions must be disciplined by law and elevated by love. When that process is completed, Random will have attained a new ethical sense that boasts a perfect and invisible suture between authority and compassion.

### III Private wrongs, private redress

Indignant at the poverty that denies him access to civil society's institutions and that injures his pride, Random often resorts to private revenge for the personal satisfaction that otherwise eludes him. This habit of behavior attests to the fact that at the outset of his adventures he neither acknowledges public authority nor considers himself a member of civil society. According to John Locke, only in the "State of Nature," where every man is "both Judge and Executioner," does revenge have the same status as justice. Civil society requires everyone to eschew personal satisfaction because "[m]en being partial to themselves, Passion and Revenge is very apt to carry them too far, and with too much heat, in their own Cases; as well as negligence, and unconcernedness, to make them too

---

[23] Claudio Guillen, "Towards a Definition of the Picaresque," in *Proceedings of the IIIrd Congress of the International Comparative Literature Association* (The Hague: Mouton & Co., 1962), pp. 252–66; rpt. in his *Literature as System* (Princeton: Princeton University Press, 1971), pp. 71–106, esp. 83–84.

remiss, in other Mens."[24] By experiencing the harmful consequences of "wild justice," Random will learn that his own safety and prosperity depend on bringing his self-love into accord with the rule of law. In the words of Adam Smith, "he must ... humble the arrogance of his self-love, and bring it down to something which other men can go along with."[25] And yet the picaresque mode demands a strong hero, one able to return in kind the knocks he takes. Smollett exploits that literary mode to show the violence necessary to rise in a putatively "civil" society. When public authority fails to satisfy him, Random takes this satisfaction upon himself.

The event that establishes Random's habitual tendency to revenge is the hero's chastisement of his schoolmaster. This dependent agent of his grandfather humiliates and injures the orphaned pupil. First, in order to hamper Random's scholastic progress (which the grandfather has interpreted as the prelude to forgery and the text identifies as a means to power), the schoolmaster locks his pupil's hand in a board that "effectually debarr'd [him] the use of [his] pen." As a consequence of this mistreatment, Random develops "antipathy and horror ... for the merciless tyrant," whose harsh punishments attest to his arbitrary character (2:5–6). After the grandfather's death, the schoolmaster "laid aside all decency and restraint, and ... abused [Random] in the grossest language his rancour could suggest, as a wicked, profligate, dull, beggarly miscreant ..." (5:15). The schoolmaster's excessive violence and the subsequent death of Random's grandfather prompt him to seek revenge. He takes it with the aid of his classmates and his Uncle Tom Bowling – an innocent "unacquainted with the ways of men in general" (3:8) – who helps to mete out "wholesome chastisement" to an "arbitrary wretch ... for the good of his soul" (5:18). In this action Bowling serves as a kind impartial spectator. While the uncle's liberal and metaphysical rhetoric diminishes the personal element in the punishment, the nephew accomplishes his ends in the spirit of popular justice and escapes.

The favorable outcome of this event establishes a precedent for Random's resorting to extra-legal redress of his grievances. But as Random leaves his Scottish village for the civil society of England, he leaves behind the communal relations that have partially legitimized his actions. Henceforth, however, his habit of private vengeance turns into an unjustifiable reflex of the class character that he wishes to establish. Like the true gentleman he believes he is and wishes others to acknowledge, he settles an early affront through the aristocratic practice of the duel.[26] In

---

24 Locke, *Two Treatises*, 2:125:396.
25 Smith, *Theory of Moral Sentiments*, p. 83. For recent studies on Smith's *Theory*, see Marshall, *The Figure of Theater*, pp. 167–92; Agnew, *Worlds Apart*, pp. 177–88, and Bender, *Imagining the Penitentiary*, n. 44 below.
26 For a survey of eighteenth-century attitudes as well as a brief history of the duel, see Donna T. Andrew, "The Code of Honour and its Critics: The Opposition to Duelling in England,

eighteenth-century England, the duel still enjoyed considerable symbolic power. Revisionist historian J. C. D. Clark calls it "the best index to, and proof of, the survival and power of the aristocratic ideal as a code separate from, and ultimately superior to, the injunctions of law and religion." Clark sees its survival as proof of continuing aristocratic cultural hegemony, for the "elite of the old society vindicated its characteristic practice; and, far from declining into ineffectiveness, the elite increased its hold over English society with time."[27]

The power of a residual aristocratic ideology is visible in *Roderick Random* even though the novel's attitude toward the practice of dueling is at best ambivalent. Random himself never expresses his opinion of dueling, but the duel produces consequences that call its ultimate efficacy into question. Tom Bowling, for example, challenges his Captain to a duel after the Captain has insulted him. Although Bowling defeats his opponent, he must flee, thereby losing his pay, part of which supported his nephew. Thus, Random's financial problems in the early part of the narrative result directly from this duel. In this respect, Smollett follows the lead of the writers who condemned the practice by pointing out that even if judges and juries were reluctant to find a charge of murder against a duelist, other dangers remained.[28] Richard Steele enumerates the dangers in his Preface to the 1710 edition of the *Tatler*: "I alone bewailed the condition of an *English* Gentleman, whose Fortune and Life are at this Day precarious; while His Estate is liable to the Demands of Gamesters, through a false Sense of Justice; and to the Demands of Duellists, through a false Sense of Honour." Gambling with one's estate is no different than gambling with one's life in the duel. The true sense of honor that must replace the false is spelled out by Steele in *Tatler* 28, which describes how a dispute over money between a lieutenant and a major-general is settled by law. Steele reflects approvingly that "the Point of Honour justly gives Way to that of Gain; and by long and wise Regulation, the richest is the bravest Man."[29] Dueling, which one writer calls "the dregs of that barbarous

---

1700–1850," *Social History* 5 (1980):409–34. Andrew writes that "the willingness to fight a duel, as well as the recognition of being a person who was 'challenge-able' defined, in great part, what it meant to be a gentleman. Thus the code of honour, by its nature, was a private or limited system of law" (415).

[27] Clark, *English Society, 1688–1832*, pp. 109, 116.

[28] J. D. Aylward quotes the judge's statement in the Crown's case against Colonel Cosmo Gordon for the murder of Lieut. Colonel Thomas: "I feel what every man who hears me must feel, that the strict and rigid rule of law, applied to the subject of deliberate duelling, is in direct opposition to the feelings of mankind and the manners of the time. Be the rule of law what it may, men to [sic] find it justifiable, commendable, and necessary to risk the decision of their differences before a tribunal they erect for themselves" (72). This duel occurred in 1783. Gordon was acquitted. "Duelling in the XVIII Century," *Notes and Queries* 189 (1945):31–34, 46–48, 70–73.

[29] Sir Richard Steele, *The Tatler*, 3 vols., ed. Donald F. Bond (Oxford: Clarendon Press, 1987). Preface, 1:5; No. 28, 14 June 1709, 1:214.

spirit which o'erspread these northern parts by the irruption of the Goths and Vandals," is no longer a measure of one's honor.[30] The much more precise measure of fortune becomes the new standard.

In his early adventures, however, before the evidence against personal vengeance has accumulated, Random's self-assertion through the duel proves his worth as an individual and constitutes him in his own mind (if not in the reader's) as a member of the elite. Thus, Random as would-be aristocratic subject attains subjective coherence through dueling. Yet even in these early moments the duel introduces a series of narrative contradictions.[31] First, it moves Random farther away from the material status that he seeks. Second, it is at odds with the sentimental nature that comes to represent the best amalgam of the old and the new for Smollett.[32] In short, although the duel appears to preserve Random from becoming one of Lovelace's bloodless, law-abiding, tame fellows, it is actually a misstep in his pursuit of status. An estate can be lost but not gained through dueling.

The circumstances of Random's first duel illustrate this contradiction. Deprived of Bowling's support, Random asks his old schoolmate Gawkey for a loan. Not only does "Squire Gawkey" deny Roderick the money, but he "betrayed [Random's poverty] to the malice of [his] cousins" (6:24). Random responds to this information in a manner appropriate to his untutored self-image: he borrows a sword and challenges the "Squire" to a duel.[33] Borrowing the sword reveals the pretense in Random's gentility even as it indicates that the pretense allows him to feel above the law; for, as Clark notes, the "conflicts [of the common people] were mere affrays, punishable at law," whereas duels were treated differently.[34] And yet in his retrospective narration, Random relates the episode with an irony that

---

30 John Cockburn, *The History of Duels* (1720; rpt., Edinburgh: Collectanea Adamantaea, vol. 25, 1888), part II, p. 45.

31 For the notion of ideological contradiction, see Pierre Macherey, *A Theory of Literary Production*, trans. Geoffrey Wall (London: Routledge & Kegan Paul, 1978), p. 122; and Terry Eagleton, *Criticism and Ideology: A Study in Marxist Literary Theory* (London: Verso, 1976), pp. 89–92.

32 Smollett gives his rendition of the restored golden age in a self-consciously pastoral scene from *Sir Launcelot Greaves*: "To be sure it was a comely sight for to see ... the buxom country-lasses, fresh and fragrant, and blushing like the rose, in their best apparel dight ... assembled on May-day, to dance before squire Launcelot, as he made his morning's progress through the village ... Lord help you! he could not rest if he thought there was an aching heart in the whole parish. Every paultry cottage was in a little time converted into a pretty, snug, comfortable habitation, with a wooden porch at the door, glass casements in the windows, and a little garden behind, well stored with greens, roots, and sallads. In a word, the poor's-rate was reduced to a meer trifle, and one would have thought the golden age was revived in Yorkshire" (31–32). In Smollett's pastoral fantasy, the golden age is a combination of old authority, new sentiment, and reduced taxes for the ratepayers.

33 G. M. Trevelyan writes that the gentleman was known in town (where challenges were more common) by wearing a sword in public. *English Social History: A Survey of Six Centuries, Chaucer to Victoria* (London: Longmans, Green and Co., 1942), p. 315.

34 Clark, *English Society, 1688–1832*, p. 113.

highlights the distance between pretense and actuality. In actuality the heroic Random has "considerable repugnance to the combat, which frequently attacked [him] in cold sweats by the way." Looking back upon the event from a position of comfort, the mature writer has learned the folly and unnaturalness of such an action. As it turns out the sword proves useless; for Gawkey leaves town rather than face combat with the fiery Random. The potentially tragic scene devolves into farce.

Not to be deprived of a victory, Random has the "whole story inserted in the news, although [he] was fain to sell a gold-laced hat to [his] landlord, for less than half-price, to defray the expence, and contribute to [his] subsistence" (6:25). In an important ideological moment, power is disassociated from violence and linked to the manipulation of public opinion. The pen promises to achieve what was denied the sword. Although Random appears to have won this "battle" and soothed his injured vanity, he has in fact only purchased a costly and pyrrhic victory. In gratifying his passion for revenge, the hero loses sight of his interests. His actions, beginning with the challenge and ending with the publication of the results of that challenge, further his impoverishment and lead to his even greater alienation from society: "I found myself deserted to all the horrors of extreme want, and avoided by mankind as a creature of a different species, or rather as a solitary being, no ways comprehended within the scheme or protection of providence" (7:25–26). Ignoring the law and spending one's capital lead to the undisguised horrors of privation and alienation. Lawless impulse has helped marginalize Random and involve him in a contradiction. He must sell his coveted gold brocade – a sign of his vanity – to support that vanity. At this point in his adventures, Random lacks a juridical conscience that can restrain his impulses.

In order to be comprehended within the schemes of providence, this creature of the road must learn boundaries. In the words of Blackstone, he must be "bound to conform [his] general behaviour to the rules of propriety, good neighbourhood, and good manners."[35] But this is a hard lesson to learn, especially when propriety demands one thing and good neighborhood another. Having travelled to London and found employment as a journeyman with a London apothecary, Random is walking abroad one night when, impelled by a "prejudice in favour of [his] country," he attacks three watchmen who have apprehended a fellow Scot. While Random keeps the watch at bay, the man he is helping runs away. This man, Random subsequently discovers, is none other than the same "Squire" Gawkey who fled once before, now a lieutenant bearing "a martial ferocity in his appearance" and lodging with the apothecary who employs Random (21:109). Random resolves to expose Gawkey once and

---

[35] Blackstone, *Commentaries*, 4:162.

for all "in order to be revenged on the cowardly wretch, for whom [he] had suffered" (21:111). But Gawkey denies that he is the man whom Random rescued, graciously "pardons" Random for his accusation, and thus wins the household to his side.

Although the insult injures Random's pride and stirs his resentment, it fades before the real dangers arising out of the affray. His encounter with the officers of the watch had the potential to end his freedom, but the conflict with Gawkey moves him even closer to the shades of the prison house.[36] When he engages an antagonist, Random little thinks that his opponent might be able to delegate his desire for satisfaction to the law's coercive arm. Gawkey, now married to the apothecary's daughter, joins with his wife in a conspiracy to frame their common enemy by planting house medicines in his chest. (The new Mrs. Gawkey has her own reasons for resenting Random.) When the apothecary finds the missing medicines in Random's room, rather than having him arrested, he dismisses him. The dismissal ill suits the conspirators, who employ the rhetoric of social obligation to argue for committing the thief to Newgate:

The captain and his lady used all the christian arguments their zeal could suggest, to prevail upon the apothecary to pursue me to destruction, and represented the injustice he did to the community of which he was a member, in letting a villain escape, who would not fail of doing more mischief in the world, when he should reflect on his coming off so easily now. (21:112–13)

The ease with which Random's inveterate and enthusiastic enemies appropriate the rhetoric of social and juridical obligation reveals that law can be an effective weapon in the struggle for social status. The perjury fails to convince the apothecary Mr. Lavement only because he feared "the cost and trouble of a prosecution to which he must bind himself," as well as dreaded how "some particulars of [Random's] confession might affect his practice." This time countervailing interests save Random from prison or worse.

The misadventure shows the reader that all moments and methods are not equally propitious for the pursuit of private vengeance. The hero fails to realize that social superiority affords his antagonists a protection that he lacks. Supported by the women of the household, the lieutenant enlists under the banner of order, adopts its rhetoric, and uses it for dishonest ends. Roderick does realize that, had the plot succeeded as the conspirators wished, it "would infallibly have brought [him] to an ignominious death" (21:111). For the time being, he is saved by a weak link in

---

[36] Random could have been arrested for assaulting the watch. "The watchmen are the ministers and assistants of the constable," writes Richard Burn, "and are under the same protection with him, and may act as he doth . . . if a person will not obey the arrest of the watchmen, they may levy hue and cry upon him that he might be taken . . ." And, "a watchman may arrest a night-walker, without any warrant from a magistrate." *Justice of the Peace*, 2:512; 1:69.

the legal chain in the figure of a pathetic, cuckolded, and avaricious apothecary and by a fault in the law itself, which can deplete some fortunes even as it protects others.[37]

Although Random escapes hanging, he does not escape the consequences of his impulsive behavior: "Thus I found myself, by the iniquity of mankind, in a much more deplorable condition than ever: ... my good name was lost, my money gone, my friends were alienated ..." (21:114). Once again a "solitary being," marked as a criminal by a law which need not directly intervene to so mark him, he has lost his good name and whatever social standing he once enjoyed. For the wayfaring adventurer seeking admission to a better life and a higher status, this episode teaches a lesson about iniquity and legality: to live with the law, one must think like it, measure one's actions by its standards, and realize that it can be used by others to further their interests. Personal vengeance may give immediate satisfaction, but the immediate proves ultimately without substance, akin to Lovelace's bubble. "Reason," as it is incarnated in a middle class that seeks to protect its interests, is the word that describes these realizations.

A better solution to the crimes and misdemeanors that others commit against him is found in the final act in Random's drama with the Gawkeys. Disowned by her parents and deserted by her now-disgraced husband, who "was broke for misbehaviour at the battle of Dettingen," Mrs. Gawkey appeals to her old enemy Random for help. "[M]oved at her distress," Random agrees to help her provided "she should do [him] the justice to clear [his] reputation, by explaining upon oath before a Magistrate, the whole of the conspiracy" (52:319–20). He strikes a private and legal agreement in order to improve his standing. Benevolence is served and self-interest furthered through a *quid pro quo*. Both parties benefit. The novel shows that reason, fairness, and concern – or "propriety, good neighborhood, and good manners" can arise when aggression is channeled into this kind of exchange. Yet this exchange succeeds because Mrs. Gawkey has nothing to lose and much to gain by agreeing to Random's demands. When Random confronts those with more power than he has, he finds that such exchanges do not work to his benefit.

---

[37] In *An Enquiry into the Causes of the Late Increase of Robbers, etc.* Fielding lists the causes for failures to prosecute. One cause is avariciousness, which moves the victim to "compound the Matter" with the criminal in order to cut losses. (1751; facs. rpt., New York: AMS Press, 1975), p. 106. See also Bernard Mandeville, *An Enquiry Into the Causes of the Frequent Executions at Tyburn and A Proposal for Some Regulations Concerning Felons in Prison* (London, 1725). In Chapter I, Mandeville writes of "theftbote," but his remarks have application to failure to prosecute for any reason. By being satisfied with the return of stolen property, victims "invite the Indigent and Lazy to pick Pockets, and render the Negligent more careless than probably they would be" (5).

## IV Authority, interest, and the hero's fortunes

If Random's propensity to "wild justice" teaches him the need for personal reform, the appearance of corrupt authority in his narrative emphasizes the need for social reform. Throughout the formative part of his adventures, Random encounters various social and juridical authorities – always self-interested and often corrupt – that threaten his freedom, which is fully restored only when he has internalized an authority that has oppressed him and when he has attained the economic status that enables him to wield that now internalized power. *Roderick Random* does not hold out the hope that the body politic can be purged of corruption once and for all. Rather, it purveys an individualist message that the upright and successful subject can protect himself and his family from such corruption when he becomes free in the sense meant by Jean-Jacques Rousseau, who writes that the "most absolute authority is that which penetrates to the inner man and is exerted no less on his will than on his actions."[38] When man and authority become one in Random, he will neither think nor act in the impulsive manner that has made him obnoxious to the stately majesty of juridically sanctioned authority.

Random's first encounter with juridical authority literally halts his progress toward attaining the independence that he lacked in Scotland. On the way to London to make his fortune, Random and his faithful companion Strap are "detained ... as evidence against" the highwayman Rifle (10:42). Random resents the delay and shows himself no friend to justice; for when Rifle escapes he reports that he feels a "great joy, as [he] was permitted now to continue [his] journey without any further molestation" (10:43). Law and the community's interest bar his progress toward his goal. Although he grudgingly recognizes the law's power to detain him, he does so not out of any sense of personal obligation to justice and order. Rather, he recognizes its power only. Like the thief Rifle, the witness Random is detained as an instrument for impersonal justice. Juridical authority – even if communal and even if free from corruption – is represented at this moment as an indiscriminate net that pulls in anyone who falls within its cast regardless of that person's interests. This characteristic of the law, which remains constant throughout the narrative, serves as a countervailing force to the narrator-hero's impulsive nature. In order to rise, Random must be "caught," brought low, and purged of his impulses by the law's considerable coercive powers.

The brush with authority on the road to London merely annoys Random, and only briefly at that. In London, however, where he has come to make his fortune in the Navy, Random's encounter with the law

---

[38] Jean-Jacques Rousseau, "Discourse on Political Economy," in *On the Social Contract*, trans. Judith R. Masters, ed. Roger D. Masters (New York: St. Martin's Press, 1978), p. 216.

takes a potentially more instructive and definitely more threatening turn. After a long day of waiting at Surgeon's Hall, Random, Beau Jackson, and some others seek some diversion. With "elevated" spirits they "sallied out, roaring and singing ... to a place of nocturnal entertainment" (17:89), where, after more drink and some modest dalliance with the women of the establishment, Beau Jackson misses his purse. No newcomer to the ways of London, the victim "seized the two Dulcineas, who sat by him, one in each hand; and swore if they did not immediately restore his money, he would charge a constable with them." His charge brings a countercharge from the brothel's owner Mrs. Harridan, who sends for the constable and accuses the whole company of "riot" and "defamation" (17:89–90). Innocent of any crime – though less innocent of the kind of expense that the narrative works to allay – Random is about to be given another lesson on the advantages of restraining his wild impulses: impulses bring juridical retribution unless one can afford the going rate that buys immunity.

Random and company display little knowledge and less respect for the influence that money can buy. The constable that answers Mrs. Harridan's summons is a good officer familiar with these ways of the world. He urges Jackson to accept his loss and come to a composition with the brothel keeper. Although Mrs. Harridan has been "often complained of as a nuisance," her business allows her to be a source of profit to the "J – t – ces, to whom she and all of her employment, pay contribution quarterly for protection" (17:90). In law the owner of a bawdy house is subject to "fine and imprisonment, the measure of which the court in their discretion may appoint; and also may superadd bodily chastisement and pillory on profligate offenders."[39] In Smollett's satire on a corrupt law that nonetheless serves an educative function, common interest between the law and the bawd allows her to assume that in a contest between her and Beau Jackson, her "oath will most signify."

Corruption in the house of justice seems about to swallow the pleasure seekers, if only temporarily. And yet, in line with the novel's ambivalent attitude toward the law, the corruption, though widespread, is not universal. The constable who mediates the conflict is an honest officer. He fulfills the spirit of his office "by maintaining good order in his neighbourhood; by punishing the dissolute and idle; by protecting the peaceable and industrious; and, above all, by healing petty differences and preventing vexatious prosecutions."[40] Although he is kind toward the young men, his kindness is ultimately made moot by the letter of the law and the procedures proper to his office. Having taken the constable's advice of coming to a composition with Mrs. Harridan, the revelers are ready to go home

[39] Burn, *Justice of the Peace*, 2:120; *Laws Respecting Women*, pp. 299–300.
[40] Blackstone, *Commentaries*, 1:8. Although Blackstone is writing of JPs, constables also held the commission of the peace. See Burn, "Justices of the Peace," *Justice of the Peace*, 2:66.

"when the constable gave [Random] to understand, he could discharge no prisoners, but by order of the justice, before whom [they] must appear" (17:91). No matter how well-disposed toward the young men the constable may be, once the law has been activated it has a power and logic independent of human agency. This independent momentum can also be exploited at any moment by those in positions of authority.

The ensuing scene before the magistrate to whom the constable brings the disputants is a comedy of errors that nearly becomes a tragedy of tragedies. Before a word can be spoken by anyone, the magistrate takes his cue from the unknown young men and the known Mrs. Harridan:

Then looking at us [the revelers], who appeared with a dejected air, he continued, "Ay, ay, thieves, I see – old offenders – O your humble servant, Mrs. Harridan! I suppose these fellows have been taken robbing your house – yes, yes, here's an old acquaintance of mine – you have used expedition (said he to [Random]) in returning from transportation; but we shall save you that trouble for the future – the surgeons will fetch you from your next transportation at their expense."

(17:91)

As a person without a settled income or established character, Random appears about to be marked by the law in the same way that French criminal procedure threatened Roxana. In another way he is a stray like Clarissa. The magistrate administers his office to the advantage of those who are known to him and who provide him with income and objects upon which to practice. It matters little that such treatment is unjust or even that the magistrate's construction of Random as an "old offender" might be challenged successfully. What matters is that law and authority work together to intimidate and incommode the protagonist so that he finds himself in an "agony of consternation," which is dispelled only after the magistrate is apprised by the constable that the disputants have reached a mutually satisfactory settlement (17:92). Random's agony, furthermore, is the price of social order as it is understood by magistrate and bawd. Had the constable not aided Random, that agony might very well have ended the protagonist's hopes.

The hero, however, has lived to reflect back on the event. Random closes the chapter with the following comment, part retrospect on and part remembrance of the weight of the law: "Thus having cloaked his own want of discernment, under the disguise of paternal care, we were dismissed, and I found myself as much lightened as if a mountain had been lifted from off my breast" (17:92). Random's reflection is remarkable for what it fails to express, for the hero represses the economic content of the scene. It is as if desiring fortune himself, he cannot make a critical association of money and cruelty, though he can represent such an association in the details of the narrative. Instead, he expresses his anger at

the magistrate's "want of discernment"; and he reflects upon the abuse of
paternalistic sentiments because he has encountered such abuses before in
his grandfather's behavior. Random confronts a structure that he does not
yet understand, a structure that functions in a crude fashion to transform
him into "a productive body and a subjected body," as Michel Foucault
describes it. The power of juridical authority "is not exercised simply as
an obligation or a prohibition on those who 'do not have it': it invests
them, is transmitted by them and through them, just as they themselves,
in their struggle against it, resist the grip it has on them."[41] *Roderick
Random* represents the slow accrual of interest on the investment that the
law has made in the protagonist, an investment that takes place under the
guidance of excessive force and arbitrary authority. The hero will eventually become a productive body just as he will learn to subject his impulses
to the laws that govern social production. At the same time, the arbitrary
character of authority will give way to a "natural" embodiment.

Random's resistance to power remains strong throughout his narrative
because like Clarissa he represents himself as a free subject. He is a proto-
type of the heroic bourgeois, a resistance fighter against absolutist oppression, following his own interests and dictates, though sometimes to excess.
His experience aboard the *Thunder* under the command of Captain
Oakhum strengthens this necessary resistance. Wrongly accused of being
a spy by the jealous ship's surgeon Mackshane, Random is stapled to the
ship's deck without being given a chance to answer the accusations. He
suffers the horror of having one man's brains splatter in his face and
another's partially disemboweled carcass nearly stifle him during a sea
fight. Whatever the result of such treatment, its intention is to make him a
tractable prisoner when his trial comes, to rob him of his wits and to
deprive him of his powers to resist. When Random is finally granted a
trial, the captain – acting as plaintiff, prosecutor, and judge – condemns
him to "dangle" after two foremastmen join the ship's surgeon in the conspiracy against the hero, who escapes the sentence only because the
surgeon Mackshane realizes that the captives "should have an opportunity of clearing [them]selves before a court-martial, and at the same
time, of making his malice and ignorance conspicuous" (31:177). Despite
this fortunate outcome, Random's resistance increases and with it comes
an understandable repugnance to the institutions that are intended to
offer equal justice to all. For this reason, he dissuades his shipmate
Morgan from pressing charges against the perjurers: "I represented to
him the precarious issue of a trial, the power and interest of his adversaries, and flattered his revenge with the hope of wreaking his resentment
with his own hands upon Mackshane after our return to England"

[41] Foucault, *Discipline and Punish*, p. 27.

(31:177). The hero turns to his tried and true nostrum: the law of personal vengeance.

Random's encounters with authority have a dual effect: they strengthen his resistance to all forms of established law and they stimulate his drive to establish himself. In short, the law works to lower his fortunes to the point where he will have to rebuild them from the very foundation. He still has not learned, for example, that the resentment that later leads him to attack another shipboard enemy, Lieutenant Crampley, on the Sussex shore almost always has unfortunate consequences. Random's violent behavior, however, cannot be attributed merely to his explosive temper or to shortsightedness in his own affairs. Established authorities also contribute to that violence. Just as I have argued that civil society produces victimization of the individual in a competitive aggregate as a means of its own cohesion, so too the juridical institution produces resentment and resistance as a justification for its coercive powers. Those coercive powers produce in turn the juridical subject who can avoid the forces' oppressive effects. Even as the novel appends a romance ending upon a hitherto grotesque mode of representation, so too the hero transforms and internalizes the law that has injured him in the past.[42] Realism chastises and romance rewards the hero, thereby solving the problem of the protagonist's unruly and self-defeating impulses. The picaro who gradually learns to live in a corrupt society does so usually at the expense of his personal integrity. In Random's case, however, survival and moral education advance together. The hero is transformed by the Marshalsea prison, where he loses his pretensions to a false gentility and is prepared to fulfill a productive function in the new capitalist order. Then, and only then, the romance endows him with a father and returns to him a lover, the necessary attributes of patriarchal authority and a public conscience bent on preserving the order and prosperity that he has attained at last.

## V The best vengeance

Random's fortunes are marked by the vicissitudes and oscillations characteristic of the picaro.[43] He acquires wealth only to lose it because of others' malice or his own imprudence. In a fiercely competitive society, the unprotected individual becomes a mark for both the cunning and the powerful. Although Random's awareness of his vulnerability grows, it alone cannot produce the conscience that will finally earn him the protection that he needs. The linking of conscience and protection is more than a reflex of the text's moral project; it is also the manner in which the

---

[42] See Fredman, "The Picaresque in Decline," pp. 204ff., for a view that the blending of the two genres is a failure.

[43] See Boucé, *Novels*, pp. 115–16 for his plot of the vicissitudes of the hero's fortunes.

text cures the law's ills by furnishing it with an ideal body. That body, furthermore, must prove capable of reproducing itself and thereby reproducing the public conscience. The antitype of this ideal has existed through most of Random's retrospective narration. Characterized by an impulsive behavior driven by resentment and a desire for social recognition, the body has managed to elude the law's trammels only through the assistance of a devoted servant who recognizes his master's inherent nobility. Strap, however, cannot provide for Random forever without inverting the hierarchical relation and introducing a kind of ideological chaos into the narrative that seeks to construct an independent proto-bourgeois hero. The crisis arrives when Random, in an action that once again contradicts the social status awaiting him, loses his and Strap's money at the gaming tables of Bath. As he returns to London, the penniless Random considers taking a final, radical step outside the law to repair his fortunes:

[W]hile we were crossing Bagshot Heath, I was seized with a sort of inclination to retrieve my fortune, by laying passengers under contribution, in some such place. – My thoughts were so circumstanced at this time, that I should have digested the crime of robbery, so righteously had I concerted my plan, and ventured my life in the execution, had I not been deterred by reflecting upon the infamy that attends detection.                                                                 (60:369)

Random's misfortunes instigate a familiar "inclination" to be revenged upon a society that refuses to acknowledge what is due him. His inclination remains a mere fantasy, however, because having circulated in that same society he watches himself being watched by others. This is a stage in Random's acquisition of a public conscience. In his discussion of Adam Smith's impartial spectator, John Bender has written that the new disciplinary regime of the Enlightenment is "based on guilt rather than shame, and marked by the introjection of impersonal norms as character."[44] Random's conscience, however, like his origins, is still split between residual and emergent orders. It is imbued as much with the residual element of shame as with the emergent deterrent of guilt. His reflection indicates that the crime itself, if it might go undetected, would be a righteous venture. Detection, on the other hand, would exclude him from the status that he seeks. Random's moral imagination at this moment is personal rather than impersonal because the norms that restrain his inclination play an instrumental role in the construction of his public character but do not affect his own self-regard. Although the application of these labels might sound paradoxical, the dichotomy between personal morality and public behavior satisfies the conservative elements in Smollett's plot by elevating visible public character over an invisible

---

[44] Bender, *Imagining the Penitentiary*, p. 221.

private interiority. In other words, the text makes the hero's motives quite clear. The shame that keeps Random from highway robbery will be transformed into bourgeois honor (merit) as he is forced to discover other means of accumulation. That bourgeois honor will be then graced with a sense of social obligation that finds expression in a new-found respect for juridical boundaries and powers.

The final stage of the hero's sentimental and juridical education begins not with highway robbery but with the fashionably effete (and thus class-bound) action of "bilking one's tailor." Random's scheme to make money by selling clothes that he has not yet paid for adds fraud to the proscribed methods of accumulation. At the same time, the selling of the suit and the subsequent loss of freedom reveals that Random's character lacks the social substance that he has strived to acquire. If clothes make the man – as life in London seems to indicate – then Random's person is the product either of a theft or an illusion. Just as borrowing the sword to duel Gawkey had failed to make him a gentleman, so defrauding a tradesman fails to buy him the opportunity to reestablish his fortunes. In each case Random has looked for assistance from extrinsic sources. And just as Clarissa learns that her God would let her depend on no one but him, Random too learns the necessity of self-reliance and of respect for the socially appointed boundaries between *meum* and *tuum*. Society's boundary school is the prison, where the body internalizes limits. Prison turns Random's fantastic identity into a nightmare.

In the Marshalsea, Random vacillates between renouncing a corrupt society entirely and preserving his attachment to it because of "the remembrance of the amiable Narcissa," the woman who represents an absolute value for him (64:397). As idealized woman, she is an exception to the aggressive behavior of the social world.[45] Her special status as both subject ignorant of competition and as desired object of the same competition allows the narrative to offer an alternative to the way of the world without withdrawing from it. Because social competition cannot be escaped anymore than one can escape society and live (*Clarissa* teaches this lesson), the alienating effects of fierce competition must be counter-vailed by a fantasy of the sufficient self living in a world that it has domesticated. "Narcissa" is little more than the hero's own gentle reflection, and thus the promise of his release from an alienating reality. "She" is at once the antidote to and the most valuable part of the civil society that has victimized him. To win her is to win ascendancy over social relations. To withdraw is to lose all: Narcissa, status, and finally self.

In order to make the means for finally realizing his goals acceptable,

---

[45] In this sense, she fulfills the narrative function of female as defined by Teresa de Lauretis in her Oedipal reading of narrative. *Alice Doesn't: Feminism, Semiotics, Cinema* (Bloomington: Indiana University Press, 1982), p. 121.

Random first loses the mental powers that have enabled him to weather his changeable fortunes.

In vain did my imagination flatter me with schemes of future happiness; surly reason always interposed, and in a moment overthrew the unsubstantial fabrick, by chastising the extravagance of my hope, and representing my unhappy situation in the right point of view: ... I seeing my money melt away, without any certainty of deliverance, and in short, all my hopes frustrated; grew negligent of life, lost all appetite, and degenerated into such a sloven, that during the space of two months, I was neither washed, shifted, nor shaved; so that my face rendered meagre with abstinence, was obscured with dirt, and overshadowed with hair, and my whole appearance squalid and even frightful ...                    (64:397)

Reason thrives in confinement, limiting imagination's power. Random's reflection, furthermore, establishes a triangular relation between reason, imagination, and money. His revels have ended; with the vanishing of the baseless fabric of his dreams has melted away all his money. Thus, both narratively and figuratively is imagination linked to the loss of money. The hero is at the point of becoming just another of the "naked miserable wretches" that inhabit the prison (61:375). But as he is reduced to the thing itself by his lost hopes, the prison also scours him of his former pretensions. Reason must now interpose in order for the hero to be supplied with an instrumental rather than a merely fantastic system of values.

It is more than a matter of plotting that Random's Uncle Bowling is the agent of those values. Bowling, as I have noted above, is the "natural" man, scornful of the distractions of fashionable society yet imbued with a moral sense. During his absence from the narrative, through hard work Bowling has repaired his own fortunes, damaged by the duel with Captain Oakhum. The rendezvous between uncle and nephew is central to the development I have been tracing, for it foreshadows the final harmony of law and individual desire. Although Bowling too has an explosive temper and a fierce pride, he escapes the law's trammels by being a productive subject. Sailing in the empire's merchant fleet, he makes his fortune trading slaves. Trading slaves as a means of accumulation is not subject to reflection because it deals with goods in demand; Random's fantastic means of attaining status, on the other hand, is subject to reflection. First out of place in and later out of step with an expanding commercial empire, the hero must resolve his "status inconsistency" by acknowledging both the importance of productive work and the law that protects its profits.

Bowling frees Random from his debts, and the nephew signs on his uncle's ship as surgeon, so to be "put ... on a method of getting a fortune in a few years, by [his] own industry" (64:400). Method entails on Random the necessity of deferring gratification voluntarily. Previously, deferral has been forced upon him; now, having experienced the hardship of enforced deferral, he chooses to put off present opportunities for wooing Narcissa in order to be in a better position to woo her in the future. The voyage is an investment; its prudence is signalled by the romance coincidence that reunites the son with his father and invests the former with the patriarchal authority of the latter. Random's authority, then, is derived from both merit and birth. Romance "locates" the father for and in Random.

Before he can assume full authority, however, his social experience must be reaccented so that his resentments can melt away now that his money mounts up. After Random recounts for his father the events of his life, he writes that his father "blessed God for the adversity I had undergone, which, he said, enlarged the understanding, improved the heart, steeled the constitution, and qualified a young man for all the duties and enjoyments of life, much better than any education which affluence could bestow" (66:415). Righteous indignation at the iniquities of competition and punishment by interested authorities has been transformed into gratitude for the education society has afforded him. Society's dual function – repressive and educational – is revealed as unitary once the individual has been moved to a position from which he can appreciate the benefits of adversity. Now qualified for the "duties and enjoyments of life," the hero can appreciate the law that protects those who enjoy such qualifications. Its social function appears fully natural.

*Roderick Random* ends with the establishment of a balance between duty and enjoyment, a balance that was still missing in Bowling's character. The return of Random's long-absent father, now called Don Rodriguez, allows him to replace the uncle as model. Drawing ideological support from the father's abstract gentility and from the sentimentality that suffuses the final chapters, the novel effects the suture between the feeling heart and the judicial head. Through his own industry and his father's, Random can now return to England, marry his Narcissa, and purchase the mortgaged paternal estate from the creditors of his profligate cousin. Full narrative closure awaits only the final dispensation of a justice free from the taint and dangers of personal vengeance. This closure is foreshadowed when Random returns with his father to their native village. A member of the family, who drove father and son from the estate, is brought before the bar of natural justice. The son acts as plaintiff, thereby allowing his father to pass judgment on a representative culprit. Because the male head of the family (the profligate fox-hunter) has already been dealt his inevitable punishment by the free play of market forces, one of the female cousins is ushered in to receive her due. She asks her cousin if he recognizes her, and Random answers:

"Yes, madam, (said I) for my own part, I shall never forget you. – Sir, this is one of the young ladies, who (as I formerly told you) treated me so humanely in my childhood!" When I pronounced these words, my father's resentment glowed in

his visage, and he ordered her to be gone, with such a commanding aspect, that
she retired in a fright, muttering curses as she went down stairs . . .     (69:433)

Don Rodriguez's resentment wears the aspect of authority and justice. He
purifies the familial Eden by expelling the inhuman(e) cousin from his
presence in the same manner that Don Rodriguez's father had polluted it
by banishing him and his young bride.[46] Whereas the grandfather acted in
a calculated manner upon an arbitrary rule that was little more than an
excuse for his avarice, the father acts according to the spontaneous dictates
of his heart. His law enjoys a direct correspondence with his feelings, and
his feelings command obedience. The father completes what Bowling had
failed to accomplish in the beginning of the novel. With his undebauched
heart, his forthright approach, and his salty tongue, Bowling could accuse
and curse; but he could not command because he lacked the patriarchal
authority tied to landed wealth. In the father, however, power and
sentiment are joined in righteous indignation and measured judgment.

*Roderick Random* ends with praise of virtuous wedlock and of a heretofore
fickle fortune. True happiness might be considered its own reward, but for
Random happiness becomes material at last. Before he left London for his
native Scotland, Random had "summoned the Squire," Narcissa's
brother, "to produce his father's will at Doctor's Commons, and employed
a proctor to manage the affair in [Random's] absence" (69:432). The
brother had claimed that the will denied Narcissa her share of the family
inheritance if she married without his consent, which he – of course –
refused to give. Fortune and the law, however, take Random's part. The
law of inheritance, which denied him and his father a rightful share of the
patrimony, will now secure his wife's inheritance for him. The end of the
novel will not recapitulate the beginning. Thus, Random learns from his
proctor that a codicil to the will removes the impediment from Narcissa's
freedom of choice at nineteen. He will certainly recover her fortune.

Random's happiness at this prospect is only exceeded by another,
greater happiness, with which he ends his tale: "I would have set out for
London immediately after receiving this piece of intelligence, but my dear
angel has been qualmish of late, and begins to grow remarkably round in
the waist; so that I cannot leave her in such an interesting situation, which
I hope will produce something to crown my felicity" (69:435). The smooth
workings of the law, set in action by the hero himself, give way to the
smoother workings of nature. All is as it should be as the hero fulfills the
terms of his mother's prophetic dream. The hero's fortunes prove the truth
of Blackstone's vision of the law: "For [God] has so intimately connected,

---

[46] See Ronald Paulson, "The Pilgrimage and the Family: Structures in the Novels of Fielding
and Smollett," in G. S. Rousseau and P-G Boucé, eds., *Tobias Smollett: Bicentennial Essays
Presented to Lewis M. Knapp* (New York: Oxford University Press, 1971), pp. 57–78, for a
discussion of the role of the family in terms of the myth of the fall.

so inseparably interwoven the laws of eternal justice with the happiness of each individual, that the latter cannot be attained but by observing the former; and, if the former be punctually obeyed, it cannot but induce the latter."[47] As he surveys his felicity from a timeless vantage far from the competition of a roguish society and secure in a patriarchal authority that gives every indication of successfully reproducing itself in the near future, the vagabond hero who has learned to work the law to his own advantage has found a public conscience and a happy justice.

[47] Blackstone, *Commentaries*, 1:40.

# 6

## Shadows of the prison house or shade of the family tree: *Amelia's* public and private worlds

Earlier, when something like the maligned bourgeois division between professional and private life still existed – a division whose passing one almost now
regrets – anyone who pursued practical aims in the private sphere was eyed
mistrustfully as an uncouth interloper.

Theodor Adorno, *Minima Moralia*, p. 23

### I Introduction

Henry Fielding's *Amelia* represents the relation between the public and
private spheres, notably the effects of the public sphere on private happiness. Taking their cue from the novel's Preface in which Fielding declares
his intention to "disclose some of the most glaring Evils, as well public as
private, which at present infest the Country," many commentators have
discussed the interrelations of public and private events in the novel.[1]
George Sherburn identifies one of the novel's two main themes as an
indictment of corrupt elites, who refuse to recognize and promote individual merit.[2] Leo Braudy writes that "[t]he reader is ... invited to look
through personal affairs into the public issues. Public and private life are
not separated in *Amelia*; we are shown instead the analogy between
them."[3] In this chapter I will argue that *analogy* is not precise enough;
rather, public events create the need for a new kind of domestic sphere,
governed by a sentimental husband, himself chastised by law and thus
enabled to defend his family against both corrupt elites in the public
sphere and pursuers of practical – that is, distinctly unsentimental – aims
in the private.

Given Fielding's education as a lawyer and practice as a magistrate, it is
not surprising that the law should be both the object of his satire and the

---

[1] Henry Fielding, *Amelia*, ed. Martin C. Battestin (Middletown: Wesleyan University Press,
1983), p. 3. All further references to this edition are included in the text. Battestin discusses
Fielding's didactic intentions in the introduction, pp. xxi–xl.

[2] George Sherburn, "Fielding's *Amelia*: An Interpretation," *ELH* 3 (1936):1–14; rpt. in *Fielding*,
ed. Ronald Paulson (Englewood Cliffs: Prentice Hall, 1962), pp. 146–57; esp. pp. 152–56.

[3] Braudy, *Narrative Form*, p. 192; see also pp. 182, 207. My reading is indebted to Braudy's.

instrument that triggers his hero's reform.[4] Cynthia Griffin Wolff argues, however, that although "Fielding attempts to offer a bridge between public and private morality in his discussion of the role of the law ..., even he must have recognized the inadequacy of his proposals."[5] Patricia Meyer Spacks arrives at a similar conclusion. Although she calls the law "the instrument of [Booth's] rescue" from the dangers of public life, she notes that like Sherburn's elites, it does not necessarily reward merit and that "Booth shows great good sense in returning with his gains" to private life in the country.[6] Terry Castle argues convincingly that *Amelia* subverts its own didactic project by "insinuat[ing] in the place of moral certainty, a tropology of ambiguity and complexity."[7] Through the masquerade – which Castle finds to be a controlling trope for the narrative – desire, judgment, and security become problematic because boundaries are unintentionally and intentionally transgressed. Finally, John Bender writes that Dr. Harrison represents the novel's disciplinary project. Working, as it were, with an authorial narrator to effect individual reform, Harrison "enacts an exemplary story with Booth as main character ... [whose] ... every move takes place in prisons or in the sanctuary of 'rules' and 'verges' pertaining to them." But like Braudy and the others, Bender concludes that *Amelia* does not fully realize this proto-panoptical disciplinary project because Harrison is split between the role of narrator and character, thereby making his interventions only partially effective because he remains visible and intrusive.[8]

Although these estimations of the success of Fielding's didactic intentions are plausible, I want to suggest another way of explaining the relation between the novel's public and private spheres. Corruption in the public sphere and honest affection in the private are dialectically necessary representational antitheses rather than the products of failed didactic intentions. In order for Fielding's text to perform the ideological labor of

[4] For Fielding's career as a magistrate, see Benjamin M. Jones, *Henry Fielding, Novelist and Magistrate* (London: Allen & Unwin, 1933) and Battestin's Introduction to *Amelia*. The definitive study of the technical role of the law in *Amelia* is Hugh Amory's unpublished dissertation, "Law and the Structure of Fielding's Novels", Columbia University, 1964, pp. 373–420. For other notes on specific connections between *Amelia* and legal reform, see Tuvia Bloch, "The Prosecution of the Maidservant in *Amelia*," *English Language Notes* 6 (1969): 269–71; and John C. Stephens, Jr., "The Verge of the Court and Arrest for Debt in Fielding's *Amelia*," *Modern Language Notes* 63 (1948):104–9. Brian McCrea argues that Fielding's attack on specific abuses in the legal system was an attempt to criticize injustice without attacking the Pelham ministry, which he supported. "Politics and Narrative Technique in Fielding's *Amelia*," *The Journal of Narrative Technique* 13 (1983):131–40, esp. 131–33.

[5] Cynthia Griffin Wolff, "Fielding's *Amelia*: Private Virtue and Public Good," *Texas Studies in Literature and Language* 10 (1968):54.

[6] Patricia Meyer Spacks, *Imagining a Self: Autobiography and Novel in Eighteenth-Century England* (Cambridge, MA: Harvard University Press, 1976), p. 292.

[7] Terry Castle, *Masquerade and Civilization: The Carnivalesque in Eighteenth-Century English Culture and Fiction* (Stanford: Stanford University Press, 1986), p. 242.

[8] Bender, *Imagining the Penitentiary*, pp. 166, 147, 193.

creating a haven from a world described by Adam Ferguson as one where a "man is sometimes found a detached and solitary being ... in competition with his fellow-creatures," corruption must remain a constant and intractable aspect of public life.[9] Private life offers satisfactions that countervail those available in the public sphere. Thus, instead of seeing public and private as two mutually exclusive spheres, they must be viewed simultaneously as connected and separate. The nuclear family is represented as the place for individual happiness because it is free from the practical – that is, instrumental or objectifying – aims of the public sphere. At the same time, however, uncouth interlopers such as Betty Harris, Miss Mathews, and Colonel James bring the public sphere's general corruption into the family. Such infiltration serves both a narrative and ideological function by providing the novel's neophyte *paterfamilias* with a motive to eradicate his passional instability and become a man of law.

At the same time that the family is constituted apart from the public, it must prove that it possesses more than a fugitive and cloistered virtue by venturing its essence against that of the public sphere. That essence is Amelia, whom Leo Braudy calls the novel's "ultimate value" and Patricia Meyer Spacks the embodiment of the myth of "noble womanhood."[10] In fact Amelia is the object of numerous valuations that fall into conflict and are subject to competition. Her body has an intrinsic value (she is desirable) and an extrinsic value (she was and will be again an heiress), both of which make her an object of masculine struggle for social dominance. Amelia's value is thus certified by the ferocity of the competition over it. She brings together a competitive public and an affective private value by embodying a secured object of competition that deserves an unflagging affection. In other words, her social value as woman and heiress is transformed into a personal value of wife and mother through the successful struggle to constitute a viable domestic sphere. What Terry Eagleton observes about the nineteenth-century realist novel applies also to *Amelia*: Fielding's work, "by casting objective social relations into interpersonal terms, constantly hold[s] open the possibility of reducing one to the other."[11] This reduction is not merely the "mystification" that Eagleton names it, however, for in addition to providing a transcendent ground of personal value in a world where value has been destabilized by competitive desires, Amelia also represents the hybridizing of social and personal relations in a bourgeois world, relations that the division of experience into hermetic spheres are meant to keep separate.

[9] Ferguson, *Essay on the History of Civil Society*, p. 19.
[10] Braudy, *Narrative Form*, p. 201. Patricia Meyer Spacks, *Desire and Truth: Functions of Plot in Eighteenth-Century English Novels* (Chicago and London: University of Chicago Press, 1990), p. 105.
[11] Eagleton, *Criticism and Ideology*, p. 121.

Juridical discourse plays a pivotal role in the dialectical relation of the public and private spheres. As in *Roderick Random*, juridical consciousness can work through an instrumental reason that defends its possessor against others with practical aims. By taxing a profligate husband with a number of costly juridical experiences, the law teaches Booth that there is a link between the expense of spirit and the loss of familial pleasures. Booth's experience as an object of the law's interest offers a cure for that which Hume has described as "incurable in human nature": the recurring instances in which a person "is seduced from his great and important, but distant interests, by the allurement of present, though often very frivolous temptations."[12] This cure installs Booth finally as a mature *paterfamilias* in a commercial society where "the bands of affection are broken."[13] His encounter with the law makes Booth realize that both satisfaction and power lie within the circumscribed sphere of family life where bands of affection remain intact.

Although a paternally protected and maternally nurtured private sphere possesses the psychological advantages of affection and autonomy for the male, it is not without its own problems. As Fielding's narrative reforms Booth, it simultaneously sets out to solve these problems as well. Lawrence Stone notes that the "erosion of outside supports [for the conjugal family] involved a reduction of sociability ... as the conjugal family turned more in upon itself."[14] The introversion of the family, suggesting an intensification of emotional life that is source both of power and satisfaction for the male, creates as well a kind of affective and physical claustrophobia as the sphere in which satisfaction can be won shrinks. In order to counteract this feeling, *Amelia's* public spaces undergo a compensatory shrinking. The inhabitants of the public sphere constantly threaten each other's autonomy. Bands of affection are displaced by adversarial relations. Bailiffs and warders, sharpers and seducers compete for ownership over increasingly smaller bits of the public sphere. In contrast to these limiting dangers, the domestic space voluntarily occupied by the nuclear family expands, and confinement is redefined. When the public sphere becomes the site of coercion – whether because of its corruption or because of competition – the family becomes the chief site of freedom and the familial character the freest choice. In the following discussion I will examine how Fielding's narrative creates an ideal domestic sphere and brings Captain Booth to acknowledge the law that bestows upon him the right and power to govern the nuclear family.

---

12 Hume, "Of the Origin of Government," *Essays*, p. 36.
13 Ferguson, *Essay on the History of Civil Society*, p. 19.
14 Stone, *Family, Sex and Marriage*, p. 397.

## II The characters of the public world

From the first, the public sphere in *Amelia* is experienced as the sphere of
violence, coercion, and non-reciprocal social relations. The reader
follows the protagonist from a street fight to an arraignment in order at
last to enter the sphere's epitome by passing through prison portals. Not
so much criminal as criminally negligent, Captain Booth indulges a
sympathetic impulse to aid a man "unequally attacked" by two others.
All are arrested by the watch, but Booth, "having no Money in his
Pocket" is unable "to make up the Matter" as the others had done and is
committed to prison by the corrupt Justice Thrasher for "beating the
Watchman in Execution of his Office and breaking his Lanthorn" (24).
The first event of the narrative establishes a causal or syntagmatic
relation between indulgence and prison as well as a metaphorical or
paradigmatic relation between money and freedom. These relations serve
two functions: they operate as foundational principles of the juridical
and economic discourses respectively, and they constitute a matrix upon
which fortunes of the inhabitants of the public sphere can be plotted. In
order to be free, a character must be in possession of the positive terms of
both relations; that is, there is a causal relation between freedom,
self-restraint, and money. Fielding's novel deploys the consequentialist
element of juridical discourse and the socially constructed essentialist
element of economic discourse (you are what you can buy) in order to
construct an alternative space of non-coercive relations in the private
sphere.

That the public sphere becomes the space of coercion indicates here as
in the other texts of this study the hybrid nature of the novel, inheritor of
residual or traditional ideologies as well as herald of emergent structures of
feeling.[15] The public sphere is characterized by corruption and excess.
Terry Castle has described the novel's opening as a series of "[e]mblematic
vignettes" in the service of an allegorical and authorially controlled
"*psychomachia*, or battle of vice and virtue."[16] In Castle's view, Fielding
attempts to play the traditional role of moral censor and satirist, intent on
exposing and – with luck – reforming public corruption. The public world
is Mandevillean, and the means of getting and spending are divorced from
moral imperatives. In the words of Louis Dumont, "each subject defines
his conduct by reference only to his own interest, and society is no more
than the mechanism – or the invisible hand – by which interests harmon-
ize. It is a mechanism that ... will justify the egoistic, asocial conduct of

---

[15] For a description of these terms, see Raymond Williams, *Marxism and Literature* (Oxford:
Oxford University Press, 1977), pp. 121–35.
[16] Castle, *Masquerade and Civilization*, pp. 202–3.

everyone."[17] According to Adam Smith the invisible hand obviates the need to regulate egoistic passions, for it leads the wealthy "in spite of their natural selfishness and rapacity, ... without intending it, without knowing it, ... [to] advance the interest of ... society."[18] In Fielding's novel, however, "selfishness and rapacity" work upon and through the individual to weaken and, in some instances, to destroy society's elemental units, whether it be the individual or the family. Whereas the classical economists saw freedom in the workings of the market, Fielding's novel sees the opposite: it sees coercive competition and corrosive corruption as the profit motive (the drive for personal aggrandizement) displaces older modes of social relation, including but not limited to paternalist ideals of service. For Booth, Adam Smith's invisible hand is attached to the wrist of a constable or a bailiff or a corrupt magistrate.

When Booth goes to the aid of the solitary man attacked by two assailants, he expresses not only an instinctive sympathy and an intuitive sense of justice, but he also embodies a quixotic devotion to the underdog who seems in danger of being deprived of life and motility. But Booth, like Roderick Random, misperceives, thereby experiencing a truth about the public sphere: all its inhabitants – victims and victimizers alike – show no gratitude for assistance. In a world that is characterized by faith in an invisible hand, there is no need for gratitude, even if that hand may at times belong to one who risks life and limb to pull one from the Hobbesian fray. Even as public corruption turns Booth's winning characteristics into liabilities, the narrative subjects these traits to a discipline that will bring them in line with the Mandevillean realities of the public world. The narrative prepares Booth for this instruction in a fairly direct manner. As he enters the prison, Booth undergoes an "*uncasing*" when he cannot pay "Garnish" demanded by his fellow prisoners.[19] Stripped of his coat, Booth becomes unaccommodated man, ready to see and feel what society's wretches feel.

The prison provides Booth with an elementary education in the consequences of various kinds of unreflected action and social knowledge, especially carnal. Blear-Eyed Moll, the first sight to greet Booth, epitomizes the consequences of an unrestrained carnality. She "measured full as much round the middle as from Head to Foot," the particular embodiment of excess that the prison is meant to contain. Her distinguishable physical attributes are travesties of those belonging to the private world's

[17] Louis Dumont, *From Mandeville to Marx: The Genesis and Triumph of Economic Ideology* (Chicago: University of Chicago Press, 1977), p. 75.

[18] Smith, *Theory of Moral Sentiments*, pp. 184–85.

[19] For a discussion of the practice of garnish in light of Victor Turner's theories of liminality, see Bender, *Imagining the Penitentiary*, pp. 26–35. Although my discussion coincides with Bender's at some points, I focus on the spectacular representations arising from the violent conjunction of public and private lives.

chaste mother: "her vast Breasts had long since forsaken their native Home, and had settled themselves a little below the Girdle." "One of the merriest Persons in the whole Prison," she is all deadly appetite: "About half a dozen ebeny Teeth fortified that large and long Canal, which Nature had cut from Ear to Ear" (27–28). Moll's body confuses nurture and deadly pleasures. Her breasts reach down to the corruption below the girdle, while above, her black teeth proclaim a hell's mouth that threatens to swallow all who share her appetites. Moll breeds death. Peter Stallybrass and Allon White have written that "the grotesque body stands in opposition to the bourgeois individualist conception of the body, which finds *its* image and legitimation in the classical."[20] That Moll's grotesque body is the first female body to enter the narrative signals that the narrative will devote its energy to negating it and replacing it with the natural mother, symbol of home and purity, life and generation.

The prison stands in the narrative as a septic final home for the insensible and the moribund. The insensible lack a private history: all we know of them is that they enjoy "themselves very merrily over a Bottle of Wine and a Pipe of Tobacco." The moribund are casualties from the destruction of the private sphere. Among them are "a Man prostrate on the Ground, whose heavy Groans, and frantic Actions, plainly indicated the highest Disorder of Mind" and a "young Woman in Rags sitting on the Ground, and supporting the Head of an old Man in her Lap, who appeared to be giving up the Ghost" (32–34). The prostrate man, committed for what the narrator calls a "small Felony," groans out his guilt for his wife, "who then lay-in, upon hearing the News [of his commitment], had thrown herself from a Window two Pair of Stairs high, by which means he had, in all Probability, lost both her and his Child" (32). He represents the consequentialist or juridical axis of the public sphere. The young woman "was committed for stealing a loaf, in order to support the former [her dying father], and the former for receiving it knowing it to be stolen" (34). Lacking money, the young woman is forced to steal, thereby forfeiting her and her father's freedom. She represents the essentialist axis. Both present Booth with the spectacle of affective relations destroyed by public forces.

In order for Booth's experiences to become instrumental reason – that is, practical tools for survival – he must acquire an understanding of the effects of the public sphere's economic and juridical principles upon personal autonomy and power. The prison spectacle presents a graphic illustration of the consequences of this interrelation. It is supplemented by an explicit statement of these principles by various juridical functionaries, among them the prison keeper: " 'When Prisoners have not wherewithal as

---

[20] Stallybrass and White, *Politics and Poetics of Transgression*, p. 22.

the Law requires to entitle themselves to Justice, why they must be beholden to other People, to give them their Liberty; and People will not to be sure suffer others to be beholden to them for nothing, whereof there is good Reason; for how should we all live if it was not for these things!'" (157). The keeper identifies a paradigmatic social relation (exchange) even as he reveals the link between money and justice. Obligation in a corrupt society is both quantitative and exploitative, intricately linked with necessity and victimization. Neither justice nor freedom is possible without the aid of others; yet justice and freedom command a premium. In *Amelia* to lack wherewithal means exposing the private world to the demands of another's self-interest. Booth is being taught that misery follows from an ignorance of the relation between credit and freedom.

The pragmatic prison keeper's lesson anticipates Adam Smith's famous remark that "[i]t is not from the benevolence of the butcher, the brewer, or the baker, that we expect our dinner, but from their regard to their own interest. We address ourselves, not to their humanity but to their self-love, and never talk to them of our own necessities but of their advantages."[21] Unlike Smith's economic treatise, however, predicated on a natural law of the harmony of interests and the market's just distribution of social goods, Fielding's *Amelia* represents the economization of society as a crisis in public service. Henry St. John, Viscount Bolingbroke, describes the ideal public servant as one "speaking rather to the good sense of others, than to their passions and interest; ... and looking on the revenue of an office to be so far public money, as it is intended for the dignity and support of that office, to which it is appropriated."[22] Speaking not of ministers as Bolingbroke had but rather of minor public servants like the prison keeper and Justice Thrasher, Edmund Burke called them "generally the scum of the earth ... unworthy of any employ whatever."[23] Those who work within the institutions of the public sphere show evidence of what Robert Alter has called the "pervasive, maddening perversity of society at large."[24] To call society perverse, however, is to mystify the mechanism that enables these functionaries to embrace the particularism sanctioned

21  Smith, *Wealth of Nations*, 1:26–27.

22  Henry St. John, Viscount Bolingbroke, "Of Good and Bad Ministers," in *The Works of Lord Bolingbroke*, 4 vols. (Philadelphia: Carey and Hart, 1841), 1:493.

23  Quoted in Holdsworth, *History of English Law*, 10:143. Burke made the statement in 1780. See also Jones: "It had proved impossible to find sufficient gentlemen to undertake the onerous and sordid work, and a practice had grown up of allowing the Westminster magistrates to repay themselves by fees taken from persons charged before them. In consequence, only inferior men could be induced to accept the office, and then only with the object of enriching themselves" (*Fielding: Novelist and Magistrate* 113).

24  Robert Alter, *Fielding and the Nature of the Novel* (Cambridge, MA: Harvard University Press, 1968), p. 172. See also Claude Rawson, *Henry Fielding and the Augustan Ideal Under Stress: "Nature's Dance of Death" and other Studies* (London: Routledge & Kegan Paul, 1972), pp. 72–73; Braudy, *Narrative Form*, p. 193; and J. Paul Hunter, *Occasional Form: Henry Fielding and the Chains of Circumstance* (Baltimore: Johns Hopkins University Press, 1975), p. 204.

by economic ideology. In the words of J. G. A. Pocock, they "discern only particular values."[25] Like the Harlowes, they operate in a diminished moral and physical universe, in which everything – including character – becomes a means to the end of accumulation. In such an impoverished world, public service becomes distasteful to the man with good nature, who then turns naturally to a private world that is free from corruption and free from the juridical and economic discourses that enable it. As corruption and the drive to accumulate limit the range of one's experience in a claustrophobic public world, the private begins to look like the sphere of true freedom.

Under the regime of an economized juridical discourse, the offices of the public sphere deprive the improvident or unfortunate of their liberty. The bailiff Bondum echoes the prison keeper's sentiments in a dialogue with Booth:

"I am for Liberty, for my part." "Is that so consistent with your Calling?" cries *Booth*, "I thought, my Friend, you had lived by depriving Men of their Liberty." "That's another Matter," cries the Bailiff, "that's all according to Law, and in the Way of Business. To be sure Men must be obliged to pay their Debts, or else there would be an End of every Thing." (314)

In justifying his business, Bondum merely repeats the principle of policing credit and securing property in a market society. Booth objects, however, to the expedient of subjecting the debtor's freedom to the creditor's avarice, malice, or resentment.[26] In claiming that by "the old Constitution of *England* ... Men could not be arrested for Debt," Booth invokes an Englishman's customary rights, just as Clarissa had in her struggle with Lovelace. His argument finds precedent and support in other eighteenth-century writers. Daniel Defoe, no enemy to commerce, supplies the precedent: "Debtors abuse Creditors, and Creditors starve and murther their Debtors; Compassion flies from human Nature in the course of universal Commerce; and *Englishmen*, who in all other Cases are men of Generosity, Tenderness, and more than common Compassion, are to their Debtors mere Lunaticks, Mad-men and Tyrants."[27] The connection between freedom and credit in a world where it is not possible to master all the contingencies of trade turns everyone into a tyrant or a cheat. Structure determines action, which is the matrix of character. Samuel Johnson provides a supporting opinion some few years later: "scarcely the most

25 Pocock, *Machiavellian Moment*, p. 464.
26 For a brief summary of the history of debt legislation in the eighteenth century, see Holdsworth, *History of English Law*, 11:595–99. For Fielding's view on imprisonment for debt, see *The Champion* (19 February 1739/40), cited by Battestin, p. 314, n. 1. M. Dorothy George claims that imprisonment for debt "had no effect at all in doing what it was supposed to do – secure the rights of property and the sanctity of the contract." *London Life in the Eighteenth Century* (1925; rpt., New York: Harper and Row, 1964), p. 310.
27 Daniel Defoe, *Review*, vol. III, no. 92.; cited in Pocock, *Machiavellian Moment*, p. 453.

zealous admirers of our institutions can think that law wise, which when men are capable of work, obliges them to beg; or just, which exposes the liberty of one to the passions of another."[28] Although Booth voices a conventional concern about the liberty of the Englishman, he must still learn that Bondum is part of a structure that legitimizes particular passions by bringing them into accord with the law. Although he cannot become limited in the way that the bailiff is in his single-minded pursuit of fees – Bondum is a juridical entrepreneur trying "to load his Prisoner with as many Actions as possible" (312) – Booth must learn the differential values that the reigning juridical structures accord to passions.

While Booth's public experiences prepare him to govern the private sphere, they also emphasize the danger that men like Bondum pose to traditional social hierarchies. In the same scene discussed above, Bondum resorts to ocular proof to assert his social status: "[Bondum] then pulled out a Handful of Guineas, saying, 'There, Sir, they are all my own; I owe no Body a Shilling. I am no Beggar, nor no Debtor. I am the King's Officer, as well as you, and I will spend Guinea for Guinea as long as you please'" (353). Money is essence for this officer, and at this moment his essence is greater than Captain Booth's. Booth reacts to this claim of superiority by collaring Bondum with an intent to punish him for insubordination. The Captain learns very quickly, however, that the office protects its holder, even if the officer violates traditional relations of deference. Threatening to charge Booth with attempted "Rescue," Bondum exclaims that "[i]f Officers are to be used in this Manner, there is an end of all Law and Justice."[29] Once again the bailiff's rhetoric is self-serving, but his threat is potent. Booth, rendered passionate by his sense of injury and powerless by his debts, is saved from Newgate only by the timely arrival of help from the private sphere in the figures of Harrison and Atkinson, aided by a public professional, attorney Murphy. That is, only by the intervention of a form of obligation that is not based on a *quid pro quo* is Booth saved from further entanglement in the law.

*Amelia* counterbalances the public spectacle of the conflict of economic passions and its threat to freedom with a private though unprotected sentimentalized romance, where gentler feelings enlarge the worthy heart.[30] Romance expels the social world's baser conflicts and replaces

---

[28] Johnson, *The Idler* 22, p. 69.

[29] See Blackstone, *Commentaries*, 4:126: "[A]ll such as are guilty of any injurious treatment to those who are immediately under the protection of a court of justice, are punishable by fine and imprisonment: as if a man assaults or threatens ... a gaoler or other ministerial officer for keeping him in custody, and properly executing his duty: which offenses, when they proceeded farther than bare threats, were punished in the Gothic constitution with exile and forfeiture of goods." Bondum's ignorance of the law seems to be emphasized here by his use of the term *rescue*, whereas *gaol-break* or *escape* would be the expected charge.

[30] On the romance element in *Amelia*, see Sheridan Baker, "Fielding's *Amelia* and the Materials of Romance," *Philological Quarterly* 41 (1962):437–49.

them with an ideal affective harmony. It also provides that harmony with
a local habitation, a hybrid space constructed through Amelia's forward-
looking vision of domestic sufficiency and Harrison's retrospective vision of
civic duty. This novelistic hybrid stands as a myth of new origin that takes
as its elements republican political theory on the one hand and bourgeois
household economy on the other. Its utopian vision provides the model of
the fully human character, in command of passions and of economic social
relations rather than reduced to a mere effect of internal and external
forces. Before considering the law's transformation of Booth, I shall turn to
an examination of this hybrid.

### III The private worlds of Amelia and Harrison

Just as the way to the public world lies through the prison portals, so too
the private world and its peerless representative first become known in
Booth's confessional tale, which serves as a prelude to his "criminal
correspondence" with fellow inmate Miss Mathews. Damaged though not
destroyed, thereafter the private sphere must prove itself able to provide
the same substantial satisfactions offered by the public. Amelia's presence
in the prison – first as a character in Booth's narrative and then as the wife
on a mission to rescue her husband – underscores the difficulty of this task.
The way into the prison is easy; it is the way out that presents numerous
difficulties.

As Booth recounts his past to Miss Mathews, he describes Amelia as one
possessing the strength to travel from her home in England to the side of
her wounded husband in Gibraltar. Amelia's wifely duty mirrors Booth's
soldierly duty in this instance. Before public and private life are inter-
mixed and thrust through the prison gates, conjugal complementarity,
unchallenged by competing pleasures, enables domestic and civic heroism.
When Amelia enters the prison, however, strength and heroism have
faded before the challenge to the sufficiency of domestic and conjugal
pleasures: "The Governor was now approaching with a long Roll of
Paper, when a faint Voice was heard to cry out hastily, 'where is he?' – and
presently a female Spectre, all pale and breathless, rushed into the Room,
and fell into Mr. *Booth's* Arms, where she immediately fainted away"
(159). When the spectral Amelia faints, the action repeats the disem-
bodiment implied in the description. The bearer of private virtues loses
her vitality in the public sphere. As she falls into Booth's arms, the wife
becomes the Eurydicean body that must be retrieved from a hell of
unrestrained physical appetites.[31] The husband alone can revive the wife,

---

[31] Peter V. LePage calls the "prison ... the constant scene," resembling a hell from which the
only escape is through Christian love. "The Prison and the Dark Beauty of 'Amelia,'" *Criticism*
9 (1967):339.

and he can do it only by hardening himself against public allurements. Booth has undergone his uncasing; now he must be clothed in the armor of sentimental affections in order to carry out the project that the narrative – with its patriarchal presuppositions – has reserved solely for him. The text demands domestic, not military, heroism of Booth.

Amelia's obvious vulnerability is the best argument for self-restraint on behalf of the male: she is the reward for his accepting the rules enjoining both sexual and economic continence. Thus it is not the mere coercive power of the law that encourages restraint, but rather that power working through the male's perception of the weak body of the female and thus upon the "affective" values carried by the male, from which values (whether patriarchal or companionate) he derives satisfaction and power. Male domination is encoded as protection, and his enjoyment of superiority rests on his conscientious performance of the protective role. Protection of others is also self-protection, for in the text's semantics woman is home and property (a meaning reinforced by deriving the Booth's family fortune from Amelia's mother rather than from the Captain's presence in the public sphere). And here is a contradiction in the text. Amelia is both the embodiment of the values that the juridical discourse claims to protect and the negation of its conditions of representation. In other words, where law is the ideal woman cannot be. She must occupy the sphere governed by benevolent paternalism rather than by liberal individualism. But even if Amelia were not the locus of value in property, she would still be the site of the law's power over her husband. Without Amelia, the law would have power over her husband's body only; with her, it has power over his psychic economy. The law enters the domestic sphere through the vulnerable and valuable body of the woman, which in the words of one critic houses "strength of principle, general benevolence for all God's creatures, the most loyal love for her husband, modest material requirements, and a conception of happiness which centers in the home ..."[32]

The power of the public sphere to weaken the value of the female is demonstrated on two other occasions when Amelia is taken for a common prostitute (395, 496).[33] In public Amelia is in danger of becoming indistinguishable from Blear-Eyed Moll or Miss Mathews. At home, however, she exercises her "Talents of Cookery, of which she was a great Mistress, as she was of every OEconomical office, from the highest to the lowest" (488), and thus creates what Jean Hagstrum has called "an Eden in the

---

[32] Sabine Nathan, "The Anticipation of Nineteenth-Century Ideological Trends in Fielding's *Amelia,*" *Zeitschrift für Anglistik und Amerikanistik* 6 (1958):394. See also Spacks, *Desire,* pp. 104–7.

[33] Castle reads the travestying of fixed identities as a subversive and liberating moment within the narrative as it subverts the "rationalist subject" (*Masquerade and Civilization* 250, *passim*).

wilderness."[34] By making this factitious Eden more lovely and ordered than the public wilderness, Amelia reconstructs the private sphere as a place of comfort and pleasure. Without demanding autonomy for herself, the woman labors to provide what the man cannot. Through her management of a sufficient if necessarily frugal domestic economy, Amelia creates an alternative to the excessive economies of the public sphere. Her political economy is communal, based on a kind of Miltonian internal plenitude distributed across a familial intersubjectivity:

Great Fortunes are not necessary to Happiness. For my own Part, I can level my Mind with any State; and for these poor little Things, whatever Condition of Life we breed them to, that will be sufficient to maintain them in. How many Thousands abound in Affluence, whose Fortunes are much lower than ours! for it is not from Nature, but from Education and Habit, that our Wants are chiefly derived ... Industry will always provide us a wholesome Meal; and I will take care, that Neatness and Cheerfulness shall make it a pleasant one.       (162)

For Amelia, the private sphere requires an unqualified rejection of the public pursuit of sophisticated luxuries. Industry rather than desire governs the family, which stands apart from if not prior to social institutions. Socially generated desires serve only to irritate the tranquil mind and interfere with its ability to adapt itself to a frugal moral economy. Amelia's familial Eden is somehow free from the desires bred by a consciousness of scarcity, a consciousness that in turn necessitates extra- or even intrafamilial competition. In an Eden regulated by its own internal satisfactions, freedom and law are one.

For all its appeal, Amelia's domestic utopia is the product of a crisis as she and Booth live without visible means of support within the verge of the court. It is also a reaction to the recent history of the pair. As a result of the husband's "childish Vanity" in buying a coach, they have suffered the resentment of their neighbors, who, prompted by envy, "declare War against [them]" (148–49). The Booths, soon penniless as a result of social and economic hostilities, are forced to flee to the city. In order, then, for Amelia's vision to be more than a response to adversity, it is supplemented by Dr. Harrison's authoritative vision, which is free from both the particularism of the public sphere and the particular domestic events of the Booths' past.

Recent critics have disagreed over the effectiveness of Harrison's authority and vision.[35] John Bender's sophisticated reading of this figure's

[34] Jean H. Hagstrum, *Sex and Sensibility: Ideal and Erotic Love from Milton to Mozart* (Chicago and London: University of Chicago Press, 1980), p. 185.

[35] Wolff finds Harrison naive and ineffectual even if able to accomplish individual acts of benevolence ("Fielding's *Amelia*" 50). John Sitter calls Harrison a weak "ancestral antique" (*Literary Loneliness in Mid-Eighteenth-Century England* [Ithaca and London: Cornell University Press, 1982], p. 199). Leo Braudy sees in Harrison a combination of resolve and sensibility appropriate to a Miltonic Christian hero (*Narrative Form* 199, 205).

function offers a different means of evaluation. Bender shows that Harrison "plays a startling number of authoritative roles in *Amelia*," both as an actor within the drama and as a quasi-authorial agent.[36] Harrison's authority might be understood also as split in another way: partly ineffectual in the public sphere and productive of positive results in the private. He fails in the public sphere at times because those "Deaf to the Voice of Reason, and superior to the Fear of Shame," only "the Rod of the Law ... [can] restrain ... within the Bounds of Decency and Sobriety," as Fielding put it in his address to the grand jurors of Westminster in 1749; or as Adam Ferguson writes some time after, "where the manners of a people are considerably changed for the worse, ... [the individual] must be referred to the whip, or the gibbet, for arguments in support of a caution, which the state now requires him to assume, on a supposition that he is insensible to the motives which recommend the practice of virtue."[37] He succeeds in the private sphere because by being allied with Amelia, he reaches Booth's conscience through his affections.

As an ideological agent, Harrison embodies and expresses an ideal of public service. He is "not the least versed in the *Chrematistic* Art," a word strange and important enough for Fielding to explain in a footnote as "[t]he Art of getting Wealth ... so called by *Aristotle* in his Politics" (375). Despite this self-confessed ignorance, Harrison proves a true and useful domestic economist, as Booth's description of his unsophisticated country parish illustrates:

His House indeed would not much attract the Admiration of the Virtuoso. He built it himself, and it is remarkable only for its Plainness ...

Nothing, however, can be imagined more agreeable than the Life that the Doctor leads in this homely House, which he calls his earthly Paradise. All his Parishioners, whom he treats as his Children, regard him as their common Father. Once in a Week he constantly visits every House in the Parish, examines, commends, and rebukes, as he finds Occasion. This is practiced likewise by his Curate in his Absence; and so good an Effect is produced by this their Care, that no Quarrels ever proceed either to Blows or Law-suits... (144–45)

Harrison emerges from Booth's description as a rustic Lycurgus, a peacemaker whose equitable judgment saves his society from litigiousness.[38] In naming Harrison the "common Father" and placing him in an idyllic pastoral setting, Booth expresses what Isaac Kramnick has called the politics of nostalgia, in which the "good of the governed is not achieved when the civil authority meets the demands and terms of contract set by

---

[36] Bender, *Imagining the Penitentiary*, p. 191. Terry Castle finds Harrison's interventions authoritarian and him insufferable (*Masquerade and Civilization* 221).

[37] Fielding, *Charge Delivered to the Grand Jury*, p. 54. Ferguson, *Essay on the History of Civil Society*, p. 240.

[38] Wolff calls Harrison "Fielding's principal advocate of order ... , a minister and representative of the highest of all laws" ("Fielding's *Amelia*" 43).

those who consent to it; it is found in the paternalism of older views in which authority comes from above and knowing what is best for the governed earns public consent."[39] Even in the city, Harrison's patriarchal authority can control fractious interests, given the right circumstances. He is able to marshal the common people's antipathies and sympathies to apprehend the lawyer Murphy and overcome the bailiff Bondum. Harrison's encounter with the mob is a telling moment in the text, for it represents the meeting of a residual, somewhat weakened, political ideal and the emergent forces that threaten social order. In having Harrison win the day by convincing the mob to take the side of justice, Fielding hints at patriarchal authority's potential to restore respect for a visibly corrupt law that has become an invitation to social resistance.[40] And since this authority draws its strength from the private sphere, that sphere becomes the antidote to the very corruption that puts it at risk.

Harrison's authority, however, is dependent upon his presence. As soon as the good Doctor leaves the country, conspicuous consumption, envy, and litigation break out. His authority must be disembodied, turned into a principle that can be internalized by the individual and institutionalized in the family. Such a principle is found in Harrison's notion of "Domestic Happiness": "'Domestic Happiness is the End of almost all our Pursuits, and the common Reward of all our Pains. When Men find themselves for ever barred from this delightful Fruition, they are lost to all Industry, and grow careless of all their worldly Affairs. Thus they become bad Subjects, bad Relations, bad Friends and bad Men'" (414–15). Domestic happiness is first and final cause in Dr. Harrison's civil society: first because it is the motor for all industry, and final because it is industry's aim. At the same time it supplements the proscriptive public conscience with the incentive of reward. In Harrison's view law intervenes only after "Men find themselves for ever barred from this delightful Fruition," for then they lack all positive incentive to be good subjects.

Although he calls "Domestic Happiness" the "End of almost all our Pursuits," Dr. Harrison also allows for the necessary deferral of this ultimate human satisfaction. Because Harrison is devoted to the civic humanism of the older order rather than to the possessive individualism of the newer, the motive for deferral is duty to one's country rather than to the increase of one's fortune. When Captain Booth fails to sell his military commission before his regiment is sent to Gibraltar, Harrison advises him to embark with the army even though Amelia is approaching her first

[39] Isaac Kramnick, *Bolingbroke and his Circle: The Politics of Nostalgia in the Age of Walpole* (Cambridge, MA: Harvard University Press, 1968), pp. 94–95.

[40] Battestin remarks that Fielding may have in mind his own partial success in subduing the mob in the Penlez riot (xxviii–xxix). See Fielding's *A True State of the Case of Bosavern Penlez, The Complete Works of Henry Fielding, Esq.*, 16 vols., ed. William Henley (New York: Croscup & Sterling, 1902), 12:277–80.

confinement: "'your Duty to your King and Country, whose Bread you have eaten, requires it; and this is a Duty of too high a Nature to admit the least Deficiency ... Remember, my Boy, your Honour is at stake; and you know how nice the Honour of a Soldier is in these Cases'" (100–1). In Harrison's view duty and honor are the elements that connect the individual – and through *him* the family – to society. Duty is positive and its own reward; honor (a social law) negative, for an injury to a soldier's honor redounds to the detriment of his family. True honor (as opposed to the gentleman's code of honor, which Dr. Harrison calls "in direct Opposition to the plain and positive Precepts of Religion" [503]) works in Harrison's system in the same way that credit does in the prison world: both are public opinions, and both affect one's social and economic status. Thus, whereas Amelia's vision of domestic happiness remains ignorant of public reason, Harrison's takes it into account as both an acknowledgment of society's power and a means of relieving the family's potentially alienating isolation.

The connection between family and society that seemed to be lacking in Amelia's simple domestic Eden is restored in Harrison's rather more complex vision of social relations and obligations. Patriarchal authority is not circumscribed by the needs or demands of domestic life; it plays an active role in the community by disciplining those who have failed to internalize the public conscience. The fully authoritative patriarch becomes a prosecutor, and as prosecutor also becomes the juridical subject, who bears and defends the public conscience. Dr. Harrison describes this dutifully prosecuting juridical subject to a young, disputatious country curate:

Indeed, as an Enemy merely, and from a Spirit of Revenge, he cannot, and he ought not to prosecute him; but as an Offender against the Laws of his Country, he may and it is his Duty so to do: ... Revenge, indeed, of all Kinds is strictly prohibited; wherefore, as we are not to execute it with our own Hands, so neither are we to make Use of the Law as the Instrument of private Malice, and to worry each other with Inveteracy and Rancour.                  (391)

In distinguishing civic responsibility from private motives, Harrison clears the way for the rehabilitation of a law that too often is an instrument of malice or resentment. (That he himself falls short of his own ideal by having Booth arrested for debt in a moment of anger indicates the difficulty in distinguishing the two motives.) Duty to one's country empowers the citizen to employ the law; the law in turn protects the individual's "Domestic Happiness," the family, and finally the society that makes it all possible. At the same time this categorical duty to prosecute is itself an ideological function of the juridical discourse, for failure to prosecute implies disregard for the law and the elevation of self-love over social, as was the case with both Clarissa and Mr. Lavement. When Booth finally acts as a civic-minded prosecutor, he will become the authoritative bearer of a domesticated public conscience.

Finally, *Amelia* softens patriarchal authority's tendency to absolutism. The novel carefully distinguishes Booth's authoritativeness from authoritarianism in order to preserve the semblance of mutuality within the domestic idyll.[41] When Booth refuses to give Amelia his reasons for wishing her to refuse Colonel James' invitation to the masquerade, he relies on paternalist sentiments for support: "This you may depend upon, *Amelia*, that your Good and Happiness are the great Objects of all my Wishes, and the End I propose in all my Actions. This View alone could tempt me to refuse you any thing, or to conceal any thing from you" (249). Amelia, however, "appeals" to her husband and asks him "whether this be not using [her] too much like a Child." The scene becomes an epitome of progressive domestic relations as wife and husband reason with one another. In this particular matter, Amelia convinces Booth to relent. On the following day he "approved her Advice, and readily gave his Consent" (254). In addition to being a reasonable (if not always wise) patriarch, Booth can be also a caring husband and nurturant father. He holds Amelia during childbirth and serves "as her Nurse" when she is ill with a cold in London (128, 179). These actions not only display his affection but also complement the intersubjectivity that is essential to Amelia's vision of familial self-sufficiency. The obvious contrasts here are to Colonel Bath, on the one hand, who, when he nurses his sister, must practice transvestism in order to accommodate his notions of masculine honor to his tender actions; and on the other hand to Miss Mathews, who describes a hedonistic and egoistic gallantry by saying that she "thought the best Husbands had looked on their Wives lying in as a Time of Festival and Jollity" (128). The patriarchal mantle that Booth assumes is cut from the cloth of social obligation and domestic affection.

Amelia and Harrison bring Booth to submission. Although Harrison is the instrumental agent of the arrest that marks the turning point in Booth's fortunes and disposition, Amelia is motive and model for Booth's reform. She pits family interests against the urge for "luxury" consumption. Knowing too well the state of their finances and depressed by the absence of her husband (who is at the gaming table), Amelia "check'd her Inclination [for a half-pint of wine] in order to save the little Sum of Sixpence; which she did the more resolutely as she had before refused to gratify her Children with Tarts for their Supper from the same Motive" (433). The selfless supporter of the private sphere, Amelia aligns her desires with the canons of natural affection. When the narrator tells us

[41] A. R. Towers calls Booth and Amelia "a picture of idealized conjugal behavior." "*Amelia* and the State of Matrimony," *Review of English Studies* n.s. 5 (1954):156.

later that Amelia needs little time to prepare to return to the country, "for when she packed up herself in the Coach, she packed up her all" (505), he refers to more than the simple fact that she has pawned all the family possessions: Amelia is free from the encumbrances of an ever-fickle and enslaving public fashion. Having internalized patriarchal law and bourgeois frugality, she is the promise of the "delightful Fruition" awaiting Booth's ultimate reform. This, too, is a crucial part of Fielding's proto-bourgeois romance, for the woman finds her all in family and husband. Given an incurable social corruption, Fielding has no choice but to provide the same aim for the male.

## IV Booth's passions and the stable identity

As long as Booth is a prey to seductresses, card-sharps, pimps, and the king's officers, his family loses more and more of its substance and he moves farther away from Harrison's "delightful Fruition." His actions contribute to the edematous growth of the public sphere at the expense of an increasingly emaciated family. When he is arrested for a debt he owes Dr. Harrison, the half-pay officer is at last forced to confront the personal and familial consequences of his fruitless public actions. He

envied every Labourer whom he saw pass by him in his Way. The Charms of Liberty against his Will rushed on his Mind; and he could not avoid suggesting to himself, how much more happy was the poorest Wretch who without Controul could repair to his homely Habitation and his Family; compared to him, who was thus violently, and yet lawfully torn away from the Company of his Wife and Children. (310)

Booth's juridically instigated epiphany is a consequence of his material situation rather than of independent reflection. A lawful violence has brought him to a new state of awareness. Until this moment, Booth has attributed his indebtedness to the belief that "every Man acted entirely from that Passion which was uppermost" (109). Wavering between the gratifications of the city and the rewards of family, he has been unable to resist Miss Mathews, the gaming table, and the lies of influence peddlers. Deprived of the "Charms of Liberty," he now recognizes that work alone keeps the "poorest Wretch" happy and free. Law threatens to impose upon him a fixed identity not of his own choosing. Whether that identity be debtor or prisoner is all one, and it is a dreary one when compared to the delightful "Company of his Wife and Children." As the prisoner Booth travels through the streets of London, he experiences first-hand the "Controul" that society imposes upon those who refuse to control themselves by internalizing the diurnal rhythms of industry and homecoming.

In Booth's remorseful reflections upon his lost freedom, realism is succeeded by a pastoral idyll in order to convey the text's reasons for promoting self-restraint over the enticements of the public sphere. Realism fixes the hero's errant ways by describing an ineluctable logic of events, a logic that structures a syntagmatic social relation between passions and confinement. The fiction's realistic elements show that Booth's passions produce an unwilled loss of liberty because they are exploited by friend and foe alike, by a Dr. Harrison and a Colonel James. Romance elements, on the other hand, reunite the son with his estranged "father," the family with its alienated patrimony, and the lover with his beloved object. In short, romance produces the freedom that rewards the character who has submitted himself to realism's discipline. This is a powerful ideological hybrid, a formal complement to the thematic connection of passion and freedom as well as the negation of money as personal essence. Booth's pastoral epiphany creates a world that at once predates and supersedes a money economy. Simple labor becomes the means to happiness and comfort, nothing more nor less. The private world's order, when combined with the threat of the loss of affection, is more than a match for the streets, assemblies, pleasure gardens, and masquerades of London. The happy laborer stands as the antithesis of social conditions as Fielding himself described them in his address to the Westminster Grand Jury: "so immoderate are the Desires of many, so hungry is their Appetite for Pleasure, that they may be said to have a Fury after it ..."[42] Fury is banished from Booth's domestic Arcadia.

In mixing romance and realism the text declares that it is not yet ready to abandon the values that inhere in the older generic forms. Labor may bring freedom, but the genteel hero cannot undergo a loss in status without turning romance into anti-romance and seriously qualifying the ideological satisfactions that romance provides the reader.[43] On the other hand, because of the way in which money has been shown to corrupt all exchanges in the public sphere, Booth cannot become a practicing bourgeois like Crusoe or Flanders, inhabitants of a world where the "duty of the individual toward the increase of his capital ... is assumed as an end in itself," as Weber remarks in his famous study of the work ethic.[44] Indeed, Booth's one unqualified virtue is his merit as an officer in the King's army, a merit that savors more of aristocratic than it does of bourgeois values. In order for the text to rescue its hero from labor or

---

[42] Fielding, *Charge Delivered to the Grand Jury*, p. 52.

[43] Fredric Jameson's view of the relation between realism and romance is also suggestive: "It is in the context of the gradual reification of realism in late capitalism that romance once again comes to be felt as the place of narrative heterogeneity and of freedom from that reality principle to which a now oppressive realistic representation is hostage" (*The Political Unconscious* 104).

[44] Weber, *Protestant Ethic*, p. 51.

trade, the narrative provides a series of juridical events to motivate the restoration of a modified patriarchal family.

The preconditions of Booth's transformation are established over the course of his first two imprisonments and brought to an end by a crucial event that signals Booth's readiness to reform: his pursuit of the family's larcenous maidservant. Other commentators have judged the compatibility of Booth's juridical aggressiveness with his character without noticing that it enables Booth to become a juridical agent who uses the law to protect his family.[45] When the Captain learns of the theft, he "expressed himself with some Passion on the Occasion, and swore he would make an Example of the Girl" (478). Passion is the key word. On the one hand, Booth seems about to violate Harrison's strictures against passion as a motive for prosecuting a crime. On the other hand, the passions that led to his incarceration at the narrative's opening are now about to be harnessed to the law and to produce the chain of events that produces his final enlargement. In addition, domestic happiness is called upon to validate the patriarch's actions. As Booth tells Amelia, the maidservant is "not only guilty of dishonesty, but of Cruelty: for she must know our Situation, and the very little we had left. She is besides guilty of Ingratitude to you, who have treated her with so much Kindness, that you have rather acted the Part of a Mother than of a Mistress" (479). Even though Betty's theft of Amelia's linens and Booth's response to the theft highlight the cash nexus that links her to the family, Booth represses that relation by casting Amelia as mother rather than mistress to Betty. In the absence of an effectual – read male – head of the family, Betty is able to pilfer some of its substance. Booth's pursuit of Betty and his intention to prosecute her is the most independent, determined, and aggressive action that he takes in the novel. He has overcome what George Sherburn has called his "psychological flaccidity."[46] His intentions are enough to mark the emergence of the reinvigorated patriarch, now aligned with the law. Finally, the narrative saves Booth from being effectively cruel even as it criticizes the law when Booth discovers that he cannot prosecute Betty for felony because the stolen goods are valued at less than forty shillings. Both Booth and the magistrate before whom he brings the maidservant find this an unwise law, but both obey it. At last, Booth brings his passions into accord with the law.

---

[45] Bloch finds it in line with Fielding's other statements on the duty to prosecute criminals ("Prosecution" 269–71). Nathan finds it incompatible with Booth's character ("Anticipation" 383). Michael Irwin, *Henry Fielding: The Tentative Realist* (Oxford: Clarendon Press, 1967), finds it an instance where Fielding's didactic intention interfered with his artistic practice (122).

[46] George Sherburn, "Fielding's Social Outlook," *Philological Quarterly*, 35 (1956); rpt. in *Eighteenth-Century English Literature*, ed. James L. Clifford (New York: Oxford University Press, 1959), p. 263.

That this episode is a pivotal point of the narrative is demonstrated by the events that follow. The magistrate, thief, and pawnbroker are no sooner dismissed than another denizen of the London underworld and the narrative's arch-criminal appears: the adulterous Miss Mathews. Booth agrees to meet her later. Seemingly steeled by his prosecutorial adventure, however, he subsequently comes to a "Determination" to end his liaison with her. Once again the consequences of this decision are quite other than Booth had envisioned, for on his way to the appointment he is arrested for a gambling debt at the suit of Colonel James. This will be his last arrest. While in the sponging house, he confesses his infidelity to Amelia and renounces his passional instability. In short order Booth has his freedom restored, and the law begins to work for rather than against him.

Although the hand of justice has dealt with Booth in an indirect way, it has brought him to acknowledge the cost of his "Immoralities" and accept the burden of responsibility for his actions. With his zealous pursuit of the family thief, Booth shows that he partakes of the "best Constitution" and that he is willing to work in the behalf of the civilized values of gratitude and subordination. His history, "corrected by the Hand of Justice," has a fortunate outcome.[47] And yet, his failure to punish the maidservant might be an indication that, for all his new-found vigor and purpose, the old world of patriarchal authority and the new world of the "chrematistic arts" lie too far apart for the good man to unite even when he uses the best instruments of both worlds.

## V Worlds apart

The denouement's rapidly unfolding events, in which good fortune is dispensed to the reformed man, have led many commentators to complain of *Amelia's* failure to arrive at a convincing solution to "some of the most glaring Evils, as well public as private, which ... infest the Country" (3).[48] Indeed, the narrative provides ample evidence that it has represented an

---

[47] All quotations are from Fielding, *Charge Delivered to the Grand Jury*, p. 63.

[48] Robert Alter finds it inconsistent with the rest of the novel (*Fielding and the Nature of the Novel* 165–66). Irwin says it "beg[s] most of the moral questions" and is a "conventional escape" (*Fielding: The Tentative Realist* 132). Eric Rothstein argues that [t]he providential ending, which compliments the prudential, is implausible and meant to be so" because the world is fallen and no social or prudential solution can be entirely satisfactory (*Systems of Order and Inquiry in Later Eighteenth-Century Fiction* [Berkeley: University of California Press, 1975], pp. 203–4). Sherburn finds a conventional comedic solution in the ending ("Fielding's *Amelia*: An Interpretation" 152–53). Wolff asks for "some vigorous, public assertion of [Booth's] goodness which would be commensurate with the public evil of his earlier life" in order to make the ending conform to an awakened expectation of verisimilitude in the reader ("Fielding's *Amelia*" 53). Braudy dissents from the majority: "... like Hume, Fielding has a great hope for the ability of law to translate private virtue into public good" (*Narrative Form* 210).

intractable problem in the conflict between "delightful Fruition" in the private sphere and self-interested competition in the public. A romance-enabled wish-fulfillment is called upon to dispel this problem. Fielding signals an awareness of this generic sleight-of-hand by having Booth prepare Amelia for the news of the recovery of her fortune by telling her of a dream he has had:

"I dreamt," said he, "this Night that we were in the most miserable Situation imaginable. Indeed in the Situation we were Yesterday Morning, or rather worse, that I was laid in a Prison for Debt, and that you wanted a Morsel of Bread to feed the Mouths of your hungry Children. At length (for nothing you know is quicker than the Transition in Dreams) Dr. *Harrison* methought came to me, with Chearfulness and Joy in his Countenance. The Prison Doors immediately flew open; and Dr. *Harrison* introduced you, gayly tho' not richly dressed. That you gently chid me for staying so long; all on a sudden appear'd a Coach with four Horses to it, in which was a Maid Servant with our two Children. We both immediately went into the Coach, and taking our Leave of the Doctor, set out towards your Country House: for yours I dreamt it was." (527)

In effect, Booth redescribes the scene when Amelia first appears in the prison and faints upon seeing him. This time, however, Dr. Harrison appears first, and with his appearance the prison doors open, marking the ultimate enlargement of the private world. Amelia arrives clothed in the joyous apparel of a gay private life rather than in the rich apparel of a luxurious public one. The coach and four is a compromise that signals a return to a comfortable social status, approved by the presence of Dr. Harrison. As social status returns, so does paternal potency to Booth: for in the first part of the dream the hungry children are Amelia's, whereas after Booth is freed they belong to both. That it is *Booth's* "dream," in which Dr. Harrison plays an important but not focal role, further emphasizes the restoration of his authority. With the help of his wife – it is her "Country House" – and with his religious and juridical conversions, Booth trades the nightmare of London unrest for the dream of country peace.

That Fielding subjects his plot to Booth's dreamwork in order to assuage any readerly discomfort over the rapid events leading to closure indicates a disjunction between the juridical discourse of the public sphere and the ethico-religious discourse of the private. Not only does each sphere have different constitutions, but each also has different subjects and ways of judging those subjects. What religion condemns, the law cannot see. To those persons whom the law singles out for punishment, religion accords mercy. Religion is the discourse of the heart; law the discourse of the "chrematistic art." This divergence of the public and private conscience has important implications for the novel's fictional subject. Although the interventions of the ubiquitous juridical discourse are limited to specific events – debt, assault, perjury, forgery, profit – the consequences of these interventions extend beyond the events that call them into being. But the law that imbues the thoughts and actions of every character with the exception of Amelia cannot endow character with a coherent way of being in the world. It can only erect certain prohibitions and establish penalties for the transgression of those prohibitions. Writing on David Hume, Leo Braudy comments that "the gradual growth of law absorbs private whim and furnishes a medium for private virtue."[49] In Braudy's reading of Hume, law is the enabling condition for making private virtue into a public force. In Fielding, however, law and virtue (encoded as religion) remain divergent. In the secular world of *Amelia*, characters are identified most frequently by a single subjective facet, which is either of value in the economic sphere or of concern to the juridical. In the patriarchal-domestic world of *Amelia*, they are known by the fitness with which they fill their designated place. Not even Dr. Harrison can bring the two worlds together.

In an ideal world, the workings of the law – ordering society and providing an occasion for Booth's conversion – would make a return to the private world unnecessary. But *Amelia* represents a public sphere that is far from ideal. As Malvin Zirker has noted, the good characters' "retirement in one sense is the abnegation of the modern commercial world. The mind can seek out its own values in the country, it may renounce the thinness of the law, the brutality of the city poor, and, indeed, nearly the whole of the conflicts between the classes, and it may ignore the sterility of economic dogma."[50] But the mind that returns to the country is one that has been impressed with the experience of the city and influenced by the juridical discourse, which offers a means of managing those experiences and opportunities so as not to be overcome in the country, as Booth and his family were once before. The mind is no longer fully its own place, then, but rather a hybrid of country republican innocence and urban com- mercial corruption. The retreat to the country allows the former influence to prevail, now strengthened by the juridical self-mastery won from the public sphere. To leave Booth in the city would introduce the possibility of moral recidivism, a return to his earlier passional instability. Such an ending would also undo the oneiric magic that restores respect for virtue, religion and law as well as the Booth family to its proper estate.

And yet, as if the text were reluctant to falsify its matter completely, it continues the dreamwork abandoned by Booth and produces the recidivist that the city and the narrative demand. Robinson, the professional cheater who has been both our and Booth's guide through the prison- house world, also makes a climactic confession and undergoes a con-

[49] Braudy, *Narrative Form*, p. 73.
[50] Malvin Zirker, *Fielding's Social Pamphlets* (Berkeley: University of California Press, 1966), p. 139.

version. Robinson is Booth's double, subject to his weaknesses, concerned with his intimate domestic affairs, and inmate of the same prison and the same sponging house at the same time as Booth. Arrested at last as a result of his own greed in extorting money from a malicious accomplice and apparently mortally ill, Robinson reveals the fraud that allows Amelia to recover her inheritance from her sister. But Robinson does not die. His death-bed repentance restores him to health, and with health comes the momentary hope that he will have the same opportunity as Booth to begin life anew with a stable identity. His restoration, however, is short-lived. Robinson is a solitary figure. He must support himself alone in a public world that places no value upon the stable identity. Only in the family can such a work of art be appreciated; thus, only within the family does self-restraint pay. But Robinson has neither family nor function, and he ends in a bad way:

The Witness for some time seemed to reform his Life, and received a small Pension from *Booth*; after which he returned to vicious Courses, took a Purse on the Highway, was detected and taken, and followed the last Steps of his old Master. So apt are Men, whose Manners have been once thoroughly corrupted, to return, from any Dawn of an Amendment, into the dark Paths of Vice. (532)

It is unclear whether Robinson's small pension adequately supplied his needs; but it is quite clear that it could not satisfy his desires. There is a sound of inevitability in the syntactic cadences with which Fielding disposes of this lonely character. As the law performs its proper function, it not only relieves society of another predator, but it also relieves Booth of a dependent of questionable worth. Booth's fate is sweeter, for he never suffered from Robinson's thorough corruption. Booth's dawn moves into the noonday of propertied patriarchy. This somber reflection on human nature, however, casts the whole project of juridically inspired personal reform in doubt. Booth and Robinson remain worlds apart, and at the conclusion of *Amelia* – as indeed throughout the narrative – we learn that a sturdy tree may rise from the grove of the law, but that tree is not the tree of life unless it be watered by private affections.

# 7

# The embattled middle: longing for authority in *The Vicar of Wakefield*

Filial obedience is the first and greatest requisite of a state; by this we become good subjects to our emperors, capable of behaving with just subordination to our superiors ... the whole state may be said to resemble one family, of which the Emperor is the protector, father, and friend.

Oliver Goldsmith, *The Citizen of the World*, Letter 42, *Works*, 2:177

## I Political stability, narrative division, and critical certainty

*Clarissa, Roderick Random*, and *Amelia* were published between 1747 and 1752, a time of relative political stability in England.[1] The years in which Oliver Goldsmith wrote *The Vicar of Wakefield*, on the other hand, were years of political unrest and ministerial instability. In 1760 George III had acceded to the throne with intentions of "cleansing the Augean stables" of national government and punishing those ministers who had usurped his grandfather's authority.[2] The new monarch never fully realized his intentions, however, in part because the 1760s saw the simultaneous growth of political parties and popular activism that contested the King's influence in national affairs. Discontent over the King's choice of the Earl of Bute to head the government and his ministry's unsuccessful prosecution of Wilkes for the *North Briton* 45 illustrate the limits to the sovereign's power.[3] These political tensions of the 60s – a crisis of authority – inform Goldsmith's fiction, including its personal solution to the problem of instability. In effect, *The Vicar* deploys a juridical subjectivity in its protagonist, but

---

[1] John B. Owen, *The Rise of the Pelhams* (London: Methuen, 1957), pp. 298–320. See also John Brewer, *Party Ideology and Popular Politics at the Accession of George III* (Cambridge: Cambridge University Press, 1976), pp. 8–9.

[2] The phrase appears, probably ironically, in *The Monitor*, 295, 14 March 1761, p. 1781. See also, John B. Owen, *The Eighteenth Century: 1714–1815* (New York: Norton, 1974), p. 169: "A naive young man of twenty-three was about to clean out the Augean stables."

[3] On Wilkes and the *North Briton* prosecution, see George Rudé, *Wilkes and Liberty: A Social Study of 1763 to 1774* (Oxford: Clarendon Press, 1962), pp. 20–36. Brewer's study is about both the changing nature of politics and the role played by the press in that change. See p. 14 for a summary of the different concepts of "party" and Chapter 5 for the emergence of the ideology of "measures not men."

props it upon the personal presence of Sir William Thornhill, who acts as the fiction's supreme magistrate.

In a recent incisive article on *The Vicar of Wakefield*, John Bender argues that Goldsmith's text "yields a fractured, paradoxical mode of narration" because of the contradictory implications of the yearning for a personal (and intrusive) form of government on the one hand and a reformist urge to reshape subjectivity through less visible and thus more effective means. For Bender, Goldsmith's text responds to the "tactical government" of the day by seeking to provide ideological solutions to political incoherence and social instability.[4] Although Bender characterizes with great precision the text's relation to events, he overlooks the important function played by the family in the text's comprehensive solution to tactical problems that are social and personal as well as political. For it is the family that the text marks as source of and solution to the destabilizing desires in the unruly subject. The individual cries out for guidance and reform not as mere individual but as family member. As in *Amelia*, the law has full reformative power only when it acts through its familial plenipotentiary.

Goldsmith's *The Vicar of Wakefield* dramatizes political unrest in familial terms. Even though the *paterfamilias* Primrose has settled notions about proper domestic management, he cannot enact those notions in his own family without transgressing the text's sentimental presuppositions and destroying the harmonious domestic idyll that the narrative struggles to maintain. In order to deal with the disjunction between theory and practice (which also plays a comic role in the Vicar's character), the text splits Primrose's patriarchal function by having him enact his governing powers in the public sphere of the prison while maintaining his benignly affective character within the private sphere of the family. When juridical authority is introduced to the family by the inevitable consequences of the family's behavior, it is mediated by an erstwhile outsider, Sir William Thornhill, whose various disguises allow him to be both within and without the affective unit. In this novel with its contrived ending Goldsmith enjoys not only the aesthetic triumph that Marshall Brown finds, but also an ideological solution in which the politics of personal power become allied with juridical punishments to create a family idyll in which desire can be contained both coercively and affectively.[5] Sir William Thornhill's personal powers, which bring stability and closure to the narrative, may be fabulous; but it is expressly this fable which gives the law its human countenance and makes it an effective instrument of political order.

Many commentators on Goldsmith's novel have sought to impose a

---

[4] John Bender, "Prison Reform and the Sentence of Narration in *The Vicar of Wakefield*," in Nussbaum and Brown, *The New Eighteenth Century*, pp. 178, 169.

[5] Marshall Brown, *Preromanticism* (Stanford: Stanford University Press, 1991), pp. 174–75.

monological reading on this dialogical text. They have aimed to fix the Vicar in one of two positions: either as an unreliable narrator and an object of authorial satire or as a paradigm of Christian virtue. This critical project, even as it reproduces the desire for stability that incites the narrative, is in direct conflict with what Mikhail Bakhtin has identified as the novel's essence: "the new zone opened by the novel for structuring literary images, namely the zone of maximal contact with the present (with contemporary reality) in all its openendedness."[6] Such openendedness results inevitably in a hybrid literary and ideological text. The dream of a pure artistic product can no more withstand the pressures of experience than can the pastoral idyll survive the material forces of commercial society. Primrose is a hybrid of affective and political demands, a product of a split between private experience and public function in much the way as the other protagonists in this study. In him can be read the growing fault lines that distance civil society from the family, a distance that opens up an area in which various and often contradictory responses to demands from different spheres contend for dominance.

Those who read *The Vicar* as satire seek critical certainty by foregrounding the Vicar's intellectual inadequacy or moral flaccidity as an indicator of the text's moral or epistemological center.[7] These critics discover a gap between the Vicar's professed views and his actual practices. Richard Jaarsma, for example, claims that Primrose is the vehicle for "one of the most savage indictments of *bourgeois* values in eighteenth-century literature."[8] By seeing Primrose's sentimental rhetoric as tainted by economic motives or by identifying the sentimental itself as pathological, the revisionist critics implicitly fault the Vicar for lacking the self-knowledge that will enable him to resist the allure of vulgar materialism or social distinction. Excessive desire for social goods or the blindness attributed to the sentimentalist ego is subjected to the discipline of satire and recontained as a pathology of character. By identifying the Vicar's desire for worldly eminence as the *radix malorum*, the critics hold out for the result that the text itself continually calls into question: the possibility of a worldly still-point, from which authority can unerringly point to the correct choice of action in all cases.

For those who employ a traditional Christian heuristic of fall and

---

[6] Bakhtin, *Dialogic Imagination*, p. 11.

[7] See, for example, W. O. S. Sutherland, *The Art of the Satirist: Essays on the Satire of Augustan England* (Austin: University of Texas Press, 1965), pp. 84–91; Ronald Paulson, *Satire and the Novel in Eighteenth-Century England* (New Haven: Yale University Press, 1967), pp. 269–75; Richard J. Jaarsma, "Satiric Intent in *The Vicar of Wakefield*," *Studies in Short Fiction* 5 (1968):331–41; Robert H. Hopkins, *The True Genius of Oliver Goldsmith* (Baltimore: The Johns Hopkins Press, 1969), pp. 166–230; John Dussinger, *The Discourse of the Mind in Eighteenth-Century Fiction*, Studies in English Literature, vol. 80 (The Hague and Paris: Mouton, 1974), pp. 148–72.

[8] Jaarsma, "Satiric Intent," p. 338.

redemption to read the novel, the Vicar is "enlarged" into a kind of transcendental signifier, a sign of Providence's hand in human affairs.[9] Like their counterpart, this group also foregrounds the Hobbesian values of a materialistic world, but it identifies them as causal links to redemption. And yet in the moment of devaluing self-interested action in the world, this camp achieves the opposite; for without that world the Vicar could never become the *magnus animus*. Walter Benjamin describes this paradox in a brief aside on the *Bildungsroman*: "By integrating the social process with the development of a person, it bestows the most frangible justification on the order determining it."[10] By casting the ways of the world as necessary to redemption, these critics perpetuate a self-misunderstanding of the text: exploitative social relations lead to ethical or spiritual maturity. These relations become the stable center of the text, the means by which the text transcends the materials of its own representations.

Thus, the two critical camps converge in finding a similar tendency in the novel – worldly concerns are degraded; spiritual are elevated – even though they arrive at the conclusion through opposite interpretations of Dr. Primrose. As a partial corrective to this view, Eric Rothstein and Howard Weinbrot have argued that law provides a unifying motif that resolves the crises besetting the Primrose family.[11] Rothstein and Weinbrot, however, like Bender, fail to take account of the various forces and discourses that frustrate any ultimate ideological unity. The Vicar and his family are caught in the skeins of multiple determinations: religious, political, economic, juridical, and sentimental. These discourses surface, disappear, and resurface at various points in the text. At times they serve as vehicles for the characters' desires, at other times as consolation for their misfortunes, and at still other times as rewards for their behavior. The rapidity with which religious piety succeeds economic value only to interact with juridical power makes Wakefield a confusing and a modern world, in which fierce competition for wealth, prominence, or pleasure is played out sometimes within a quasi-pastoral setting. When Goldsmith restores the family to a fully pastoral condition, he attempts to stabilize his narrative by embodying in Sir William Thornhill a transcendent natural law, located outside the family and yet efficacious within it. The failure of this strategy to resolve all the ambiguities and collapse the polarities of the

---

9   See, for example, Battestin, *Providence of Wit*; Oliver W. Ferguson, "Dr. Primrose and Goldsmith's Clerical Ideal," *Philological Quarterly* 54 (1975):323–32; Mary Elizabeth Green, "Oliver Goldsmith and the Wisdom of the World," *Studies in Philology* 77 (1980):202–12; Raymond F. Hilliard, "The Redemption of Fatherhood in *The Vicar of Wakefield*," *Studies in English Literature* 23 (1983):465–80; Thomas R. Preston, "The Uses of Adversity: Worldly Detachment and Heavenly Treasure in *The Vicar of Wakefield*," *Studies in Philology* 81 (1984):229–51.

10   Walter Benjamin, "The Storyteller: Reflections on the Works of Nikolai Leskov," in *Illuminations*, trans. Harry Zohn, ed. Hannah Arendt (New York: Schocken Books, 1969), p. 88.

11   Eric Rothstein and Howard D. Weinbrot, "*The Vicar of Wakefield*, Mr. Wilmot, and the 'Whistonean Controversy,'" *Philological Quarterly* 55 (1976):231.

work into a seamless unity reveals at once the limits of authority and the libidinal forces that remain resistant to the public conscience.

Goldsmith himself, like his hero Primrose, might be taken as an example of one in whom the theory of restraint and the practice of consumption were at odds. His biographer claims that the author "had a growing awareness of his influence as a social critic," and Goldsmith's journalism provides evidence that he believed that the writer must act as an adjutant to the law even though he had no illusions about his society's willingness to reward such labor.[12] In the persona of Lien Chi Altangi, Goldsmith describes the writer's responsibilities in a country where "the luxurious man stands in need of a thousand different artists to furnish out his happiness":[13] "as every country grows more polite, ... writers become more necessary, as readers are supposed to increase ... That man, though in rags, who is capable of deceiving even indolence into wisdom, and who professes amusement while he aims at reformation, is more useful in refined society than twenty cardinals with all their scarlet ..."[14] The "refined society" that results from commercial expansion brings with it a host of political problems, as Goldsmith writes elsewhere: "Foreign commerce ... tends rather to the accumulation of immense wealth in the hands of some, than to a diffusion of it among all; it is calculated rather to make individuals rich, than to make the aggregate happy."[15] Thus, the writer's task is set: to furnish out the happiness of the luxurious man, to stand as auxiliary to the law, and to find a fiction that will balance the disintegrative with the integrative aspects of luxury. The way to political stability runs through the personal experience that will create "a just equipoise of the passions," a harmony of self-love and social, of *otium* and *negotium*.[16]

Goldsmith fulfills this function in his fictions through the persona of a benevolent patriarch who cleanses the social stables of vice, indolence, and imprudence. Sir William Honeywood of *The Good Natur'd Man* and Sir William Thornhill of *The Vicar* – landed virtue shining from their surnames – guide, protect, and reform those under their influence. Sir William Honeywood's scheme for reforming his imprudent nephew resembles the pattern that I have educed in both *Roderick Random* and *Amelia*: "Now, my intention is to involve him in fictitious distress, before he has plunged himself into real calamity. To arrest him for that very debt, to clap an officer upon him, and then let him see which of his friends will

[12] Ralph M. Wardle, *Oliver Goldsmith* (1957; rpt., Hamden: Archon Books, 1969), p. 122.
[13] Oliver Goldsmith, *The Citizen of the World*, in *The Collected Works of Oliver Goldsmith*, 5 vols., ed. Arthur Friedman (Oxford: Clarendon Press, 1966), Letter 11, 2:52.
[14] Goldsmith, *The Citizen of the World*, Letter 57, 2:238.
[15] Goldsmith, *The Revolution in Low Life*, 3:197.
[16] Goldsmith, *The Citizen of the World*, Letter 47, 2:201.

come to his relief."[17] This pattern is present in *The Vicar* as well, embodied in the neoclassical virtues of self-reliance, restraint, subordination of passions, and recognition of interests. Like Sir William Honeywood, Goldsmith involves his readers in the fictitious distress of the Primroses in order to demonstrate the dangerous consequences of indulging desire in a competitive world.

In his own life, however, Goldsmith never fully mastered the difficult art of acting prudently, as his friend Samuel Johnson reports upon hearing of Goldsmith's death: "Chambers you find, is gone far, and poor Goldsmith is gone much further. He died of a fever exasperated, as I believe, by the fear of distress. He had raised money and squandered it, by every artifice of acquisition and folly of expence. But let not his frailties be remembered; he was a very great man."[18] Johnson's description of his dead friend hints at the latter's need for the timely arrival of a Honeywood to save him from the "folly of expence." Boswell reports another of Johnson's postmortem pronouncements that is of interest: "Goldsmith had no settled notions upon any subject; so he talked always at random. It seemed to be his intention to blurt out whatever was in his mind, and see what would become of it."[19] In the absence of an authority who could settle his notions once and for all, Goldsmith becomes the victim of intellectual impulse. *The Vicar of Wakefield* registers the wish for an authority to restrain such impulse and for a domestic sphere in which that restraint can signify. In addition to these authoritarian and bourgeois dreams, *The Vicar* also looks to a cooperative society, in which order comes from a kind of utopian social functionalism that answers the need for labor and provides the means of leisure too. But this utopian moment is brief and "bracketed," as it were, contained by the coercive walls of the prison. Problems of power return unsolved at the conclusion. Goldsmith could settle neither all his debts nor all his notions, but then the settlement of such difficulties still eludes most determined juridical auxiliaries.

## II Infinite desire demands fabulous patriarchy

In order to settle notions and order affairs, the eighteenth-century novels that I have discussed chastise their protagonists' desire and ultimately bring instrumental reason into harmony with a socially transcendent affection. *Roderick Random* and *Amelia* reform the husband because, in the words of John Brenkman, "a social relation in which the practices of

[17] Goldsmith, *The Good Natur'd Man*, Act I, 5:20.
[18] "To Bennet Langton," 5 July 1774, Letter 358, *The Letters of Samuel Johnson. With Mrs. Thrale's Genuine Letters to Him*, 3 vols., ed. R. W. Chapman (Oxford: Clarendon Press, 1952), 1:410.
[19] James Boswell, *The Life of Johnson*, 6 vols., ed. George B. Hill; rev. by L. F. Powell (Oxford: Clarendon Press, 1934), 3:252.

exchange make *any* other object or situation or person susceptible to an (economic) designation that at once makes its value *the same for all individuals* and turns it into *something to be possessed*" demands a husband who can protect his charges from the hunger for possession that threatens essence and authenticity.[20] In *The Vicar of Wakefield*, however, the dangers of unrestrained appetites come from within as well as from without the family. Unlike Narcissa or Amelia, the women of the Vicar's family have desires of their own, which demand regulation by a husband, in part because they are represented as too weak or too innocent to regulate themselves. Were the Vicar really the lawgiver he claims to be (33), all the calamities except the departure from Wakefield itself might have been averted. But as Oliver Ferguson has noted, "the Primrose household is more a democracy than a republic."[21] The Vicar fails to lay down the law because such rigor is incompatible with the affective ties that define the family. The law can be brought to bear on the Vicar's or his son's extravagance, thereby effecting their reform; but the women, lacking the interiority that comes from an active engagement in the public sphere, remain impervious to its corrective powers. Thus, *The Vicar of Wakefield* presents a different kind of problem for the juridical subject by representing resistance to the very principles of juridical subjectivity within the family.

This different problematic – the containment of desire within the affective unit – is represented allegorically in the scene in which the Primrose women convince the Vicar to commission an itinerant painter to execute a family portrait. After Primrose's wife and daughters discover that a neighboring family, with whom they "had long a sort of rivalry in point of taste," has had its portrait painted, they argue for the same distinction with the following results: "notwithstanding all I could say, and I said much, it was resolved that we should have our pictures done too."[22] His use of the passive voice is a virtual abdication of responsibility for the outcome of this project. The results are telling. The family is "perfectly satisfied," except for one small point. The portrait

was so very large that we had no place in the house to fix it. How we all came to disregard so material a point is inconceivable; ... The picture, therefore, instead of gratifying our vanity, as we hoped, leaned, in a most mortifying manner, against the kitchen wall, where the canvas was stretched and painted, much too large to be got through any of the doors ...                        (83)

Although their vanities fit within the picture frame, the frame itself has no place within the house. The portrait sits useless in the kitchen, where, one

[20] Brenkman, *Culture and Domination*, p. 115.     [21] Oliver Ferguson, "Dr. Primrose," p. 326.
[22] Oliver Goldsmith, *The Vicar of Wakefield*, 4:82. All further citations to the novel are from this edition (unless otherwise noted) and appear in the text. The volume number has been omitted.

might assume, its pretensions will soon be obscured by the smoke of more material activities. In addition to being an obvious commentary on vanity, the scene literalizes the difficulty of containing desire. Embedded in the portrait as described is a crisis of representation; for although desire can find a place within the crude and incoherent allegorical scene, it does not "fit" within a domestic economy. It is an excess that produces "mortification" in the household.

In order to protect the family from such excess, the public conscience must be inscribed upon its members without, however, destroying the family's essential affective nature. This proviso attached to the introjection of the public conscience complicates an already difficult problem. Could the juridical discourse enable Primrose to assume the authority that Random and Booth assume at the *end* of their narratives, then the law would in fact succeed in bestowing a stability on the possessive and envious world represented in the novel. As it oscillates between the juridical and the sentimental discourses, the narrative is unable to solve the problem. Both discourses are present: both pull in opposite directions, as romance and realism fall into conflict. This oscillation and its ensuing conflicts are expressed in the Vicar's actions at different times. When officers come to arrest him for debt, he rebukes his parishioners for their intention to rescue him. By deferring to the officers' authority, he appears to be a model juridical subject. The same is true when he lays down the law to his fellow inmates in prison.

The Vicar's model juridical subjectivity is only apparent, however, for it lacks an essential component: a respect for "temporalities," or those very interests that fall under the law's cognizance:

The temporal concerns of our family were chiefly committed to my wife's management, as to the spiritual I took them entirely under my own direction. The profits of my living, which amounted to but thirty-five pounds a year, I made over to the orphans and widows of the clergy of our diocese; for having a sufficient fortune of my own, I was careless of temporalities, and felt a secret pleasure in doing my duty without reward. (21–22)[23]

Although this self-satisfied neglect of temporal concerns frees the Vicar from the endemic hunger after material possessions, it is also the source of his weakness as *paterfamilias*. Primrose's opinion that "the honest man who married and brought up a large family, did more service than he who continued single, and only talked of population" suggests that he holds principles that would make him a responsible provider of familial subsistence (18). In actuality, however, the family's needs involve him in conflict with its members, a conflict that threatens the all-important

---

[23] Eric Rothstein and Howard Weinbrot discuss the legal meaning of the term *made over*. They see it as a cause of the Vicar's removal from Wakefield ("The Vicar of Wakefield" 226–27).

familial harmony. And so he relegates material matters to his wife, both in order to avoid such conflict as well as to be able to pursue his immaterial means of distinction, for he too is not without desire for social eminence.

It is not quite correct to say that the Vicar has a hunger for *immaterial* rewards, for recognition brings with it a pleasure that is in part physical. Rather, the Vicar has an aversion to financial transactions because they bring him into conflict with his family. When he is not dealing with temporalities that fall into conflict with his pastoral ideal of domestic life or with his secret pleasures, the Vicar fulfills the duties of the husbandman admirably, as when he and his son Moses "pursue [their] usual industry abroad" (33). His disparagement of temporalities turns out to be a disparagement of cash relations, which make everything "susceptible to an (economic) designation," and thus purchasable given the means. Such potential availability of all pleasures disrupts settled social relations and fuels the women's desire. (In this case, the text projects these destabilizing desires onto a culturally convenient, pre-constructed object.) The Vicar's nostalgia for a simpler world drives the affective and juridical discourses into mutually exclusive spheres. In the pastoral world where there is little call for law, affective relations are impervious to economic factors. But because the text is committed in part to a representation of a complex social organization with its multiple discourses of law, economy, and political authority, the pastoral simplification serves to highlight the disjunction between public competition and family harmony. The Vicar is the site of this disjunction. He cannot take "sides," for he is of the family that defines itself in part through its economic fantasies.

Responding to the ineffectiveness of the Vicar's patriarchal authority, some commentators have proposed the hybrid character Burchell/ Thornhill as a solution to the problematic I have been discussing.[24] The figure's nominal dualism, however, calls into doubt its ability to function as an ideal solution. The disguised Thornhill (Burchell) fails to influence the family, as he tells the Vicar when he finds the Primrose family in prison: " 'I partly saw your delusion then, and as it was out of my power to restrain, I could only pity it!' " (164–65). Affection without authority is powerless. The empowered Sir William Thornhill, on the other hand, can no longer be viewed as an equal within the domestic economy, as Burchell could. Only because Burchell survives as an afterimage in Thornhill's shadow is his integration into the family acceptable. The split in this character can be read as a yet unbridgeable gap between sentiment and

[24] See, for example, David Durant: "the worldly happy ending sees the Vicar replaced as hero by the superman Burchell." "*The Vicar of Wakefield* and the Sentimental Novel," *Studies in English Literature* 17 (1977):485. See also John Dussinger, who accords the Vicar a "physical disability" that keeps him from rescuing Sophia and causes him to rely on the " 'healthy' and level-headed" Burchell (*Discourse of Mind* 153).

power, freedom and domination, and non-coercive and authoritarian
social relations. In order to resolve the uncertainties and allay the anxieties of the world of desire that modernizes Goldsmith's pastoral fable,
patriarchal authority must misrepresent itself. To solve by misrepresentation, however, is to create additional problems, especially in a civil
society in which all vie for limited personal satisfaction by any means
available, including misrepresentation.

## III Competition, disguise, and the endangered middle

*The Vicar of Wakefield's* "women" are not alone in having strong desires.
The Vicar seeks distinction in his pamphlets against deuterogamy; his
eldest son seeks his fortune in the exercise of various occupations. Ned
Thornhill wants to seduce the pretty daughters of his tenants. Jenkinson
looks for a quick profit from the naive country bumpkin. Even Sir
William, while disguised as Burchell, wants others to accept his advice. All
in all, each character enters the public sphere to compete for profit,
distinction, or pleasure. And because the antipastoral world of the public
sphere is characterized by scarcity, competition is always at someone's
cost. Those who occupy the middle station are most vulnerable to the
dangers of expense because they confront a double threat from the
cunning of social inferiors and the anger of social superiors.

When social superiors enter the Primrose's homely habitation, they
trigger a natural desire for imitation. This desire has the potential to
disfigure the legibility of the social structure by reproducing its marks of
distinction. The material base of the social structure, however, can defend
its signifying practices against counterfeiting by making the action costly.
The middle order, especially, is unable to sustain the level of expenditure
necessary for distinction. In Goldsmith's fictional world, social superiors
control the wealth that the middle order would need to draw upon to
finance its extravagant desires. In short, through their control of status
markers *and* the means to acquire such markers, the social elite acts the
role of Sir William Honeywood without his benevolent intentions. When
the family of the middle order spends beyond its means, the elites can fall
upon it with a "tenfold weight" (102). At the same time, the "fall" appears
to be the fault of the insufficiently sentimentalized family, which invites
ruin by choosing the allure of luxury rather than the comfort of familial
affections. The consequences of this choice – indebtedness – bring the
juridical power into the private sphere.

When law enters the family, it functions both as a means of oppression
and as an argument to discipline the desire for distinction. Although the
former function is subject to criticism while the latter is one of the
narrative's ideological aims, both work toward the same end: the preser-

vation of social hierarchy. The innocent actions of the Vicar's two youngest sons, who are fascinated by Squire Thornhill's appearance at his first
visit, reveal that the social hierarchy needs both coercive and ideological
support: "my little ones ... fondly stuck close to the stranger. All my
endeavours could scarce keep their dirty fingers from handling and tar-
nishing the lace on [Ned Thornhill's] cloaths, and lifting up the flaps of his
pocket holes, to see what was there" (37). In expressing an untutored
curiosity for pretty things, the Vicar's children shrink the deferential
distance that the lace, and the clothes, and the flaps of the pocket holes are
intended to create. The power and effect of their curiosity is reflected in
the Vicar's description: he is "scarce" able to restrain their "dirty fingers"
from handling the magnificence before them. Goldsmith's text represents
the desire for status goods as an innocent urge, an infant fascination with
the materiality of the sign rather than an adult yearning for the social
power of the signifier.

With this "genuine touch of nature" Goldsmith has revealed an important conflict.[25] Spontaneous admiration for the indices of success excites
imitation. Imitation, however, especially when its object is the "trifling
circumstance" of "mere outside" (20), threatens to dilute the authority of
social status by reproducing its signs, thereby scrambling the codes of an
already promiscuous society. In effect, imitation necessarily entails misrepresentation. As juridical subject and father of the sentimental household,
it is the Vicar's duty to discourage imitation. When Squire Thornhill
returns to the Primrose cottage accompanied by "Miss Skeggs and Lady
Blarney" – two women of questionable character who misrepresent
"proper ladies" – it becomes apparent to the Vicar that he is even less able
to control the imitative desires of his grown children than he was of his
little ones: "I now began to find that all my long and painful lectures upon
temperance, simplicity, and contentment, were entirely disregarded. The
distinction lately paid us by our betters awaked that pride which I had
laid asleep, but not removed" (56). Once the counterfeit ladies perform
the physical pleasures of distinction in the sentimental household, lessons
on the abstract consolations of "temperance, simplicity, and contentment"
lose what little persuasive power they had. Ideology needs support from
coercive forces that will introduce even greater suffering as a means of
countervailing the mental unease that incites the urge to imitate.

Coercive power enters the sentimental household in the person of the
agents of Squire Thornhill, who earlier loaned the Vicar 100 pounds to be
used to buy his son George a commission in the army. Unlike Olivia's
unsuccessful suitor, farmer Williams – who enjoys his independence
because he "owed his landlord [Thornhill] no rent, and little regarded his

<hr />

[25] The phrase appears in slightly different form in a contemporary review of *The Vicar*, in the
   *Critical Review* 21 (1766):440.

indignation" (86) – Primrose's indebtedness has put him in the Squire's power. After having seduced and abandoned Olivia, Thornhill attempts to use this economic advantage to extort from Primrose his approval of the Squire's marriage to the wealthy Miss Wilmot. Primrose refuses, and the Squire has him imprisoned for debt (137–38), an action that he has little trouble justifying when he later meets his uncle in Primrose's prison cell: "'with regard to [the Vicar's] being here, my attorney and steward can best inform you, as I commit the management of business entirely to them. If he has contracted debts and is unwilling or even unable to pay them, it is their business to proceed in this manner, and I see no hardship or injustice in pursuing the most legal means of redress'" (170–71). Although Sir William finds his nephew's action "equitable" rather than "generous" and reproves him for subjecting the Vicar to the "subordinate tyranny" of his agents, he finds nothing illegal in the business. Even when the young squire's explanation is subsequently revealed to be self-serving, the revelation does not discredit the processes of confinement, which have been all according to law and business, as Bondum might say. The Vicar's imprisonment shows with what ease delegated legal power can fall on the imprudent sentimental family. And even though the text reveals the young Squire to be nothing more than a corrupt viceroy, liable to recall by the benevolent supreme magistrate, it cannot recall the moment in which power threatens the sentimental family.

That the law is liable to be exploited by the powerful while still appearing impartial makes a supreme magistrate an ideological necessity for the author who seeks to create an equitable society. Not only is the benevolent supreme magistrate or monarch a necessary corrective to the blind rule of law, but he is also the necessary supplement to the patriarch's power, which is limited by the demands of affection. Given these necessities, it is no surprise that the Vicar himself – the site of this double need – articulates the function of the supreme magistrate. According to Primrose, in a modern commercial nation the great, who derive power from their exclusive control of foreign commerce, seek "to diminish kingly power as much as possible; because whatever they take from that is naturally restored to themselves" (100). Like Ned Thornhill, they make "dependants, by purchasing the liberty of the needy or the venal," who are used against the "middle order of mankind [wherein] are generally to be found all the arts, wisdom, and virtues of society" (101–2). In this state, characterized by conflict of status groups, the magistrate's interests coincide with the middle order, who are too weak to threaten his supremacy yet not so weak as to be useless to him in his struggle to keep power from being monopolized by the commercial magnates. Thus, the monarch protects the middle orders, who in turn are obliged to "preserve the prerogative and privileges of the one principal governor with the most sacred circumspection" (102). In Primrose's political theory, the monarch has no agenda of his own; he exists merely as a necessary political fiction, an agent of the "people," who would otherwise be enslaved by a class of petty tyrants. This necessary and supreme fiction keeps England from becoming like "Holland, Genoa, or Venice, where the laws govern the poor, and the rich govern the law" (102). Like the writer, then, the monarch is a necessary adjutant to an inhuman law. As Goldsmith writes elsewhere, Britons' "freedom consists in their enjoying all the advantages of democracy with this superior prerogative borrowed from monarchy, *that the severity of their laws may be relaxed without endangering the constitution.*"[26]

This necessary political fiction takes shape in *The Vicar of Wakefield* in the bearer of the public conscience, a local monarch who knows the law's limits and thus introduces affection for his charges into the public conscience. Such a solution works as long as the keeper of the public conscience provides no grounds for suspecting him of acting according to self-interest. But the narrative violates this requirement by inserting the supreme magistrate into a family that is itself riven by conflict and by giving him particular affections for one member of that family. In short, by humanizing the supreme magistrate, the text suggests that the transcendent figure is a misrepresentation. As a penniless suitor, Burchell has no authority. That is, as soon as the monarch descends into the political arena where all compete as equals for limited goods, he loses his transcendent powers. This indicates that his powers are not personal but situational. When Burchell goes against the Primrose family interests, he is unceremoniously dismissed by Mrs. Primrose, with the hesitant but finally willing collusion of the Vicar:

I was not displeased at bottom that we were rid of a guest from whom I had much to fear. Our breach of hospitality went to my conscience a little: but I quickly silenced that monitor by two or three specious reasons, which served to satisfy and reconcile me to myself ... Conscience is a coward, and those faults it has not strength enough to prevent, it seldom has justice enough to accuse.          (71)

In acquiescing to Burchell's expulsion, Primrose shows that the conscience is an indifferent monitor without the support of the supreme magistrate. In order to fulfill the text's twofold need, authority must act overtly outside the family to protect it rather than make covert demands from within. As the Vicar says later in his oration on monarchy, power is tolerable only when it remains "at the greatest distance from the greatest number of people" (99). The problem that the Vicar faces in his family is duplicated in the provisional political solution to endemic instability.

The expulsion of the disguised bearer of the public conscience indicates textual resistance to its internalization. It is as if in accord with the

[26] Goldsmith, *The Citizen of the World*, Letter 50, 2:210.

pastoral nature of the representation the narrative strives to preserve a state of politico-moral infancy, in which the guardian power protects but does not punish, aids but never demands, guides but does not force the tottering steps that seek their own willful way. And yet the consequences of the failure to internalize the public conscience indicate the great dangers of this failure. Burchell does not depart without introducing the threat of coercive power, which is armed to punish the unwary, imprudent, or impudent. After Burchell has been "dismissed," one of Primrose's small sons discovers his letter case containing a copy of a letter that Burchell wrote to Skeggs and Blarney. The family persuades the Vicar to break open the case and read the letter. When it is discovered that the letter warns the women to avoid the family, they think Burchell their enemy. Burchell comes to take leave of the family, is confronted with the discovery, and reacts with an alarming fierceness to the family's resentment: "'And how came you,' replied he, with looks of unparallelled effrontery, 'so basely to presume to break open the letter? Don't you know, now, I could hang you all for this? All that I have to do, is to swear at the next justice's, that you have been guilty of breaking open the lock of my pocket-book, and so hang you all up at his door'" (80). Burchell's threat indicates both the Vicar's vulnerability and authority's power. Furthermore, the Vicar's reaction to the threat – it "raised [him] to such a pitch, that [he] could scarce govern [his] passion" – proves that he needs the very guidance that he dismisses (80). Burchell misrepresents true power by endowing it with a benevolent restraint. This misrepresentation may also explain the reluctance to internalize, for once the law has been so internalized, mercy is not always an appropriate response to infraction or a wise policy to follow. As Goldsmith writes elsewhere, "the people are generally well pleased with a remission of punishment, and all that wears the appearance of humanity; it is the wise alone who are capable of discerning that impartial justice is the truest mercy: they know it to be difficult, very difficult at once to compassionate, and yet condemn an object that pleads for tenderness."[27] Once the rules of the pastoral world are suspended and a indulgent paternalism no longer has a suitable place, the superior orders (who have taken the father's place) pose a grave danger to the desiring middle.

The dangers from the lower orders that also populate the antipastoral world arise from the failure of a universally recognized authority to create a stable hierarchical system founded upon a standard of absolute value. In this ideal system each person would know her or his place. Thus, each would be impervious to the enticements of the marketplace's relative values. In other words, need would coincide with social entitlements. That

---

[27] Goldsmith, *The Citizen of the World*, Letter 38, 2:163.

Wakefield lacks this utopian authority has been registered by Martin Battestin, who comments that "the Vicar's vanity and pride distort his vision of reality, leading him to mistake the semblance for the truth of things."[28] *The Vicar of Wakefield* demonstrates, however, that in the competitive marketplace the relative value of things can and often must be taken for their absolute truth. What Battestin calls vanity is a moment within a market transaction, a form of need that helps to determine exchange value. Such vanity, moreover, is liable to be exploited by the needy and resourceful lower orders.

While trying to sell his horse at a country fair, Primrose discovers the relative nature of value. He is drawn into the circuit of exchange by his family's desire for distinction, a desire that is itself as relative as the value of the horse he tries to sell. After failing to find a buyer, he begins to adopt the attitudes of those whom he has tried to interest in the horse:

> By this time I began to have a most hearty contempt for the poor animal myself, and was almost ashamed at the approach of every customer; for though I did not entirely believe all the fellows told me; yet I reflected that the number of witnesses was a strong presumption they were right, and St. Gregory, upon good works, professes himself to be of the same opinion.          (72)

The law of the marketplace confuses the man inexperienced with temporalities. By summoning St. Gregory to his aid, the Vicar introduces a moral authority into economic calculations. This inappropriate mixture of discourses has predictable results, as the Vicar becomes liable to exploitation by one who can manipulate the same scholarly discourse. When Primrose retires to a tavern with a fellow cleric and there meets the cheat Jenkinson disguised as a venerable man of "green old age," he easily moves from one inappropriate authority to another. Just as the counterfeit Skeggs and Blarney had enacted genteel manners in the Primrose household, so too Jenkinson enacts pious and scholarly traits in the tavern. When Jenkinson contracts to buy the subjectively devalued horse with a bill drawn on the Vicar's neighbor Flamborough, the Vicar agrees readily because the experiences of the fair have opened the Vicar to Jenkinson's spurious authority.

Jenkinson tricks Primrose by counterfeiting erudition and sentiment. This event proves that authority must protect the accounts of the innocent middle order. Primrose encounters another counterfeit as he searches for his eloped daughter Olivia. On the promiscuous highway he has little to guide him but ceremony and habit, which prove to be dependable guides only in a known and stable environment. That Primrose is duped again reinforces the narrative anxiety evoked by anonymous social relations working against the traditional safeguards – such as gratitude, obligation,

---

[28]Battestin, *Providence of Wit*, p. 206.

and law – that support the established order. This time the counterfeit is a butler who usurps the custom of the manor and engages the Vicar in a debate on the best form of government. Shocked by the butler's republican rhetoric, Primrose gives a spirited apology for monarchy. Not only do the butler's actions constitute yet another instance of misrepresentation in a text where true authority cannot be identified, but Primrose's response reveals the internal split that drives the narrative forward in search for a solution to its contradictions. His response proves him a fierce monarchist in national politics and a republican in domestic life. A tyrant is necessary, but he must be kept at a distance: "as I naturally hate the face of a tyrant, the farther off he is removed from me, the better pleased am I" (99). And yet by keeping authority at this remove, the Vicar is subject to danger from the "rabble," who easily ape their betters, especially when those betters are marked only by their dress and discourse. By "occupying" the manor in the absence of the true lord, the servants make concrete the text's fears of anarchy and mob rule. The "elegant supper" shared by Primrose and the counterfeit lord of the manor stands as a symbolic appropriation of authority and an actual expropriation of property: that is, as a dangerous criminal act. As long as authority remains distant, the middle order remains at risk. The text must bring authority back into the family, thereby establishing a means of guiding the family's desires. In the pastoral world of the Primrose family, a world that finally turns on the utopian vision of comic harmony, authority and law must remain at once within and without.

The confusions and instability of an anonymous society point to the need for a juridical order administered by an unimpeachable authority. The calamities that befall Primrose and his family from above and below repeat the simple point that status mobility threatens as much as it promotes individual happiness and social harmony. Law alone cannot guard the middle ranks because it can be turned against them. Even when the law provides security, it cannot create the positive ties that are an essential part of the pastoral vision. *The Traveller*, written probably around the same time as *The Vicar*, describes this situation eloquently:

> That independence Britons prize too high,
> Keeps man from man, and breaks the social tie;
>
> Nor this the worst. As nature's ties decay,
> As duty, love, and honour fail to sway,
> Fictitious bonds, the bonds of wealth and law,
> Still gather strength, and force unwilling awe.[29]

The natural order is displaced by an inadequate fiction that fails to create community. In *The Vicar of Wakefield* Goldsmith personalizes the law's

[29] Goldsmith, *The Traveller*, ll. 339–352, *Works*, 4:263–64.

power in order to construct a human fiction superior to that which the forces of law and wealth weave daily into the fabric of society. If his fiction appears superior to the existing one, then it does so by providing a vision of society in which each individual fulfills a determinate social role under an omniscient and benevolent legislator-magistrate. In this supreme fiction, produced by the painful contingencies of a developing market society, a transcendent authority erases the barrier between law and equity.

## IV Proper occupations and an unsettling joke

By bringing the family to the public conscience and erasing its bothersome desires within the prison, *The Vicar of Wakefield* constructs its supreme political fiction. And by producing in Sir William Thornhill a transcendent authority with immanent affective interests that diminish both its alien and tyrannical nature, Goldsmith's sentimental novel plays an affirmative role in the culture of his time.[30] John Bender has noted this affirmative role and shown how "*The Vicar of Wakefield* partakes of a reformist discourse, conducted in the broadly shared vocabulary of sensationalist empiricism."[31] Aimed at modifying individual behavior for the most part and institutional practices to a degree, this reformist discourse produces a disciplined subject without questioning the structures of power that effect this construction. Yet in addition to this affirmative discourse of reform, the text also produces a utopian moment that points beyond the disciplinary relations of market society to a different kind of social organization based on social functions rather than on status mobility. This is a fleeting moment, however, not unburdened by problems of its own. The Vicar's incarceration suggests that the internalized public conscience can provide the means for an orderly, harmonious, and cooperative society as long as it is supplemented by a supreme magistrate who possesses the power and the wisdom to know when to intermit the rigors of the law.

Juridical authority proper enters the narrative when the bailiffs come to take Primrose to prison for his debt to Squire Thornhill. Primrose obeys the officers' commands, and he rebukes his rebellious parishioners for their intentions to rescue him. His obedience, best contrasted with Random's and Booth's resistance, indicates that he already respects the law and its officers. Prison must bring him to respect the temporalities that the law serves. Primrose's respect for the officers is not ill-placed, and it begins the text's utopian moment. The officers carry out their duties with compassion, taking special care with Olivia, who is "enfeebled by a slow fever, which had begun for some days to undermine her constitution" (140). In helping Olivia, the bailiff meliorates the law's coercive power, in effect

[30] For a discussion of affirmative culture, see Brenkman, *Culture and Domination*, pp. 4–18.
[31] Bender, "Prison Reform," p. 180.

civilizing it through particular administration. Once imprisoned, Primrose also finds the gaoler and his servants "civil enough." The Vicar tells of the former's kindness after his son Moses has procured lodgings for the women of the family: "He [Moses] obeyed; but could only find one apartment, which was hired at a small expence, for his mother and sisters, the gaoler with humanity consenting to let him and his two little brothers lie in prison with me" (144). At bottom of these officers' humanitarian actions are the generic demands of sentimental fiction. This formal demand, however, also produces an alternative solution to the problems of individualism. Through a settled occupation defined by service rather than by the unsettling operations of the market, the officer performs a social task and satisfies the needs of all concerned. Minor officials may never have been like the way Goldsmith represents them, but these narrative agents hint at the integrative function of humanized labor.[32]

A stray remark from a repentant Jenkinson – the "green" old man who had gulled Primrose at the country fair – signals the text's next movement toward a utopian resolution of all conflicts. When the Vicar is surprised at Jenkinson's actual age, the trickster describes how he acquired his talents of disguise: "I . . . have learnt the art of counterfeiting every age from seventeen to seventy. Ah sir, had I but bestowed half the pains in learning a trade, that I have in learning to be a scoundrel, I might have been a rich man at this day" (143). Jenkinson claims that worldly happiness is more likely to follow from a fixed socioeconomic identity than from a succession of counterfeitings. When a person deliberately rejects a settled occupation (and with it a stable character), Jenkinson's tale implies, restraint inevitably falls upon him with tenfold weight. One may choose the liberating function of a social occupation or involuntary servitude in prison. Jenkinson's remorse begins the gradual blending of utopian and affirmative moments in *The Vicar*, a synthesis that explains in part its popularity. Labor liberates, but it is a labor without sweat (all pains are in the learning of it), a labor that certifies the individual as a proper juridical subject and leads him to leisure.

Prison brings Primrose to an awareness of the material demands of life, an awareness that had previously been deadened by his sententious rhetoric. The Vicar's practical instructions to his son Moses give some evidence of this new awareness:

---

32  See Johnson, *Idler* 38 (6 January 1759): "the corrosion of resentment, the heaviness of sorrow, the want of exercise, and sometimes of food, the contagion of diseases from which there is no retreat, and the severity of tyrants against whom there can be no resistance, and all the complicated horrors of a prison, put an end every year to the life of one in four of those that are shut up from the common comforts of human life" (2:118–19). For a recent history of English prisons, see Sean McConville, *A History of English Prison Administration: Volume I, 1750–1877* (London: Routledge & Kegan Paul, 1981), esp. pp. 49–77. See also Bender, *Imagining the Penitentiary*, pp. 11–40.

"And as for you, my son," continued I, "it is by the labour of your hands we must all hope to be supported. Your wages, as a day labourer, will be full sufficient, with proper frugality, to maintain us all, and comfortably too. Thou art now sixteen years old, and hast strength, and it was given thee, my son, for very useful purposes; for it must save from famine your helpless parents and family. Prepare then this evening to look out for work against to-morrow, and bring home every night what money you earn, for our support."                                    (144)

Despite the habitual pathos in the Vicar's rhetoric, the speech indicates a revaluation of temporalities, an acceptance of the necessity of entering the circuit of exchange in order to support the family in its new situation. Exchange relations are thus ratified by sentimental exigencies. By mastering temporalities, moreover, the aim of oppression will be defeated; for the wages of the "day labourer" can lead the family into a sufficient, frugal, and comfortable promised land. Sufficiency, frugality, and comfort are the signs of freedom in the text. At this moment a religiously accented economic discourse dispels oppression and holds out the promise of a paradise of affective relations within the competitive public sphere.

The next step in the Vicar's transvaluation of temporalities occurs when he undertakes to reform the other prisoners. Upon being first committed to prison, Primrose observes his fellow inmates "forgetting thought in merriment or clamour" (141). Like the inmates of Booth's and Random's prisons, they have degenerated to an existence marked by "execrations, lewdness, and brutality" (144). Moved by the wasteful spectacle, Primrose dedicates himself to their reformation, thereby unifying the split between his spiritual and temporal functions. Prior to his incarceration, the Vicar has boasted about the effectiveness with which he performed his pastoral duties. Never, however, has the reader witnessed him executing the professional part of his triadic function of priest, husbandman, and father.[33] In the prison, the exercise of that profession becomes "a duty incumbent upon [him]." As he pursues his own "great gain" in saving the prisoners' "precious" human souls, Primrose begins "to think of doing them temporal services also" by turning "idle industry" to profitable activity. Some of the prisoners begin "to work at cutting pegs for tobacconists and shoemakers, the proper wood being bought by a general subscription, and when manufactured, sold by [the Vicar's] appointment; so that each earned something every day: a trifle indeed, but sufficient to maintain him" (149). Under the pressure of a necessity that is part moral and part material, the Vicar returns order to the prison by means of his

[33] The only other instance in which the Vicar performs his pastoral duty is narrated rather than dramatized. In that instance he is preoccupied by the absence of his family, who have decided to travel to church by horse: "I waited near an hour in the reading desk for their arrival; but not finding them come as expected, I was obliged to begin, and went through the service, not without some uneasiness at finding them absent" (59).

entrepreneurial initiative. And yet he is no capitalist, for the labor and the capital are fully social, provided by and returning to the prisoners with the Vicar acting the role of factor. Noticeably absent from this scene are the destructive effects of competition. The Vicar remakes the conditions of labor even as he disciplines the workers: "I did not stop here, but instituted fines for the punishment of immorality, and rewards for peculiar industry. Thus in less than a fortnight I had formed them into something social and humane, and had the pleasure of regarding myself as a legislator, who had brought men from their native ferocity into friendship and obedience" (149). To alter slightly a phrase borrowed from Mrs. Primrose: authority is as authority does. He has led the men from natural depravity through industry to a respect for property and – one assumes – property's corollary, the law. His work of reformation has a dual effect, for as he socializes the prisoners through production, he also repairs his own patriarchal authority, which has been damaged by experience. As legislator within the prison, Primrose remains *primus inter pares*. His reclamation of his function of leader, furthermore, affirms the existing hierarchies and its structures of authority even as it introduces a new freedom from want in the workers' ownership of the means of production.

Thus Goldsmith's novel blends authoritarian and proto-socialist solutions to problems stemming from market society's powerful forces and competitive relations. The prison, however, cannot be the final scene of the narrative because it is hostile to the full enjoyment of affective ties. *The Vicar of Wakefield* is no Newgate pastoral. Prison life is a life of labor without leisure; whatever leisure the prisoners enjoy is qualified by their lack of freedom of movement. And so, in order to remove the family from the prison and return them to a suitable domestic idyll, the narrative produces a final crisis: the arrest and imprisonment of George Primrose. In this last juridical calamity, the text reveals the uneasy marriage of law and affection. George Primrose's arrest serves two functions: it enlarges the Vicar's sympathy by providing him with the opportunity for what most commentators have recognized as his moment of triumph as a priest;[34] and it necessitates the ministrations of Sir William Thornhill, who appears armed with natural law and equity, prepared to harrow the prisons and judge the living and the (supposed) dead.[35]

Thornhill's reappearance constitutes the text's ideological solution to

---

[34] "He becomes like the transcendent preacher in *The Deserted Village*" (Oliver Ferguson, "Dr. Primrose", p. 331). "[I]n prison Primrose has his finest hour. Here, he too is free to be most authentically human, to be radically *Christian*." Robert Hopkins, "Social Stratification and the Obsequious Curve: Goldsmith and Rowlandson," in *Studies in the Eighteenth Century. Papers Presented at the Third David Nichol Smith Memorial Seminar, Canberra, 1973*, eds. R. F. Brissenden and J. C. Eade (Toronto: University of Toronto Press, 1976), p. 64.

[35] Both Battestin, *Providence of Wit*, p. 210; and Preston, "The Uses of Adversity," p. 245, note the association of Burchell with Christ.

intractable problems even as it indicates the insufficiency of its pastoral representation of labor. As Burchell, the knight exhibits the heroic physical attributes of the natural aristocrat. He saves Sophia twice, once from drowning and once from abduction. The transformation that turns Mr. Burchell into Sir William Thornhill preserves the romance strength of the former even as it modernizes it in the political power of the latter. The Vicar describes this textual movement as a shift in self-representation: "The poor Mr. Burchell was in reality a man of large fortune and great interest, to whom senates listened with applause, and whom party heard with conviction; who was the friend of his country, but loyal to his king" (168). In other words, Sir William Thornhill reconciles all knotty contemporary contradictions within himself. He is a publicly recognized true patriot. Even the gaoler knows him, and he allows Jenkinson to leave prison with two servants in order to search for Sophia's abductor: " 'Your promise is sufficient [security],' replied the [gaoler], 'and you may at a minute's warning send them over England whenever your honour thinks fit' " (169).

Sir William's word is law informed by wisdom. Although initially deceived by his nephew, Sir William is apprised of his villainy through a private investigation he holds in the prison. He sees justice done by enlarging George Primrose, whose action of sending a challenge to the nephew is capital according to a "late act of parliament":[36] " 'All [Ned Thornhill's] guilt is now too plain, and I find his present prosecution was dictated by tyranny, cowardice, and revenge; at my request, Mr. Gaoler, set this young officer, now your prisoner, free, and trust to me for the consequences. I'll make it my business to set the affair in a proper light to my friend the magistrate who has committed him' " (173). Sir William's discernment supersedes positive law, and his power and influence free "the young officer," who would then have been free to serve his country had not the restoration of his fortune made that particular form of service unnecessary.

The rest is history, managed by the master comedian Thornhill. By his behavior in the prison the Vicar has shown a new respect for temporalities. Like Random and Booth, he appears at least momentarily better fitted to rule his family. With order restored the narrative itself turns "fanciful" as Sir William's presence brings health and wealth to all. Or almost all, for the return of the pastoral scene is also a return of the repressed fears associated with the indistinguished space of woman's will. As the tale moves toward conventional comic closure, the brides protest too much about the sequence in which the marriages should be performed. Olivia,

---

[36] The phrase is from the first edition. It was dropped by Goldsmith in the second. In the Oxford English Novels edition of *The Vicar*, Friedman points out that no such law ever existed (London: Oxford University Press, 1974), p. 207.

punished for her sexual transgression with the status of a "matron," "still remembers [Thornhill] with regret" (183). At the wedding feast, George proposes indiscriminate seating arrangements, but his mother "was not perfectly satisfied, as she expected to have the pleasure of sitting at the head of the table and carving all the meat for all the company" (184). These minor commotions and dissatisfactions gently molest the newly instituted hierarchy and injure the general harmony effected by Sir William, the "son-in-law" who dispenses charity and reprimands to the Vicar's almost rebellious parishioners, and who embodies the harmony of political, legal, economic, and sentimental discourses. Turning to comedy to stabilize and close his fictional world, Goldsmith also brings anti-authoritarian laughter back to the now-extended Primrose family.[37]

According to Primrose there is much laughter at the wedding feast, but he chooses to relate a single joke only: "One jest I particularly remember, old Mr. Wilmot drinking to Moses, whose head was turned another way, my son replied, 'Madam, I thank you.' Upon which the old gentleman, winking upon the rest of the company, observed that he was thinking of his mistress" (184). The joke is evidence of that unruly something that eludes control. That the identity of the speaker should be mistaken at all recalls the other cases of mistaken identity, which had more grievous con-sequences. That Mr. Wilmot should be mistaken for a woman, the only man reproved by Sir William for his "immoderate passion for wealth," recalls that the narrative represents woman as the source of an ever-disruptive desire. Finally, that Moses (a future lawgiver?) might be thinking of his mistress suggests that this inexhaustible and destabilizing desire is not confined to women. And yet, the text may be doing nothing more nor less than indicating that the stuff of comedy is inexhaustible, the joke of our order-obsessed societies.

But this joke is not quite the end of the novel. It ends with the entire family seated by "a chearful fire-side." The women lose representation here in the curious detail of the final seating arrangements: "My two little ones sat upon each knee, the rest of the company by their partners." Absorbed into a community now organized by marriage (And what of Olivia?), the Vicar can ruminate upon "gratitude in good fortune" and "submission in adversity." This balanced period captures the hopes of the

---

[37] Narrative and ideological closure is also effected through linguistic means. Compare the following two passages, the first describing the Primrose's first dinner away from Wakefield, the second about the wedding feast:

A feast also was provided for our reception, at which we sat chearfully down; and what the conversation wanted in wit, was made up in laughter. (32)

I can't say whether we had more wit amongst us now than usual; but I am certain we had more laughing, which answered the end as well. (184)

A return to pre-Squire Thornhill days is implied in the second quotation, but rural amusement is recuperated at this moral feast prepared by Squire Thornhill's cook.

book even while it leaves as its last mark the signs of conflict and oppression. Family and law are complementary only in this timeless tableau, a tableau that displaces the female-inspired portrait that exceeded the capacity of the household. But it is the pleasure of just such a timeless moment that produces a longing for the day when all are emplaced by a law that is a friend to labor and leisure too.

# 8

# *Caleb Williams*: negating the romance of the public conscience

In society, no man possessing the genuine marks of a man can stand alone. Our opinions, our tempers and our habits are modified by those of each other. This is by no means the mere operation of arguments and persuasives; it occurs in that insensible and gradual way which no resolution can enable us wholly to counter-act. He that would attempt to counteract it by insulating himself will fall into a worse error than that which he seeks to avoid. He will divest himself of the character of a man, and be incapable of judging his fellow men, or of reasoning upon human affairs.

On the other hand, individuality is of the very essence of intellectual excellence. He that resigns himself wholly to sympathy and imitation can possess little of mental strength or accuracy ... he is incapable of the enterprise of a hero, or the severity of a philosopher. Mankind cannot be benefited by him.[1]

## I Introduction

I have chosen to end this study with William Godwin's *Things as They Are; or, The Adventures of Caleb Williams* because it is the negation of both the fortunate and unfortunate juridical narrative paradigms found in the other novels of this study. Despite their criticism of social conditions, the other novels end by generally affirming society's juridical structures and recommending, as it were, the subject appropriate to such structures. Even *Roxana* attributes its heroine's ultimate disintegration to her violation of natural and revealed laws rather than to the contractual negotiations that endow her with a false sense of juridical immunity. William Godwin's novel, on the other hand, ascribes its hero's misfortune to the discursive structures that the other works affirm: individual right and juridical power. Those rights and powers neither protect Williams from enemies nor provide him with domestic pleasures as a reward for successful internalization of juridical principles. Instead, the discursive systems of liberal individualism produce a guilty subject, self-indicted for juridical crimes against an adversary who also uses juridical powers for self-protection. In short, instead of constructing a disciplined and empowered

---

[1] Godwin, *Enquiry*, p. 757.

subject, juridical discourse in *Caleb Williams* brings on the collapse of the novel's eponymous subject-in-formation.

The formation and collapse of Williams as juridical subject indicates a self-conscious critique of one master narrative available to eighteenth-century fiction. This critique, situated between radical individualism and communitarian social relations, adumbrates class antagonisms that will be increasingly foregrounded in succeeding English narratives. In this short concluding chapter, I shall not look forward to this new narrative paradigm; instead, I will trace the narrative logic of Williams' disintegration. His formation begins with an autobiographical apology – a common strategy for subject formation – that becomes a brief confession before its abrupt disintegration.

Williams' self-formation begins with his admission of a desire to participate in the socio-political life of his day. Like the Primrose boys' actions, Williams' desire takes the form of a drive to touch and investigate in order finally to know. His will to knowledge and power, however, does not play itself out in Arcadia or in *terra incognita*. Rather, Williams enters a territory already marked with signs of possession. From the first motion of his will, he encounters suspicion, resentment, and resistance. That resistance takes the form of a punitive public conscience, embodied initially in an aristocratic character, who uses the law when he feels that his honor and social status are threatened by Williams' investigations. Later, society's juridical structures relieve the aristocratic Count Falkland of the burden of defending himself by taking over the prosecution of Williams' alleged criminal behavior. Solitary; subjected to surveillance, confinement, and persecution; and finally himself the agent of a disciplinary and punitive public conscience, Williams becomes the vehicle for the negation of the public conscience as a means of social integration. And that moment reveals a contradiction between theoretical freedom in a self-determining individualism and actual coercion in a hierarchical society policed by juridical power.

In the other novels when social relations had been redefined and restricted to the domestic sphere, narrative contradictions were displaced by the creation of a juridico-patriarchal sphere inhabited by gendered subjects enjoying various measures of empowerment. Even in Samuel Richardson's *Clarissa* juridical relations were partially rehabilitated in Belford, and the heroine was translated to a metaphysical state where patriarchal power is free from corruption. In this manner Richardson's novel offers its readers a double purification of the juridical ideal. Like *Clarissa*, *Caleb Williams* also reveals the need for more just social relations, in which the rights of the weak are protected against infringement by the powerful. Unlike *Clarissa*, however, *Caleb Williams'* unmitigated tragedy demonstrates that rights alone are not enough. If juridical power is to protect rather than deform, injure, and destroy, it must be grounded in what Jean Cohen calls "political sociality, or the capacity of self-determination through interaction with others regarding the affairs of the community."[2] In Godwin's words, if a person is not to be "incapable of judging his fellow men, or of reasoning upon human affairs," then that person ought to be ruled by a law that does not rest upon the assumption that all who come before it wish for nothing more than to "stand alone."

## II Rational individualism in Godwin's *Enquiry*

In his *Enquiry Concerning Political Justice*, Godwin describes a dialectical relation between the individual and society. Character is subject to social modification even as it contributes to the transformation of the society that molds it. In order to resist the tyranny of intellectual error, a person must live apart from civil society. Through solitary meditation the individual makes the heroic – or as Godwin writes "angelic" – effort to divest her or himself of the prejudice and self-interest that are error's adjutants.[3] Intellectual independence, however, must not come at the cost of a self-cultivated alienation from society. By nature the human being is social; by choice and effort a person distances her or himself in order to help remove the idols that thwart social betterment. Various forces work against the maintenance of the division between independence of the intellect and participation in society. Godwin's true hero maintains this distinction without falling prey to either an unquestioning conformism or a Romantic isolationism.

By dividing human nature into social and mental domains, and by making the mind the antagonist of error, Godwin in effect creates rational individualism. The rational individual resists both the idols of the marketplace and the idols of the domestic hearth; that is, this intellectual hero as rational individual resists the weaknesses in possessive and affective individualisms. Governed neither by economic nor by sentimental imperatives, the self retreats occasionally to a paradise within, from which flow the moral and intellectual streams that will reclaim the fallen world. The retreat is not permanent. The philosopher-hero returns, engaging in debate and persuasion to help overcome the "cold reserve that keeps man at a distance from man."[4] By "constantly and carefully enquiring into the deserts of all," the rational individual advances the "general good" and makes society fitter for human habitation.[5]

---

[2] Cohen, *Class and Civil Society*, p. 31.

[3] "[T]he soundest criterion of virtue is to put ourselves in the place of an impartial spectator, of an angelic nature, suppose, beholding us from an elevated station, and uninfluenced by our prejudices, conceiving what would be his estimate of the intrinsic circumstances of our neighbor, and acting accordingly" (Godwin, *Enquiry*, pp. 173–74).

[4] Godwin, *Enquiry*, p. 288.    [5] Ibid., pp. 172, 165–66.

Despite the obvious differences between this philosophical plot and the novelistic plots discussed in this study, the philosopher's *reason* is analogous to the novelist's *marriage*. Whether in "my Father's House," "my Narcissa," restored family prosperity, or the wedding feast presided over by the supreme magistrate, all the novelists plot the conditions in which their characters can realize their full potential in the comfort of unalienated and harmonious personal relations. Even Roxana looks forward to the moment when she will leave behind the hazards of trade and share innocent leisure with Amy and the Dutch Merchant. Yet the similarity of narrative aim – utopian longings for comfort – should not obscure the different sort of pleasure that awaits Godwin's rational individual in the improved society. The rational hero's pleasure comes from living in a way that "expands the understanding, supplies incitements to virtue, fills us with a generous consciousness of our independence, and carefully removes whatever can impede our exertions."[6] Not only does Godwin's hero never come to rest, but she or he continually battles troublesome evils of conformism. Self-determination – or the "generous consciousness of ... independence" – practically precludes the internalization of juridical discourse that marriage in the other plots demands.

To attain this consciousness, which in turn generates salutary social effects, requires constant and often solitary mental exertion against other individuals' error-bred desires and the irrational institutions that support those desires. If there is a siege mentality in both the *Enquiry* and in *Caleb Williams*, it is primarily fostered by institutional reproduction of an erroneous *status quo*. Godwin describes the law's part in this ideological reproduction in the *Enquiry*:

"I have deeply reflected," suppose, "upon the nature of virtue, and am convinced that a certain proceeding is incumbent on me. But the hangman, supported by an act of parliament, assures me I am mistaken." If I yield my opinion to his *dictum*, my action becomes modified, and my character also.

... Men are so successfully reduced to a common standard by the operation of positive law that, in most countries, they are capable of little more than, like parrots, repeating what others have said.[7]

As law perpetuates erroneous behavior, so the public conscience modifies action and character. It forestalls and eventually destroys the emergence of the rational individual, who exists only in potential. *Caleb Williams* is the story of the abortive emergence of this rational individual, undone by the destructive public conscience. It shows how positive law, struggle between status groups, and social desires construct character and instigate actions "in that insensible and gradual way which no resolution can enable us wholly to counteract." According to the common standard which governs

---

[6] Ibid., p. 176.       [7] Ibid., pp. 205–6.

all lives, "men" use juridical power to further their fortunes in a war for social position. Instead of communication in a rationalized Eden, there is charge and countercharge in a bellicose civil society. Not only is society not bettered, but the individual becomes fixed and formulated in a juridical wilderness, forever exiled from rational individualism's nurturant, contemplative oasis.

## III A juridical wilderness

Critics have read *The Adventures of Caleb Williams* as a fictionalized rendition of Godwin's political philosophy and as an exploration of the mysteries of the human mind.[8] More recently some critics have claimed the novel as an instance of the "textuality" of experience.[9] In these post-structuralist readings the self is always already fragmentary, a product of various and contradictory discursive forces. In a chapter from the *Enquiry* entitled "The Characters of Men Originate in Their External Circumstances,"

---

[8] For the political readings, see Harvey Gross, "The Pursuer and the Pursued: A Study of *Caleb Williams*," *Texas Studies in Literature and Language* 1 (1959):401–11. David McCracken, "Godwin's Literary Theory: The Alliance between Fiction and Political Philosophy," *Philological Quarterly* 49 (1970):113–33; and "Introduction," *Caleb Williams*, by William Godwin (New York: Norton, 1977), p. xii. Heather and Ian Ousby, "'My Servant Caleb': Godwin's *Caleb Williams* and the Political Trials of the 1790s," *University of Toronto Quarterly* 14.5 (1974):47–55. For the psychological readings, see Robert Kiely, *The Romantic Novel in England* (Cambridge, MA: Harvard University Press, 1972), pp. 81–97. Kiely finds that in Godwin's finest novelistic moments "the old-fashioned abstractions give way to perceptions of human nature which have little to do with political systems or dreams of utopian republics" (87). Kenneth Graham, "The Gothic Unity of *Caleb Williams*," *Papers on Language and Literature* 20 (1984):47–59. Graham argues, "[t]hat Godwin's novel leaves Caleb in a condition of self-contempt and disillusionment represents a victory of art over politics and adventure" (49). Michael DePorte, "The Consolations of Fiction: Mystery in *Caleb Williams*," *Papers on Language and Literature* 20 (1984):154–64. DePorte writes that Godwin's novel demonstrates the impossibility of finding a fiction capable of explaining and ordering human passions (161–62). All three authors either minimize or ignore Williams' origin and the nature of the conflict between him and Falkland. For readings linking personal and political issues, see Rudolf F. Storch, "Metaphors of Private Guilt and Social Rebellion in Godwin's *Caleb Williams*," *ELH* 34 (1967):188–207. For Storch, "social justice is an abstract idea, which is not likely to be self-generating even as an ideal force, but draws its energies from sources within the individual mind, which are usually disguised and symbolically displaced" (189). Alex Gold, Jr., "It's Only Love: The Politics of Passion in Godwin's *Caleb Williams*," *Texas Studies in Literature and Language* 19 (1977):135–60. Gold writes that "for Godwin, *all* love is the product of repressive social institutions and the enemy of equality, independence and harmony" (137).

[9] Jerrold E. Hogle, "The Texture of Self in Godwin's *Things as They Are*," *Boundary 2* 7.2 (1979):261–81. See also Jacqueline Miller, "The Imperfect Tale: Articulation, Rhetoric, and Self in *Caleb Williams*," *Criticism* 20 (1978):366–82. According to Miller, Caleb fails to create a self with his own language because Falkland monopolizes linguistic authority. Rothstein, *Systems of Order and Inquiry*, pp. 208–42, finds that Caleb models his own experience upon texts that he has read. Hogle's and Rothstein's arguments coincide at many points. Although I agree with their main premises of Caleb's proclivity to imitation, I show below that Williams' choice of "rhetorical systems" is not arbitrary but rather determined by his aspirations and social resistance to those aspirations.

Godwin himself provides partial justification for the post-structuralist readings. He writes that "[v]arious external accidents, unlimited as to the period of their commencement, modify in different ways the elements of the animal frame."[10] Godwin's modification becomes the critics' belated textuality: for them, *Caleb Williams* reproduces dominant discursive formations of the time. And yet, as Edward Said writes, repetition entails upon all novelistic characters a "task ... to be different, so heavily do paternity and routine weigh upon them."[11] Taken from this imperative, Caleb Williams' narrative is more than a mere pastiche of rhetorical systems and discursive forces. Although Williams uses the discursive weapons available to him in his struggle for privilege and power, his narrative is a moment of rebellion against the old order rather than repetition without difference. His resources include plots of romantic fiction as well as the juridical powers and forensic practices of the legal system. One provides him with the fantasy of domination and the other with the means *and* the justification for enacting that fantasy. Like Random's narrative, the romance plot and juridical competence hold out hope for historical change in the form of the ascendancy of a new class. Unlike Random's narrative, however, Williams' confessional tale does not end in his empowerment.

Rather than being the scripture of a new age, Williams' narrative is an apologia, what Georges Gusdorf has called "the final chance to win back what was lost."[12] In pursuit of eminence, Williams loses his reputation as well as the innocence of curiosity, emulation, and ambition. Branded as a criminal and commonplace social climber by his enemies, Williams must write a confession to recuperate his lost exceptionality. He extols the mental powers that distinguished him from the mute, inglorious company of his origin. His "inquiring mind," he writes, urged him into patterns of "improvement," thus creating a "distance from man" and from the common amusements of the place of his birth. Williams presents his native distinction as the first awakenings of a robust rational individualism. His tale begins as if it were the genealogy of Godwin's philosopher-hero:

I was somewhat above the middle stature ... uncommonly vigorous and active. My joints were supple, and I was formed to excel in youthful sports. The habits of my mind however were to a certain degree at war with the dictates of my boyish vanity. I had considerable aversion to the boisterous gaiety of the village gallants, and contrived to satisfy my love of praise with an unfrequent apparition at their amusements. My excellence in these respects however gave a turn to my meditations. I delighted to read of feats of activity, and was particularly interested by

[10] Godwin, *Enquiry*, p. 108.
[11] Said, "On Repetition," in *The World, the Text, and the Critic*, p. 117.
[12] Georges Gusdorf, "Conditions and Limits of Autobiography," tr. James Olney, in *Autobiography: Essays Theoretical and Critical* (Princeton: Princeton University Press, 1980), p. 39.

tales in which corporeal ingenuity or strength are the means resorted to for supplying resources and conquering difficulties.[13]

Williams' "uncommon" attributes include a mind at war with conventional amusements and a body "formed to excel." His love of reading sets him apart from the unreflecting "village gallants," while his supple joints preserve him from the appearance of effeminacy or the odor of the scholarly lamp. In short, he presents himself as one possessing the "enterprise of a hero" and "the severity of a philosopher." These possessions enable him to lift the heavy weight of his paternity and of customary village life.

Williams' talents and innate sense of superiority provide him with an easy victory over the "boisterous gaiety of the village gallants." For his other tasks he draws strength from an "invincible attachment to books of narrative and romance," which provide him with a precedent for overcoming the more formidable obstacle of his social superior and employer Squire Falkland. In Williams' story Falkland is represented both as an object of conscious imitation and as an obstacle to the narrator's own aggrandizement.[14] Like Williams, Falkland "avoided the busy haunts of men; nor did he seem desirous to compensate for this privation by the confidence of friendship." Unlike Williams, Falkland's "benevolence" earns him the gratitude of his community even as he carefully maintains a demeanor that causes him to be "regarded ... upon the whole with veneration as a being of superior order" (6–7). Falkland is the ideal authority: generous, aloof, and revered. His single flaw is his overly passionate devotion to aristocratic ideology: "Among the favourite authors of his early years were the heroic poets of Italy. From them he imbibed the love of chivalry and romance ... He believed that nothing was so well calculated to make men delicate, gallant, and humane, as a temper perpetually alive to the sentiments of birth and honour" (10). This temper, in the words of Falkland's philosopher-friend Mr. Clare, is an "error" (34).

Williams' early introduction of Falkland's "error" through the mouth of an impartial and respected witness sets the terms of the novel's conflict and establishes the object of his quest: to displace the reigning power, whose error makes him vulnerable to irrational and destructive passions. The personal struggle also functions as a political allegory of a struggle between

---

13 William Godwin, *Caleb Williams*, ed. David McCracken (New York: W.W. Norton, 1977), p. 4. All subsequent references to *Caleb Williams* are from this edition and appear parenthetically in the text. Until the fifth edition (1831), the last revised by Godwin, the title page read *Things as They Are; or, The Adventures of Caleb Williams*. See p. 342. Godwin's change suggests a revision of his original, radical conception of the determining force of social conditions.

14 Storch, "Metaphors," p. 195; Kiely, *Romantic Novel*, pp. 91–92; McCracken, Intro., p. xxi; and Hogle, "Texture of Self," pp. 264–65, note correspondences between Williams and Falkland.

bourgeois rationalism and aristocratic irrationality in the figures of a village youth "somewhat above the middle stature ... uncommonly vigorous and active" and a local landlord of "small stature, with an extreme delicacy of form and appearance" (5).[15] The stakes are nothing less than the command of society's juridical structures of power. If those structures are to be administered equitably, they must be freed from passions like Falkland's. By presenting himself as the ideal administrator of a law that has victimized him, Williams seeks to prepare his entry into that law through writing an incontrovertible defense of his actions. In other words, Williams begins his apologia with the intention of demonstrating beyond a shadow of a doubt both his innocence and his superior powers of penetration. As the action progresses, however, and as the time between event and its recording grows ever shorter, Williams becomes less and less able to support the distinction that he attempts to draw between victim and victimizer.

The personal struggle between Williams and Falkland begins with the narrator's quest for certain knowledge about an incident in Falkland's past. After hearing that Falkland had been exonerated of the charge of murdering his local rival Barnabas Tyrrel, Williams, prompted by circumstantial evidence, begins to wonder whether it were "possible after all that Mr. Falkland should be the murderer?" (107). In order to satisfy his curiosity, the narrator writes that "I determined to place myself as a watch upon my patron" (107), remarkable for the "coldness of his address and the impenetrableness of his sentiments" (6). The opportunity to penetrate Falkland's reserve arrives when Falkland, acting in his capacity as local justice of the peace, hears a complaint of murder. As Falkland interrogates the accused, Williams resolves to observe the proceedings, hoping to settle his doubts about the Squire's role in the murder of Tyrrel: "I will watch [Falkland] without remission. I will trace all the mazes of his thought. Surely at such a time his secret anguish must betray itself. Surely, if it be not my own fault, I shall now be able to discover the state of his plea before the tribunal of unerring justice" (126). By observing a proceeding at which he would not usually be present and by arrogating to himself powers of penetration that belong properly to a metaphysical court, Williams adopts inquisitorial practices of his own. He justifies those actions by invoking an "unerring justice," thereby according himself an unimpeachable integrity.

Williams describes Falkland's behavior when he discovers his secretary in the hearing-room. Falkland "turned from red to pale, and from pale to red. I perfectly understood his feelings, and would willingly have with-

---

[15] For the applicability of class struggle to eighteenth-century narratives, see my "Social Class, Character, and Narrative Strategy in *Humphry Clinker*," *Eighteenth-Century Life* 10.3 (1986):172–85.

drawn myself. But it was impossible; my passions were too deeply engaged; I was rooted to the spot; though my own life, that of my master, or almost of a whole nation had been at stake, I had no power to change my position" (126). Williams cannot withdraw because he has alienated his will to a juridical process that moves toward a seemingly inexorable conclusion. His temporary paralysis results from the interrelations of the passion to know, the techniques available for attaining such knowledge, and the pleasures to be derived from the success of the inquest. By intuiting that he is about to discover the justice's secret from his countenance, Williams is filled with the fantastic pleasures of power and control. Such pleasures momentarily suspend his present power of willing because they produce the expectation of a yet-more-powerful pleasure or a more pleasurable power.

Hearing the accused murderer speak of his remorse, Falkland "could endure it no longer. He suddenly rose, and with every mark of horror and despair rushed out of the room" (129). As Falkland rushes from the hearing chamber, Williams' suspense is released into a burst of triumph. His opponent has been vanquished from the juridical precincts. Williams himself remains until the hearing is concluded, thus displacing in his own mind the presiding justice. At the conclusion of the hearing, Williams retreats to the garden to savor his victory. His reaction to his "discovery" shows the extent to which knowledge and power interact to create the pleasures of the juridical subject:

I hastened into the garden, and plunged into the deepest of its thickets. My mind was full almost to bursting. I no sooner conceived myself sufficiently removed from all observation, than my thoughts forced their way spontaneously to my tongue, and I exclaimed in a fit of uncontrollable enthusiasm: "This is the murderer! the Hawkinses were innocent! I am sure of it! I will pledge my life for it! It is out! It is discovered! Guilty upon my soul!" (129)

Various commentators have noted the erotically charged nature of this outburst.[16] The erotics of detection are doubly potent, for in addition to providing personal gratification they also destroy Falkland as Williams' romantic ideal, thereby enabling Williams to step into the vacated place of power.

Thus, class antagonisms, ambition, pleasure, and self-preservation all contribute to the protagonist's obsessive curiosity. The "element of mystery in all passion," which one critic has found in the novel, remains inscrutable only as long as Williams' motives and actions are dissociated from the "various external accidents" that mandate aggressive and

---

[16] See Gold, "It's Only Love," pp. 150–53. Hogle calls the scene an "orgasm of textual penetration" ("Texture of Self" 271).

antagonistic behavior in order to achieve social eminence.[17] To be sure, the socio-historical context that the accidents provide cannot entirely account for human passions, but it grounds them in individual desires within a hierarchical society whose structure has been weakened by market relations. In his critique of the central thesis of Michel Foucault's *Discipline and Punish*, Frank Lentricchia offers an alternative to Foucault's explanation of the dynamics of power relations, an explanation that mystifies passion and power by representing humans as "instinctually violent creatures who are prone to the expression of a will to dominate, independent of all socio-political formations." Foucault's construction of the disciplinary society, Lentricchia asserts, racked with "a universal violence circulating through ... exploiters and exploited alike," is "inno-cent ... of class conflict and other historical categories ..."[18] In the light of historical categories, then, Williams' and Falkland's violent passions can be understood as consequences of living in a market society in which juridical powers can be used to protect one's position against the inevitable challenges that arise. Their actions represent neither a "metaphysical will to dominate" nor a "universal violence circulating through ... exploiters and exploited alike." Rather, they are inevitable consequences of an understandable desire for autonomy and social prominence.

Although Lentricchia offers a valuable corrective to Foucault's totaliz-ing theory of power, it is important to note that Caleb Williams' fortunes indicate the way in which juridical power reproduces itself in its victims and comes to attain the appearance of just such a totalizing force. The system's power to perpetuate existing relations is realized in Williams' repetition of Falkland's actions. And yet it is in that very repetition that Godwin's novel offers its strongest critique of things as they are. As Williams' autobiographical romance becomes a Newgate narrative, and as Williams himself becomes both defendant and plaintiff, the novel reveals the effects of a juridical society on the "elements of the animal frame." Godwin's novel breaks with the mid-century narratives of this study, for it represents the law as a system that keeps the individual from a peaceful and sociable life. As Raymond Williams writes, Godwin's novel is revolution-ary in the way that it presents "first, a version of social relations as dependence, pressure and pursuit, and second, a transcendence of moral contrast by a new process in which both hunter and hunted, persecutor and persecuted, are dynamically though of course differently formed and impelled by a general condition which is common to both."[19]

---

[17] DePorte, "Consolations," p. 159.

[18] Frank Lentricchia, "Reading Foucault (I): (Punishment, Labor, Resistance)," *Raritan* 1.4 (1982):11.

[19] Raymond Williams, "The Fiction of Reform," in *Writing in Society* (London: Verso Editions, n.d.), p. 146. My debt to Williams' reading is obvious.

Understanding the general condition that produces the differential effects of juridical power and social status, both of which are inter-dependent, can thus dispel some of the mystery that shrouds the passions of Williams and Falkland. Social status affords safety and comfort to its possessor. Juridical powers protect that status. Desire for comfort, in turn, produces the obsessive subject devoted to mastery of the juridical pro-cedures that protect status and insure comfort. Even though Falkland and Williams vow to have nothing to do with institutional tyranny, they both find juridical techniques necessary to their survival. Williams' surveillance of his employer produces its counterpart in Falkland, as Williams tells us shortly after the hearing: "I was his prisoner: and what a prisoner! All my actions observed; all my gestures marked. I could move neither to the right nor the left, but the eye of my keeper was upon me. He watched me; and his vigilance was a sickness to my heart. For me there was no more of freedom, no more of hilarity, of thoughtlessness, or of youth" (143). The narrative shift from romantic fantasies of supersession to novelistic repre-sentations of entrapment is enabled by a logic of domination that underlies hierarchical social orders. Falkland's aristocratic status, emblematic of irrational order, is supported by quasi-juridical techniques. He embodies that "spirit and character of government [that] intrudes itself into every rank of society" (1).

After his first escape from this intrusive power, Williams tries to distance himself from the "odious scene" of oppression: "I looked back with abhorrence to the subjection in which I had been held ... I resolved, and this resolution has never been entirely forgotten by me, to hold myself disengaged from this odious scene, and never fill the part either of the oppressor or the sufferer" (156). Caught in the web of an opposing juridical power, Williams is soon forced to abandon both his lingering romance fantasies and his noble resolutions in order to protect himself and vindicate his "honour and character." He enters a juridical battle. Just as it does with the other protagonists of this study, the law of self-preservation forces Williams to become a juridical subject despite a resolution to reject the juridical instruments that oppress him. In Godwin's sophisticated view of social relations, it is impossible to resist fully the "insensible and gradual" influences of experience. That is, in order to be neither oppressor nor sufferer, Williams must subject himself to the jurisdiction of a local court.

When Williams returns to vindicate himself from a charge of theft, he learns that evidence not unlike that fabricated by the Gawkeys to incriminate Roderick Random has been fabricated to incriminate him. Although it appears inevitable that he will be committed to prison to await trial for the theft, Falkland refuses to commit his secretary to prison and explains his decision in the following way: "I will obey the dictates of my own mind. I will never lend my assistance to the reforming mankind by axes and gibbets; I am sure things will never be as they ought, till honour and not law be the dictator of mankind, till vice is taught to shrink before the resistless might of inborn dignity, and not before the cold formality of statutes" (175). This aristocratic gesture reflects Falkland's attempt to distance himself from the workings of a law that does not have his full support. And yet, he has used the law as a means of producing the spectacle that will discredit Williams and preserve his own reputation. In doing so, he has started a process that must continue independently of his will. As in *Roderick Random*, once the law has begun its operations, others in society will see to it that it proceeds inexorably to its end. In this instance, Forester, Falkland's brother, demands that Williams be committed to prison while he awaits trial on the charges.

The efforts of the two antagonists to have no part or lend no assistance to social oppression or juridical violence prove fruitless because the structures of power work independently of individual interests. Although Williams possesses what he considers to be incontrovertible proof of Falkland's guilt, he discovers that his knowledge only makes him liable to the state's coercive power. When he charges Falkland with subornation of perjury at his hearing for theft, Forester brands Williams a "[v]ile calumniator! ... the abhorrence of nature, the opprobrium of the human species" (174). Williams regards this charge as another instance of the ways in which "[w]ealth and despotism easily know how to engage ... laws as the coadjutors of their oppression" even though Forester acts from the disinterested motive of preserving order and respect for the law (72).

As an abhorrence, the law claims Williams as its own peculiar charge. After suffering persecution, betrayal, and imprisonment, and after finding himself confronted once again by "the remorseless fangs of the law" (273), Williams decides that he has no recourse but to "turn the tables upon [his] accuser" by revealing before a magistrate the "astonishing secrets" in his possession (275). He discovers, however, that the law works for Falkland even without his consent because it is designed to protect the position he occupies. When Williams reveals his "astonishing secrets," an offended magistrate speaks the law's great concern for preserving authority: "Whether or no the felony with which you stand charged would have brought you to the gallows, I will not pretend to say. But I am sure this story will. There would be a speedy end to order and good government, if fellows that trample upon ranks and distinctions in this atrocious sort, were upon any consideration suffered to get off" (276). When Williams had first attempted to escape Falkland's surveillance by resigning his position as secretary, the squire had threatened to crush him "with the same indifference that I would any other little insect." As for Williams, he could do nothing against Falkland: "Do not imagine I am afraid of you! I wear an armour, against which all your weapons are impotent" (153). That armor turns out to be composed of the adamantine substance of the law.

Williams' appearance before the magistrate is only one in a series of "markings" that serve to ostracize him from all human community. He has been called a "demon" by Forester (173). While in prison, he acknowledges that he "must be marked as long as [he] lived for a villain" (192–93). He earns the scorn of a benevolent old man, who tells Williams that "[t]here was no criminal on the face of the earth, no murderer, half so detestable, as the person who could prevail upon himself to utter the charges [he] had done by way of recrimination against so generous a master" (249). Finally convinced that he will never be able to vindicate his honor in a corrupt society, Williams chooses the conventional consolation of a life within the private sphere, a consolation that had first occurred to him in prison: "Henceforth I will be contented with tranquil obscurity, with the cultivation of sentiment and wisdom, and the exercise of benevolence within a narrow circle" (193). Prison makes Williams choose the same pleasures that Random and Booth learned to value. From romantic fantasies and Newgate realities Williams has arrived at domestic sentiments, far from which his now sobered desires will never want to stray. But Williams' narrative recapitulates the history of eighteenth-century narrative paradigms in order to negate the novel's teleology and to explode the juridical means that enable that teleology. There will be no retreat to a domestic utopia at the end of this narrative. Denied the consolation of affective individualism by persistent persecution in the form of Falkland's agent Gines, Williams learns that the division between public and private spheres is an ideological phantasm. As a notorious ingrate, Williams is driven from abode to abode until no hospitable spot remains for him. Realizing that the law has left an indelible mark upon him, he exclaims "[s]olitude, separation, banishment! ... few men, except myself, have felt the full latitude of their meaning" (303). This moment of insight produced by pain reveals the repressed fear of the eighteenth-century novel and makes Williams' condition analogous to Robinson's in *Amelia*. Exiles from both the public and the private spheres, they enter a wilderness incapable of sustaining life.

Williams' ultimate isolation, however, must be attributed not only to his victimization by another obsessive juridical subject but also to his own quest for distinction. In order to break the repetition of country life and throw off the burdensome weight of his paternity, Williams felt compelled to mark himself off from the very community that he now seeks to rejoin. And just as he distanced himself from the village gallants, so too he distances himself from his fellow inmates in prison, despite the fact that he recognizes injustice in the law's administration: "I had no power of withdrawing my person from a disgustful society in the most chearful and valuable part of the day; but I soon brought to perfection the art of withdrawing my thoughts, and saw and heard the people about me for just as short a time and as seldom as I pleased" (186). Williams has no sympathy for his fellow sufferers. Lacking that sympathy, he makes no attempt to understand their behavior. When he breaks prison and falls in with Mr. Raymond's band of outlaws, his feelings are similar:

> The character and manners of the men among whom I lived were disgusting to me. Their brutal ignorance, their ferocious habits and their coarse behaviour, instead of becoming more tolerable by custom, hourly added force to my original aversion.
>
> ... I sighed for that solitude and obscurity, that retreat from the vexations of the world and the voice even of common fame, which I had proposed to myself when I broke prison.                                                                                                          (229–30)

Coercively excluded from much of society, Williams voluntarily excludes himself from the rest in order to maintain the illusion of superiority. The burden of his radical isolation finally forces him back to the foul shop of the law for one last attempt at gaining relief. Instead of relief he finds that the law only increases his alienation.

The law that has refused to lead Williams up the long carnival road to Tyburn also refuses to release him. In Godwin's novel, the law's coercive power is not its only effective instrument. It also works through the hero's desires for a happy social life. After alienating him from others, it alienates him from himself by drawing him back again and again into juridical action. Whereas in the other fictions the public conscience was an integrative force that enabled its bearer to function profitably, in *Caleb Williams* it is disintegrative. The disintegration is completed when Williams is driven for the last time to the law to seek redress. The last resort coincides with a change in the narrative. Williams' carefully crafted retrospective apology becomes a hurried transcription of events as they happen. Denied the felicities of any sort of narrative paradigm – whether romantic, Newgate, or sentimental – Williams writes to the moment merely to finish his tale. He summons Falkland to reply to a charge of murder before a magistrate. The Falkland who answers the summons has "the appearance of a corpse ... [and] seemed not to have three hours to live" (318–19). Shocked by his former master's appearance, Williams attempts to rationalize his action: "It appeared therefore to my mind to be a mere piece of equity and justice, such as an impartial spectator would desire, that one person should be miserable in preference to two, that one person rather than two should be incapacitated from acting his part, and contributing his share to the general welfare" (319). Williams' use of the utilitarian calculus is a miscalculation, as he himself realizes, for he has neither been an impartial spectator to events nor has he been actively involved in promoting the general welfare. Instead, he has erroneously calculated his rise to distinction without examining the instruments of that rise. Having witnessed Falkland's disintegration, however, he confesses his own entanglement in the web of law: "Hitherto I have only been miserable; henceforth I shall account myself base! Hitherto, though hardly treated by mankind, I stood acquitted at the bar of my conscience. I had not filled up the measure of my wretchedness" (320). Although the public conscience absolves Williams, his own conscience finds him guilty of having treated Falkland inhumanely through the law. Falkland dies three days later, and the conflict ends with the destruction of both antagonists.

Although Williams is chastened by his defeat, he does not learn from it. His next to last reflection recapitulates his earliest contempt for "human affairs": "But of what use are talents and sentiments in the corrupt wilderness of human society? It is a rank and rotten soil from which every finer shrub draws poison as it grows" (325). Williams has harvested the final bitter fruit of his conquest by adopting the scorn of the man he has conquered. Once again, however, there is a difference in this textual repetition; for Williams does not enjoy the illusory superiority that sustained Falkland in his isolation. When Williams writes that "I began these memoirs with the idea of vindicating my character. I have now no character that I wish to vindicate," he declares that neither romantic nor juridical subjectivity supports him (326). In *Caleb Williams* both discourses construct a human subject in radical isolation from others. In this wilderness, character is either a fantasy or a point of purchase for the law's power. Neither aristocratic nor bourgeois ideology provides the subject with sociable autonomy.

Godwin had little respect for the law that "tends, no less than creeds, catechisms and tests, to fix the human mind in a stagnant condition, and to substitute a principle of permanence in the room of that unceasing progress which is the only salubrious element of mind."[20] His attitude toward the law, however, results in a contradictory attitude toward the society that produces and is sustained by it. Those contradictions are clearly visible in *Caleb Williams*, and they are responsible for the impasse that the hero reaches at the end. One way of solving this impasse is to view society as a voluntary aggregate, from which one can withdraw at will: "We ought to be able to do without one another," Godwin writes in the *Enquiry*. "He is the most perfect man to whom society is not a necessary of life, but a luxury, innocent and enviable, in which he joyfully indulges."[21]

[20] Godwin, *Enquiry*, p. 688.
[21] Ibid., p. 761. David McCracken writes that "Godwin was the confident spokesman for personal freedom, for the rights and duties of individual men. He had no trust in groups of

Despite his philosophical views, his fiction proves that society is more than an indulgence. The solitary mind acting alone cannot free itself from error, nor can the individual thrive outside the community.

*The Adventures of Caleb Williams* is indeed a novel that "deconstructs" character, and in deconstructing character criticizes the social forces and relations that construct the juridical subject. Like most deconstructive maneuvers, it has little to offer in the place of adversarial conditions presided over by an adversarial institution, except perhaps the utopian ideal that Williams calls an open heart (323). Although this too is an ideological solution to the novel's various social conflicts, it is not without value. The open heart qualifies the way in which juridical techniques must be used. An open heart, moreover, does not expend its spirit in guarding against wasteful impulse or conniving competitors. In *Things as They Are* we have only a scant hint of that utopia, hardly even a Pisgah sight. Instead, we stand in the "corrupt wilderness of human society," hearing the confession of one who has "divest[ed] himself of the character of a man, and [who is] incapable of judging his fellow men, or of reasoning upon human affairs." And yet the human voice that produces hope from its pain lingers, faint and marginalized, speaking from the depths of its own alienation, crying out in the wilderness of its exile, inviting others to take up the labor of imagining new communities, inviting others to write a romance that will humanize the public conscience.

men, not even in groups of right-thinking men and especially not in revolutionaries" ("Introduction" vii).

# Bibliography

Aarsleff, Hans. "The State of Nature and the Nature of Man in Locke." *John Locke: Problems and Perspectives: A Collection of New Essays*. Ed. John W. Yolton. Cambridge: Cambridge University Press, 1969. 99–136.

Adorno, Theodor. *Minima Moralia: Reflections from a Damaged Life*. Trans. E. F. N. Jephcott. London: Verso, 1974.

Adorno, Theodor, and Max Horkheimer. *Dialectic of Enlightenment*. Trans. John Cumming. London: Verso, 1979.

Agnew, Jean-Christophe. *Worlds Apart: The Market and the Theater in Anglo-American Thought, 1550–1750*. Cambridge: Cambridge University Press, 1986.

Albert, Theodore G. "1. The Law vs. Clarissa Harlowe. 2. Pastoral Argument of *The Sound and the Fury*. 3. Melville's Savages." Diss. Rutgers University, 1976.

Alter, Robert. *Fielding and the Nature of the Novel*. Cambridge, MA: Harvard University Press, 1968.

Althusser, Louis. *Lenin and Philosophy and Other Essays*. Trans. Ben Brewster. New York and London: Monthly Review Press, 1971.

Amory, Hugh. "Law and the Structure of Fielding's Novels." Diss. Columbia University, 1964.

Andrew, Donna T. "The Code of Honour and its Critics: The Opposition to Duelling in England, 1700–1850." *Social History* 5 (1980):409–34.

Appleby, Joyce Oldham. *Economic Thought and Ideology in Seventeenth-Century England*. Princeton: Princeton University Press, 1978.

Armstrong, Nancy. *Desire and Domestic Fiction: A Political History of the Novel*. New York: Oxford University Press, 1987.

Arwaker, Edmund. *Thought Well Employ'd; or, the Duty of Self Observation in the Care and Regulation of Life according to the Royal Pattern*. London, 1695.

Atiyah, P. S. *The Rise and Fall of Freedom of Contract*. Oxford: Clarendon Press, 1979.

Aylward, J. D. "Duelling in the XVIII Century." *Notes and Queries* 189 (1945):31–34, 46–48, 70–73.

Backscheider, Paula R. *Daniel Defoe: Ambition and Innovation*. Lexington: University Press of Kentucky, 1986.

Bacon, Francis. *Essays, Advancement of Learning, New Atlantis, and Other Pieces*. Ed. Richard Foster Jones. New York: Odyssey Press, 1937.

Baker, J. H. *An Introduction to English Legal History*. London: Butterworths, 1971.

Baker, Sheridan. "Fielding's *Amelia* and the Materials of Romance." *Philological Quarterly* 41 (1962):437–49.

Bakhtin, M. M. *The Dialogic Imagination: Four Essays.* Trans. Caryl Emerson and Michael Holquist. Ed. Michael Holquist. Austin: University of Texas Press, 1981.

Battestin, Martin. *The Providence of Wit: Aspects of Form in Augustan Literature and the Arts.* Oxford: The Clarendon Press, 1974.

Beasley, Jerry. "*Roderick Random*: The Picaresque Transformed." *College Literature* 6 (1979):211–20.

Beattie, J. M. *Crime and the Courts in England, 1660–1800.* Oxford: Clarendon Press, 1986.

Bender, John. *Imagining the Penitentiary: Fiction and the Architecture of Mind in Eighteenth-Century England.* Chicago and London: University of Chicago Press, 1987.

"Prison Reform and the Sentence of Narration in *The Vicar of Wakefield*." *The New Eighteenth Century: Theory, Politics, English Literature.* Eds. Felicity Nussbaum and Laura Brown. New York and London: Methuen, 1987. 168–88.

Benjamin, Walter. *Illuminations.* Trans. Harry Zohn. Ed. Hannah Arendt. New York: Schocken Books, 1969.

Berman, Harold J. *Law and Revolution: The Formation of the Western Legal Tradition.* Cambridge, MA and London: Harvard University Press, 1983.

Birdsall, Virginia Ogden. *Defoe's Perpetual Seekers: A Study of the Major Fiction.* Lewisburg: Bucknell University Press, 1985.

Bjornson, Richard. *The Picaresque Hero in European Fiction.* Madison: University of Wisconsin Press, 1977.

Black, Jeremy. "Introduction." *British Politics and Society from Walpole to Pitt, 1742–1789.* Ed. Jeremy Black. London: Macmillan, 1990. 1–28.

Blackstone, William. *Commentaries on the Laws of England.* "A Facsimile of the First Edition." 4 vols. Chicago and London: University of Chicago Press, 1979.

Blewett, David. *Defoe's Art of Fiction: "Robinson Crusoe," "Moll Flanders," "Colonel Jack" & "Roxana."* Toronto: University of Toronto Press, 1979.

Bloch, Ernst. *Natural Law and Human Dignity.* Trans. Dennis J. Schmidt. Cambridge, MA and London: MIT Press, 1986.

Bloch, Tuvia. "The Prosecution of the Maidservant in *Amelia*." *English Language Notes* 6 (1969):269–71.

Boardman, Michael. *Defoe and the Uses of Narrative.* New Brunswick: Rutgers University Press, 1983.

Bobbio, Norberto "Gramsci and the Conception of Civil Society." *Gramsci and Marxist Theory.* Ed. Chantal Mouffe. London: Routledge & Kegan Paul, 1979. 21–47.

Bonfield, Lloyd. *Marriage Settlements, 1601–1740: The Adoption of the Strict Settlement.* Cambridge: Cambridge University Press, 1983.

Boorstin, Daniel. *The Mysterious Science of the Law.* 1941. Gloucester, MA: Peter Smith, 1973.

Boswell, James. *The Life of Johnson.* 6 vols. Ed. George B. Hill. Rev. by L. F. Powell. Oxford: Clarendon Press, 1934.

Boucé, Paul-Gabriel. *The Novels of Tobias Smollett.* Trans. Antonia White. London and New York: Longman, 1976.

Braudy, Leo. *Narrative Form in History and Fiction: Hume, Fielding, and Gibbon.* Princeton: Princeton University Press, 1970.

Brenkman, John. *Culture and Domination.* Ithaca and London: Cornell University Press, 1987.

Brewer, John. *Party Ideology and Popular Politics at the Accession of George III.* Cambridge: Cambridge University Press, 1976.

Brooks, Peter. *Reading for the Plot: Design and Intention in Narrative.* New York: A. A. Knopf, 1984.

Brown, Homer O. "*Tom Jones*: The 'Bastard' of History." *Boundary 2* 7.2 (1979):201–33.

Brown, John. *Estimate of the Manners and Principles of the Times.* 2 vols. London, 1757.

Brown, Marshall. *Preromanticism.* Stanford: Stanford University Press, 1991.

Bunn, James H. "Signs of Randomness in *Roderick Random.*" *Eighteenth-Century Studies* 14 (1981):452–69.

Burn, Richard. *The Justice of the Peace and Parish Officer.* 2 vols. London, 1755.

Carroll, John, ed. *Selected Letters of Samuel Richardson.* Oxford: Clarendon Press, 1964.

Castle, Terry J. "'Amy, Who Knew My Disease': A Psychosexual Pattern in Defoe's *Roxana.*" *ELH* 46 (1979):81–96.

*Clarissa's Ciphers: Meaning and Disruption in Richardson's "Clarissa."* Ithaca and London: Cornell University Press, 1982.

*Masquerade and Civilization: The Carnivalesque in Eighteenth-Century English Culture and Fiction.* Stanford: Stanford University Press, 1986.

Cheshire, G. C., and C. H. S. Fifoot. *The Law of Contract.* 7th edn. London: Butterworths, 1969.

Clark, J. C. D. *English Society 1688–1832: Ideology, Social Structure and Political Practice during the Ancien Regime.* Cambridge: Cambridge University Press, 1985.

Clay, Christopher. "Marriage, Inheritance, and the Rise of Large Estates in England, 1660–1815." *Economic History Review*, 2nd series, 21 (1968):503–18.

Cockburn, John. *The History of Duels.* 1720. Collectanea Adamantaea. Vol. 25. Edinburgh, 1888.

Cohen, Jean L. *Class and Civil Society: The Limits of Marxian Critical Theory.* Amherst: University of Massachusetts Press, 1982.

Colletti, Lucio. *From Rousseau to Lenin: Studies in Ideology and Society.* Trans. John Merrington and Judith White. London: New Left Books, 1972.

Collins, Hugh. *Marxism and Law.* Oxford and New York: Oxford University Press, 1984.

Corrigan, Philip, and Derek Sayer. *The Great Arch: English State Formation as Cultural Revolution.* Oxford: Basil Blackwell, 1985.

Cotterrell, Roger. "The Development of Capitalism and the Formalisation of Contract Law." *Law, State and Society.* Eds. Bob Fryer, et al. London: Croom Helm, 1981. 54–69.

Coward, Rosalind, and John Ellis. *Language and Materialism: Developments in Semiology and the Theory of the Subject.* London and New York: Routledge & Kegan Paul, 1977.

Damrosch, Leopold, Jr. *God's Plot and Man's Stories: Studies in the Fictional Imagination from Milton to Fielding.* Chicago and London: University of Chicago Press, 1985.

Davis, Lennard. *Factual Fictions: The Origins of the English Novel.* New York: Columbia University Press, 1983.

de Lauretis, Teresa. *Alice Doesn't: Feminism, Semiotics, Cinema.* Bloomington: Indiana University Press, 1982.

Defoe, Daniel. *Complete English Tradesman in Familiar Letters.* 2nd edn. London, 1727.

  *Conjugal Lewdness; or, Matrimonial Whoredom.* 1727. Gainesville: Scholars' Facsimiles and Reprints, 1967.

  *Defoe's Review.* 22 vols. Ed. Arthur W. Secord. 1938. New York: AMS Press, 1965.

  "Everybody's Business is Nobody's Business." 1725. *The Novels and Miscellaneous Works of Daniel De Foe.* 7 vols. London, 1854.

  *The Life and Strange Surprizing Adventures of Robinson Crusoe.* Ed. J. Donald Crowley. Oxford: Oxford University Press, 1972.

  *A Plan of the English Commerce.* 2nd edn. 1730. New York: Augustus Kelley, 1967.

  *Roxana, the Fortunate Mistress.* Ed. Jane Jack. 1964. Oxford and New York: Oxford University Press, 1981.

DePorte, Michael. "The Consolations of Fiction: Mystery in *Caleb Williams.*" *Papers on Language and Literature* 20 (1984):154–64.

Dews, Peter. *Logics of Disintegration: Post-Structuralist Thought and the Claims of Critical Theory.* London: Verso Books, 1987.

Dijkstra, Bram. *Defoe and Economics: The Fortunes of "Roxana" in the History of Interpretation.* London: Macmillan Press, 1987.

*A Dissertation on the Law of Nature, the Law of Nations, and the Civil Law in General.* London, 1723.

Doederlein, Sue Warrick. "Clarissa in the Hands of the Critics." *Eighteenth-Century Studies* 16 (1983):401–14.

Doody, Margaret. *A Natural Passion: A Study of the Novels of Samuel Richardson.* Oxford: Clarendon Press, 1974.

Dumont, Louis. *Essays on Individualism: Modern Ideology in Anthropological Perspective.* Chicago and London: University of Chicago Press, 1986.

  *From Mandeville to Marx: The Genesis and Triumph of Economic Ideology.* Chicago: University of Chicago Press, 1977.

Durant, David. "*The Vicar of Wakefield* and the Sentimental Novel." *Studies in English Literature* 17 (1977):477–91.

Dussinger, John. *The Discourse of the Mind in Eighteenth-Century Fiction.* Studies in English Literature, vol. 80. The Hague and Paris: Mouton, 1974.

Eagleton, Terry. *Criticism and Ideology: A Study in Marxist Literary Theory.* London: Verso, 1976.

  *The Ideology of the Aesthetic.* Oxford: Basil Blackwell, 1989.

  *The Rape of Clarissa: Writing, Sexuality, and Class Struggle in Samuel Richardson.* Minneapolis: University of Minnesota Press, 1982.

Eden, Kathy. *Poetic and Legal Fiction in the Aristotelian Tradition.* Princeton: Princeton University Press, 1986.

Fabel, Robin. "The Patriotic Briton: Tobias Smollett and English Politics, 1756–1771." *Eighteenth-Century Studies* 8 (1974):100–14.

Faller, Lincoln B. *Turned to Account: The Forms and Functions of Criminal Biography in Late Seventeenth- and Early Eighteenth-Century England.* Cambridge: Cambridge University Press, 1987.

Feinman, Jay M., and Peter Gabel. "Contract Law as Ideology." *The Politics of Law: A Progressive Critique.* 2nd edn. Ed. David Kairys. New York: Pantheon Books, 1990. 373–86.

Ferguson, Adam. *An Essay on the History of Civil Society.* Intro. Louis Schneider. New Brunswick and London: Transaction Books, 1980.

Ferguson, Oliver W. "Dr. Primrose and Goldsmith's Clerical Ideal." *Philological Quarterly* 54 (1975):323–32.

Fielding, Henry. *Amelia.* Ed. Martin C. Battestin. Middletown: Wesleyan University Press, 1983.

*A Charge Delivered to the Grand Jury, at the Sessions of the Peace Held for the City and Liberty of Westminster, etc. On Thursday, the 29th of June 1749.* London, 1749.

*The Complete Works of Henry Fielding, Esq.* 16 vols. Ed. William Henley. New York: Croscup & Sterling, 1902.

*An Enquiry into the Causes of the Late Increase of Robbers, etc.* 1751. New York: AMS Press, 1975.

Flanders, W. Austin. *Structures of Experience: History, Society, and Personal Life in the Eighteenth-Century British Novel.* Columbia: University of South Carolina Press, 1984.

Flynn, Carol. *Samuel Richardson: A Man of Letters.* Princeton: Princeton University Press, 1982.

Foucault, Michel. *Discipline and Punish: The Birth of the Prison.* Trans. Alan Sheridan. New York: Random House, 1979.

*The History of Sexuality. Volume 1: An Introduction.* Trans. Robert Hurley. New York: Random House, 1978.

"Prison Talk." *Power/Knowledge: Selected Interviews and Other Writings, 1972–1977.* Trans. Colin Gordon, Leo Marshall, John Mepham, Kate Soper. Ed. Colin Gordon. New York: Pantheon Books, 1980. 37–54.

Fredman, Alice Green. "The Picaresque in Decline: Smollett's First Novel." *English Writers of the Eighteenth Century.* Ed. John H. Middendorf. New York and London: Columbia University Press, 1971. 189–207.

Freud, Sigmund. "Character and Anal Erotism." *The Freud Reader.* Ed. Peter Gay. New York: Norton, 1989. 293–97.

Furbank, P. N., and W. R. Owens. *The Canonisation of Daniel Defoe.* New Haven and London: Yale University Press, 1988.

Geertz, Clifford. *Local Knowledge: Further Essays in Interpretive Anthropology.* New York: Basic Books, 1983.

George, Dorothy M. *London Life in the Eighteenth Century.* 1925. New York: Harper and Row, 1964.

Godwin, William. *Caleb Williams.* Ed. David McCracken. New York: Norton, 1977.

*Enquiry Concerning Political Justice.* Ed. Isaac Kramnick. Harmondsworth: Penguin Books, 1976.

Gold, Alex, Jr. "It's Only Love: The Politics of Passion in Godwin's *Caleb Williams.*" *Texas Studies in Literature and Language* 19 (1977):135–60.

Goldberg, Rita. *Sex and Enlightenment: Women in Richardson and Diderot.* Cambridge: Cambridge University Press, 1984.

Goldsmith, Oliver. *The Collected Works of Oliver Goldsmith.* 5 vols. Ed. Arthur Friedman. Oxford: Clarendon Press, 1966.

   *The Vicar of Wakefield.* Ed. Arthur Friedman. London: Oxford University Press, 1981.

Gonson, Sir John. *The Charge of Sir John Gonson, Knt., to the Grand Jury of the City and Liberty of Westminster.* 4th edn. London, 1740.

Graham, Kenneth. "The Gothic Unity of Godwin's *Caleb Williams.*" *Papers on Language and Literature* 20 (1984):47–59.

Gramsci, Antonio. *Selections from the Prison Notebooks.* Ed. and trans. Quintin Hoare and Geoffrey Nowell Smith. New York: International Publishers, 1971.

Green, Mary Elizabeth. "Oliver Goldsmith and the Wisdom of the World." *Studies in Philology* 77 (1980):202–12.

Gross, Harvey. "The Pursuer and the Pursued: A Study of *Caleb Williams.*" *Texas Studies in Literature and Language* 1 (1959):401–11.

Grotius, Hugo. *De Jure Belli ac Pacis.* 2 vols. Trans. Francis W. Kelsey. Oxford: Clarendon Press, 1925.

Guillen, Claudio. "Towards a Definition of the Picaresque." *Proceedings of the IIIrd Congress of the International Comparative Literature Association.* The Hague: Mouton & Co., 1962. 252–66. Rpt. in his *Literature as System: Essays toward the Theory of Literary History.* Princeton: Princeton University Press, 1971. 71–106.

Gusdorf, Georges. "Conditions and Limits of Autobiography." Trans. James Olney. *Autobiography: Essays Theoretical and Critical.* Ed. James Olney. Princeton: Princeton University Press, 1980. 28–48.

Habakkuk, H. J. "Marriage Settlements in the Eighteenth Century." *Transactions of the Royal Historical Society,* 4th series, 32 (1950):15–30.

Habermas, Jürgen. *The Structural Transformation of the Public Sphere: An Inquiry into a Category of Bourgeois Society.* Trans. Thomas Burger with Frederick Lawrence. 1962. Cambridge, MA: MIT Press, 1989.

Hagstrum, Jean H. *Sex and Sensibility: Ideal and Erotic Love from Milton to Mozart.* Chicago and London: University of Chicago Press, 1980.

Hale, Sir Matthew. *Historia Placitorum Coronae. The History of the Pleas of the Crown.* London, 1736.

   *The History of the Common Law of England.* Ed. and intro. Charles M. Gray. Chicago and London: University of Chicago Press, 1971.

Harding, Alan. *A Social History of English Law.* Harmondsworth: Penguin Books, 1966.

Hawkins, William. *A Treatise of the Pleas of the Crown.* 2 vols. 8th edn. London, 1824.

Hay, Douglas. "Property, Authority, and the Criminal Law." *Albion's Fatal Tree: Crime and Society in Eighteenth-Century England.* Eds. Douglas Hay, et al. New York: Pantheon Books, 1975. 17–63.

Hegel, G. W. F. *Hegel's Philosophy of Right.* Trans. T. M. Knox. London: Oxford University Press, 1967.

Held, David. *Introduction to Critical Theory: Horkheimer to Habermas.* Berkeley and Los Angeles: University of California Press, 1980.

Hentzi, Gary. "Holes in the Heart: *Moll Flanders, Roxana,* and 'Agreeable Crime.'" *Boundary 2* 18.1 (1991):174–200.

Hill, Christopher. *Change and Continuity in Seventeenth-Century England.* Cambridge, MA: Harvard University Press, 1975.

"Clarissa Harlowe and her Times." *Essays in Criticism* 5 (1955):315–40.

*Intellectual Origins of the English Revolution.* Oxford: Clarendon Press, 1965.

Hilliard, Raymond F. "The Redemption of Fatherhood in *The Vicar of Wakefield.*" *Studies in English Literature* 23 (1983):465–80.

Hirschman, Albert O. *The Passions and the Interests: Political Arguments for Capitalism before its Triumph.* Princeton: Princeton University Press, 1977.

Hobbes, Thomas. *Leviathan.* Ed. Richard Tuck. Cambridge Texts in the History of Political Thought. Cambridge: Cambridge University Press, 1991.

Hogle, Jerrold E. "The Texture of Self in Godwin's *Things as They Are.*" *Boundary 2* 7.2 (1979):261–81.

Holdsworth, W. S. A *History of English Law.* 12 vols. Boston: Little, Brown, and Company, 1922–38.

Holmes, Geoffrey. *British Politics in the Age of Ann.* London: Macmillan, 1967.

Home, Henry, Lord Kames. *Historical Law Tracts.* 2 vols. Edinburgh, 1753.

Hopkins, Robert H. "Social Stratification and the Obsequious Curve: Goldsmith and Rowlandson." *Studies in the Eighteenth Century. Papers Presented at the Third David Nichol Smith Memorial Seminar, Canberra, 1973.* Eds. R. F. Brissenden and J. C. Eade. Toronto: University of Toronto Press, 1976. 55–71.

*The True Genius of Oliver Goldsmith.* Baltimore: The Johns Hopkins Press, 1969.

Horwitz, Morton J. *The Transformation of American Law, 1780–1860.* Cambridge, MA and London: Harvard University Press, 1977.

Howell, T. B., ed. *A Complete Collection of State Trials.* 34 vols. London, 1816–31.

Hume, David. *Essays Moral, Political and Literary.* Oxford: Oxford University Press, 1963.

*The History of England from the Invasion of Julius Caesar to The Revolution in 1688.* 6 vols. Indianapolis: Liberty Classics, 1983.

*A Treatise of Human Nature.* Ed. L. A. Selby-Bigge. 2nd edn. rev. by P. H. Nidditch. Oxford: The Clarendon Press, 1978.

Hunter, J. Paul. *Before Novels: The Cultural Contexts of Eighteenth-Century Fiction.* New York: Norton, 1990.

*Occasional Form: Henry Fielding and the Chains of Circumstance.* Baltimore: Johns Hopkins University Press, 1975.

"'The Young, the Ignorant, and the Idle': Some Notes on Readers and the Beginnings of the English Novel." *Anticipations of Enlightenment in England, France, and Germany.* Eds. Alan Charles Kors and Paul J. Korshin. Philadelphia: University of Pennsylvania Press, 1987. 259–82.

Hutcheson, Francis. *Illustrations on the Moral Sense.* Ed. Bernard Peach. Cambridge, MA: Harvard University Press, 1971.

Irwin, Michael. *Henry Fielding: The Tentative Realist.* Oxford: Clarendon Press, 1967.

Jaarsma, Richard J. "Satiric Intent in *The Vicar of Wakefield.*" *Studies in Short Fiction* 5 (1968):331–41.

Jacob, Giles. *The Law Dictionary.* London, 1809.

Jameson, Fredric. *The Political Unconscious: Narrative as a Socially Symbolic Act.* Ithaca: Cornell University Press, 1981.

Johnson, Samuel. *A Dictionary of the English Language.* London: Times Books, 1979.

   *The Idler and Adventurer.* Eds. W. J. Bate, John M. Bullitt, and L. F. Powell. New Haven and London: Yale University Press, 1963.

   *The Letters of Samuel Johnson. With Mrs. Thrale's Genuine Letters to Him.* 3 vols. Ed. R. W. Chapman. Oxford: Clarendon Press, 1952.

Jones, Benjamin M. *Henry Fielding, Novelist and Magistrate.* London: Allen & Unwin, 1933.

Kauffman, Linda S. *Discourses of Desire: Gender, Genre, and Epistolary Fictions.* Ithaca and London: Cornell University Press, 1986.

Kay, Carol. *Political Constructions: Defoe, Richardson, and Sterne in Relation to Hobbes, Hume, and Burke.* Ithaca and London: Cornell University Press, 1988.

Kiely, Robert. *The Romantic Novel in England.* Cambridge, MA: Harvard University Press, 1972.

Knapp, Lewis M., ed. *The Letters of Tobias Smollett.* Oxford: Clarendon Press, 1970.

   *Tobias Smollett, Doctor of Men and Manners.* Princeton: Princeton University Press, 1949.

Kramnick, Isaac. *Bolingbroke and his Circle: The Politics of Nostalgia in the Age of Walpole.* Cambridge, MA: Harvard University Press, 1968.

LaCapra, Dominick. *Rethinking Intellectual History: Texts, Contexts, Language.* Ithaca and London: Cornell University Press, 1983.

Landau, Norma. *The Justices of the Peace, 1679–1760.* Berkeley: University of California Press, 1984.

Langbein, John H. "Albion's Fatal Flaws." *Past and Present* 98 (1983):96–120.

   "The Criminal Trial before the Lawyers." *The University of Chicago Law Review* 45 (1978):263–316.

   *Torture and the Law of Proof: Europe and England in the Ancien Régime.* Chicago & London: University of Chicago Press, 1977.

*The Laws Respecting Women.* 1777. New York: Oceana Publications, 1974.

Lentricchia, Frank. "Reading Foucault (I): (Punishment, Labor, Resistance)." *Raritan* 1.4 (1982):5–32.

LePage, Peter V. "The Prison and the Dark Beauty of 'Amelia.'" *Criticism* 9 (1967):337–54.

Levy, Anita. *Other Women: The Writing of Class, Race, and Gender, 1832–1898.* Princeton: Princeton University Press, 1991.

Lieberman, David. *The Province of Legislation Determined: Legal Theory in Eighteenth-Century Britain.* Ideas in Context. Cambridge: Cambridge University Press, 1989.

Little, David. *Religion, Order, and Law: A Study in Pre-Revolutionary England.* New York: Harper and Row, 1969.

Locke, John. *Two Treatises of Government.* Ed. Peter Laslett. New York: New American Library, 1963.

Lukács, Georg. *The Theory of the Novel*. Trans. Anna Bostock. Cambridge, MA: MIT Press, 1971.

McConville, Sean. *A History of English Prison Administration: Volume I, 1750–1877*. London: Routledge & Kegan Paul, 1981.

McCracken, David. "Godwin's Literary Theory: The Alliance between Fiction and Political Philosophy." *Philological Quarterly* 49 (1970):113–33.

McCrea, Brian. "Politics and Narrative Technique in Fielding's *Amelia*." *The Journal of Narrative Technique* 13 (1983):131–40.

Macfarlane, Alan. *The Culture of Capitalism*. Oxford: Basil Blackwell, 1987.

   *The Origins of English Individualism: The Family, Property and Social Transition*. New York: Cambridge University Press, 1979.

Macherey, Pierre. *A Theory of Literary Production*. Trans. Geoffrey Wall. London: Routledge & Kegan Paul, 1978.

MacIntyre, Alasdair. *After Virtue: A Study in Moral Theory*. London: Gerald Duckworth, 1981.

McKeon, Michael. *The Origins of the English Novel, 1600–1740*. Baltimore and London: Johns Hopkins University Press, 1987.

McLynn, Frank. *Crime and Punishment in Eighteenth-Century England*. London and New York: Routledge, 1989.

Macpherson, C. B. *The Political Theory of Possessive Individualism, Hobbes to Locke*. Oxford: Clarendon Press, 1962.

Maine, Sir Henry Sumner. *Ancient Law*. London: J. M. Dent, 1917.

Mandeville, Bernard. *An Enquiry Into the Causes of the Frequent Executions at Tyburn*. London, 1725.

   *The Fable of the Bees*. 2 vols. Ed. F. B. Kaye. 1924. Indianapolis: Liberty Classics, 1988.

Marshall, David. *The Figure of Theater: Shaftesbury, Defoe, Adam Smith, and George Eliot*. New York: Columbia University Press, 1986.

Marx, Karl. *Capital: A Critique of Political Economy. Volume 1*. Trans. Samuel Moore and Edward Aveling. Ed. Frederick Engels. New York: International Publishers, 1967.

   *The Marx-Engels Reader* 2nd edn Ed. Robert C. Tucker. New York: Norton, 1978.

Miller, D. A. *The Novel and the Police*. Berkeley: University of California Press, 1988.

Miller, Jacqueline. "The Imperfect Tale: Articulation, Rhetoric, and Self in *Caleb Williams*." *Criticism* 20 (1978):366–82.

Milton, Philip. "David Hume and the Eighteenth-Century Conception of Natural Law." *Legal Studies* 2 (1982):14–33.

*The Monitor*, 295, 14 March 1761, p. 1781.

Moore, John Robert. *A Checklist of the Writings of Daniel Defoe*. 2nd. edn. Hamden: Archon Books, 1971.

Nathan, Sabine. "The Anticipation of Nineteenth-Century Ideological Trends in Fielding's *Amelia*." *Zeitschrift für Anglistik und Amerikanistik* 6 (1958):382–409.

Neale, R. S. "'The Bourgeoisie, Historically, Has Played a Most Revolutionary Part.'" *Feudalism, Capitalism and Beyond*. Eds. Eugene Kamenka and R. S. Neale. New York: St. Martin's Press, 1975. 85–102.

Nenner, Howard. *By Colour of Law: Legal Culture and Constitutional Politics in England, 1660–1689*. Chicago and London: University of Chicago Press, 1977.

Nicholson, Linda J. *Gender and History: The Limits of Social Theory in the Age of the Family*. New York: Columbia University Press, 1986.

Novak, Maximillian E. *Defoe and the Nature of Man*. Oxford: Oxford University Press, 1963.

*Economics and the Fiction of Daniel Defoe*. Berkeley and Los Angeles: University of California Press, 1962.

"Review of Dijkstra, *Defoe and Economics: The Fortunes of 'Roxana' in the History of Interpretation*." *Modern Philology* 87.1 (1989):89–92.

"The Unmentionable and the Ineffable in Defoe's Fiction." *Studies in the Literary Imagination* 15.2 (1982):85–102.

Olsen, Frances E. "The Family and the Market: A Study of Ideology and Legal Reform." *Harvard Law Review* 96 (1983):1497–1578.

Ousby, Heather, and Ian Ousby. "'My Servant Caleb': Godwin's *Caleb Williams* and the Political Trials of the 1790s." *University of Toronto Quarterly* 14.5 (1974):47–55.

Owen, John B. *The Eighteenth Century: 1714–1815*. New York: Norton, 1974.

*The Rise of the Pelhams*. London: Methuen, 1957.

Parker, Alice. "Tobias Smollett and the Law." *Studies in Philology* 39 (1942):545–58.

Pateman, Carole. "Feminist Critiques of the Public/Private Dichotomy." *The Disorder of Women: Democracy, Feminism, and Political Theory*. Cambridge: Polity Press, 1989. 118–40.

*The Sexual Contract*. Cambridge: Polity Press, 1988.

Paulson, Ronald. "The Pilgrimage and the Family: Structures in the Novels of Fielding and Smollett." *Tobias Smollett: Bicentennial Essays Presented to Lewis M. Knapp*. Eds. G. S. Rousseau and P-G Boucé. New York: Oxford University Press, 1971. 57–78.

*Satire and the Novel in Eighteenth-Century England*. New Haven: Yale University Press, 1967.

Peterson, Spiro. "The Matrimonial Theme of Defoe's *Roxana*." *PMLA* 70 (1955):166–91.

Plucknett, T. F. T. *A Concise History of the Common Law*. 5th edn. Boston: Little, Brown, 1956.

Pocock, J. G. A. *The Ancient Constitution and the Feudal Law: A Study of English Historical Thought in the Seventeenth Century. A Reissue with a Retrospect*. Cambridge: Cambridge University Press, 1987.

"Early Modern Capitalism – The Augustan Perception." *Feudalism, Capitalism and Beyond*. Eds. Eugene Kamenka and R. S. Neale. New York: St. Martin's Press, 1975. 62–83.

*The Machiavellian Moment: Florentine Political Thought and the Atlantic Republican Tradition*. Princeton: Princeton University Press, 1975.

Polanyi, Karl. *The Great Transformation: The Political and Economic Origins of Our Time*. Boston: Beacon Press, 1957.

Pollak, Ellen. *The Poetics of Sexual Myth: Gender and Ideology in the Verse of Swift and Pope*. Chicago: University of Chicago Press, 1985.

Porter, Roy. "English Society in the Eighteenth Century Revisited." *British Politics and Society from Walpole to Pitt, 1742–1789.* Ed. Jeremy Black. London: Macmillan, 1990. 29–52.

    *English Society in the Eighteenth Century.* Harmondsworth: Penguin, 1982.

Preston, Thomas R. "The Uses of Adversity: Worldly Detachment and Heavenly Treasure in *The Vicar of Wakefield.*" *Studies in Philology* 81 (1984):229–51.

Pufendorf, Samuel. *De Jure Naturae et Gentium.* 2 vols. Trans. C. H. and W. A. Oldfather. Oxford: Clarendon Press, 1934.

Punter, David. "Smollett and the Logic of Domination." *Literature and History* 2 (October 1975):60–83.

Radzinowicz, Leon. *A History of Criminal Law and its Administration from 1750.* 4 vols. London: Stevens & Sons, 1948.

Rapaczynski, Andrezj. *Nature and Politics: Liberalism in the Philosophies of Hobbes, Locke, and Rousseau.* Ithaca and London: Cornell University Press, 1987.

Rawson, Claude. *Henry Fielding and the Augustan Ideal Under Stress: "Nature's Dance of Death" and other Studies.* London: Routledge & Kegan Paul, 1972.

Reed, Joseph W., Jr. "A New Samuel Richardson Manuscript." *Yale University Library Gazette* 42 (1968):215–31.

Renner, Karl. *The Institutions of Private Law and their Social Functions.* Trans. Agnes Schwarzschild. Ed. and Intro. O. Kahn-Freund. London: Routledge & Kegan Paul, 1949.

Richardson, Samuel. *Clarissa, or the History of a Young Lady.* 8 vols. Oxford: Shakespeare Head Press, 1930.

    *Clarissa, or the History of a Young Lady.* 4 vols. New York and London: Everyman's Library, 1932.

    *"Clarissa": Preface, Hints of Prefaces, and Postscript.* The Augustan Reprint Society, No. 103. Intro. R. F. Brissenden. Los Angeles: William Andrews Clark Memorial Library, 1964.

Richetti, John J. *Daniel Defoe.* Boston: Twayne, 1987.

    *Defoe's Narratives: Situations and Structures.* Oxford: Clarendon Press, 1975.

    *Popular Fiction before Richardson: Narrative Patterns, 1700–1739.* Oxford: Clarendon Press, 1969.

    "Representing an Under Class: Servants and Proletarians in Fielding and Smollett." *The New Eighteenth Century: Theory, Politics, English Literature.* Eds. Felicity Nussbaum and Laura Brown. New York and London: Methuen, 1987. 84–98.

Rosenblum, Michael. "Smollett as Conservative Satirist." *ELH* 42 (1975):556–79.

Ross, Angus. "The 'Show of Violence' in Smollett's Novels." *Yearbook of English Studies* 2 (1972):118–29.

Rothstein, Eric. *Systems of Order and Inquiry in Later Eighteenth-Century Fiction.* Berkeley: University of California Press, 1975.

Rothstein, Eric, and Howard D. Weinbrot. "The Vicar of Wakefield, Mr. Wilmot, and the 'Whistonean Controversy.'" *Philological Quarterly* 55 (1976): 225–40.

Rousseau, G. S. "Review Essay. Revisionist Polemics: J. C. D. Clark and the Collapse of Modernity in the Age of Johnson." *The Age of Johnson*, vol. 3. Ed. Paul Korshin. New York: AMS Press, 1989. 421–50.

"Smollett and the Picaresque: Some Questions about a Label." *Studies in Burke and his Time* 12 (1971):1886–1904. Rpt. in *Tobias Smollett: Essays of Two Decades.* Edinburgh: T. & T. Clark, 1982. 53–73.

Rousseau, Jean-Jacques. "Discourse on Political Economy." *On the Social Contract.* Trans. Judith R. Masters. Ed. Roger D. Masters. New York: St. Martin's Press, 1978. 209–40.

Rubin, Gayle. "The Traffic in Women: Notes on the 'Political Economy' of Sex." *Toward an Anthropology of Women.* Ed. Rayna R. Reiter. New York: Monthly Review Press, 1975. 157–210.

Rudé, George. *Wilkes and Liberty: A Social Study of 1763 to 1774.* Oxford: Clarendon Press, 1962.

Said, Edward. *The World, the Text, and the Critic.* Cambridge, MA: Harvard University Press, 1983.

Schochet, Gordon J. *Patriarchalism in Political Thought: The Authoritarian Family and Political Speculation and Attitudes Especially in Seventeenth-Century England.* New York: Basic Books, 1975.

Schonhorn, Manuel. *Defoe's Politics: Parliament, Power, Kingship, and "Robinson Crusoe."* Cambridge Studies in Eighteenth-Century Literature and Thought 9. Cambridge: Cambridge University Press, 1991.

Scott, Sarah. *A Description of Millenium Hall.* New York: Penguin Books, 1986.

Sekora, John. *Luxury: The Concept in Western Thought, Eden to Smollett.* Baltimore and London: Johns Hopkins University Press, 1977.

Shanley, M. L. "Marriage Contract and Social Contract in Seventeenth Century English Political Thought." *The Western Political Quarterly* 32.1 (1979):79–91.

Sherburn, George. "Fielding's *Amelia*: An Interpretation." *ELH* 3 (1936):1–14. Rpt. in *Fielding: A Collection of Critical Essays.* Ed. Ronald Paulson. Englewood Cliffs: Prentice Hall, 1962. 146–57.

"Fielding's Social Outlook." *Philological Quarterly*, 35 (1956):1–23. Rpt. in *Eighteenth-Century English Literature: Modern Essays in Criticism.* Ed. James L. Clifford. New York: Oxford University Press, 1959. 251–73.

Shklar, Judith. *Legalism.* Cambridge, MA: Harvard University Press, 1964.

Simpson, A. W. B. "The Horwitz Thesis and the History of Contracts." *Legal Theory and Legal History: Essays on the Common Law.* London and Ronceverte: Hambledon Press, 1987. 203–71.

Sitter, John. *Literary Loneliness in Mid-Eighteenth-Century England.* Ithaca and London: Cornell University Press, 1982.

Smith, Adam. *An Inquiry into the Nature and Causes of the Wealth of Nations.* 2 vols. Eds. R. H. Campbell and A. S. Skinner. 1976. Indianapolis: Liberty Classics, 1981.

*The Theory of Moral Sentiments.* Eds. D. D. Raphael and A. L. Macfie. 1976. Indianapolis: Liberty Classics, 1982.

Smollett, Tobias. *The Adventures of Ferdinand Count Fathom.* Ed. Jerry C. Beasley. Athens and London: University of Georgia Press, 1988.

*The Adventures of Roderick Random.* Ed. Paul-Gabriel Boucé. Oxford: Oxford University Press, 1979.

*The Adventures of Sir Launcelot Greaves. Together with The History & Adventures of an Atom.* Oxford: The Shakespeare Head Press, 1926.

Spacks, Patricia Meyer. *Desire and Truth: Functions of Plot in Eighteenth-Century English Novels*. Chicago and London: University of Chicago Press, 1990.

*Imagining a Self: Autobiography and Novel in Eighteenth-Century England*. Cambridge, MA: Harvard University Press, 1976.

St. John, Henry, Viscount Bolingbroke. "Of Good and Bad Ministers." *The Works of Lord Bolingbroke*. 4 vols. Philadelphia: Carey and Hart, 1841.

Stallybrass, Peter, and Allon White. *The Politics and Poetics of Transgression*. Ithaca: Cornell University Press, 1986.

Starr, G. A. *Defoe and Casuistry*. Princeton: Princeton University Press, 1971.

"Sympathy *v.* Judgement in Roxana's First Liaison." *The Augustan Milieu: Essays presented to Louis A. Landa*. Eds. Henry Knight Miller, Eric Rothstein, G. S. Rousseau. Oxford: Clarendon Press, 1970. 59–76.

Staves, Susan. *Married Women's Separate Property in England, 1660–1833*. Cambridge, MA and London: Harvard University Press, 1990.

Steele, Sir Richard. *The Tatler*. 3 vols. Ed. Donald F. Bond. Oxford: Clarendon Press, 1987.

Stephens, John C., Jr. "The Verge of the Court and Arrest for Debt in Fielding's *Amelia*." *Modern Language Notes* 63 (1948):104–9.

Sterne, Laurence. *The Life and Opinions of Tristram Shandy, Gentleman*. 3 vols. Eds. Melvyn New and Joan New. Gainesville: University Presses of Florida, 1978, 1984.

Stone, Lawrence. *The Family, Sex and Marriage in England, 1500–1800*. New York: Harper & Row, 1977.

Storch, Rudolf F. "Metaphors of Private Guilt and Social Rebellion in Godwin's *Caleb Williams*." *ELH* 34 (1967):188–207.

Stuber, Florian. "Clarissa and Her World: Form and Content in Richardson's *Clarissa*." Diss. Columbia University, 1980.

Sutherland, W. O. S. *The Art of the Satirist: Essays on the Satire of Augustan England*. Austin: University of Texas Press, 1965.

Tanner, Tony. *Adultery in the Novel: Contract and Transgression*. Baltimore and London: The Johns Hopkins University Press, 1979.

Thompson, E. P. *Whigs and Hunters: The Origin of the Black Act*. New York: Pantheon Books, 1975.

Tigar, Michael E., and Madeleine R. Levy. *Law and the Rise of Capitalism*. New York: Monthly Review Press, 1977.

Towers, A. R. "*Amelia* and the State of Matrimony." *Review of English Studies* n.s. 5 (1954):144–57.

[Tradesman of the City]. *The nature of contracts consider'd, as they relate to the third and fourth subscriptions, taken in by the South Sea Company*. London, 1720.

*A Treatise of Feme Coverts: Or the Lady's Law*. Intro. Lance E. Dickson. 1732. South Hackensack, New Jersey: Rothman Reprints, 1974.

Trenchard, John, and Thomas Gordon. *Cato's Letters: Essays on Liberty, Civil and Religious, and Other Important Subjects*. 6th edn. 4 vols. London: 1755. New York: Da Capo Press, 1971.

Trevelyan, G. M. *English Social History: A Survey of Six Centuries, Chaucer to Victoria*. London: Longmans, Green, 1942.

"The Trial of Frederick Calvert, Esq.; Baron of *Baltimore* ... for a Rape on the Body of *Sarah Woodcock*." London, 1768.

Tuck, Richard. "The 'Modern' Theory of Natural Law." *The Languages of Political Theory in Early-Modern Europe*. Ed. Anthony Pagden. Ideas in Context. Cambridge: Cambridge University Press, 1987. 99–119.

*Natural Rights Theories: Their Origin and Development*. Cambridge: Cambridge University Press, 1979.

Tully, James. *A Discourse on Property: John Locke and his Adversaries*. Cambridge: Cambridge University Press, 1980.

Vincent, H. P. "Tobias Smollett's Assault on Gordon and Groom." *Review of English Studies* 16 (1940):183–88.

Wardle, Ralph M. *Oliver Goldsmith*. 1957. Hamden: Archon Books, 1969.

Warner, William Beatty. *Reading "Clarissa": The Struggles of Interpretation*. New Haven and London: Yale University Press, 1979.

Watt, Ian. *The Rise of the Novel: Studies in Defoe, Richardson and Fielding*. Berkeley and Los Angeles: University of California Press, 1957.

Weber, Max. *The Protestant Ethic and the Spirit of Capitalism*. Trans. Talcott Parsons. New York: Charles Scribner's Sons, 1958.

White, Hayden. "The Value of Narrativity in the Representation of Reality." *Critical Inquiry* 7.1 (1980). Rpt. in his *The Content of the Form: Narrative Discourse and Historical Representation*. Baltimore and London: The Johns Hopkins University Press, 1987. 1–25.

Williams, E. Neville. *The Eighteenth-Century Constitution, 1688–1815: Documents and Commentary*. Cambridge: Cambridge University Press, 1960.

Williams, Raymond. "The Fiction of Reform." *Writing in Society*. London: Verso Editions, n.d. 142–49.

*Marxism and Literature*. Oxford: Oxford University Press, 1977.

Wilt, Judith. "He Could Go No Farther: A Modest Proposal about Lovelace and Clarissa." *PMLA* 92 (1977):19–32.

Winner, Anthony. "Richardson's Lovelace: Character and Prediction." *Texas Studies in Literature and Language* 14 (1972):53–75.

Wolff, Cynthia Griffin. "Fielding's *Amelia*: Private Virtue and Public Good." *Texas Studies in Literature and Language* 10 (1968):37–55.

Zirker, Malvin R., Jr. *Fielding's Social Pamphlets: A Study of "An Enquiry into the Causes of the Late Increase of Robbers" and "A Proposal for Making an Effectual Provision for the Poor."* Berkeley: University of California Press, 1966.

Zomchick, John P. "'A Penetration which Nothing Can Deceive': Gender and Juridical Discourse in Some Eighteenth-Century Narratives." *Studies in English Literature* 29 (1989):535–61.

"Social Class, Character, and Narrative Strategy in *Humphry Clinker*." *Eighteenth-Century Life* 10.3 (1986):172–85.

# Index

Printed in the United Kingdom
by Lightning Source UK Ltd.
132438UK00002B/327/A